James T. Shotwell
and the
Rise of Internationalism
in America

James T. Shotwell, 1948. Courtesy the Carnegie Endowment for International Peace

James T. Shotwell and the Rise of Internationalism in America

Harold Josephson

Rutherford • Madison • Teaneck
Fairleigh Dickinson University Press

London: Associated University Presses

Associated University Presses, Inc.
Cranbury, New Jersey 08512

Associated University Presses
108 New Bond Street
London W1Y OQX, England

Library of Congress Cataloging in Publication Data

Josephson, Harold, 1942–
James T. Shotwell and the rise of internationalism in America.
Bibliography: p.
1. Shotwell, James Thomson, 1874–1965. I. Title.
D413.S56J67 327'.1'0924 74–2874
ISBN 0–8386–1524–4

PRINTED IN THE UNITED STATES OF AMERICA

For my Mother and Lila

Contents

Preface

The signing of the United Nations Charter on June 26, 1945, marked the triumph of internationalist thought in America. For more than two decades individuals and groups had waged a fierce campaign to convince the American people that only world organization could prevent another holocaust. The coming of World War II had strengthened their arguments and had helped convince most Americans of the necessity for a United Nations.

This study deals with the career and thought of James Thomson Shotwell, one of the leading protagonists of internationalism and collective security in the United States. Like many contemporary activist-intellectuals, Shotwell rejected the traditional role of professional scholars. He had a strong commitment to teaching and academic scholarship, but he also became deeply involved in popular movements and with the politics of persuasion. Until 1917, he largely ignored public issues and concentrated on teaching medieval and modern European history at Columbia University. When the United States entered the war, however, he suspended his academic career and helped establish the National Board for Historical Service. Within a few months he found himself working on President Woodrow Wilson's Inquiry, seeking solutions to problems that would affect the destiny of the world and the lives of millions of people. The experience changed his entire outlook and profoundly altered his personal interests. No longer content teaching classes or scrutinizing medieval manuscripts, he turned his attention to the question of war and the possibilities of its elimination. Now he concerned himself with influencing presidents, persuading prime ministers, drawing up drafts of treaties, lobbying in Washington and in Geneva, and convincing the American electorate that something positive could be done to bring an end to international anarchy.

To his activism, Shotwell added a strong sense of optimism. Although he constantly emphasized the need for a "practical" approach to social, economic, and political problems, he was essentially an idealist. He fully believed that through rational thought, commitment, and dedication, man could remake the world in which he lived. Throughout his life this remained his primary assumption and guiding principle. It would be easy to criticize him for his idealistic approach to world affairs, but I have chosen not to do so. Accepting him as he was, I have tried to evaluate his contributions to the American peace movement and to the general debate over the direction of American foreign policy. Finally, I have tried to keep in mind that Shotwell never achieved more than secondary importance as a molder of public opinion or as a State Department adviser. He was one of the leading theorists of collective security in America, but for the most part his influence was marginal. More important were his ideals and his deep commitment to peace. These made his life worth recording and justify this biography.

Acknowledgments

I am indebted to numerous individuals for making this study possible. The debt of gratitude which I owe Professor Merle Curti of the University of Wisconsin is immeasurable. I thank him not only for raising many fundamental questions and offering valuable recommendations, but for his encouragement and inspiration as well. I also wish to thank Mrs. Vivian D. Hewitt of the James Thomson Shotwell Library at the Carnegie Endowment for International Peace in New York City and Mrs. Lorraine Penninger and the reference staff at the Atkins Library of the University of North Carolina at Charlotte for their patience and assistance. The staff members of the Butler Library and the Oral History Research Office at Columbia University, the Manuscript Division of the Library of Congress, the National Archives, the State Historical Society of Wisconsin, the Yale University Library, and the University of Chicago Library all provided valuable help and eased my way through the various collections I had to consult for this study.

Many people were kind enough to share with me their reminiscences of Dr. Shotwell and the internationalist movement. I especially wish to thank Ms. Helen Harvey Shotwell and Mrs. Margaret Summers for freely giving of their time to discuss their father and for opening up previously closed papers. Others who granted me interviews and provided valuable information were Clark Eichelberger, Mrs. Carol Lubin, Joseph E. Johnson, Margaret Olson, Anne Winslow, and Leslie Paffrath. William A. Williams, Robert A. Divine, Llewellyn E. Pfankuchen, and Marvin Zahniser read the manuscript at various stages of preparation and offered many helpful suggestions. Research grants from the University of Wisconsin, the Carnegie Endowment for International Peace, and the University of North Carolina at Charlotte aided me in traveling and preparing the manuscript. For her criticism of the manuscript, for her aid in the proofreading, and for her constant good cheer, my wife, Lila, has my deepest appreciation.

James T. Shotwell and the Rise of Internationalism in America

1
A Pioneer Heritage

Deep within the Catskill Mountains, about halfway between New York and Albany, nestles the village of Woodstock. Started as an arts and crafts colony at the turn of the century, Woodstock had attracted over the years many artists, writers, and musicians. On August 6, 1954, several of the town's leading celebrities, as well as many guests who had traveled up from New York for the occasion, gathered at the home of James T. Shotwell to honor him on his 80th birthday. Shotwell always enjoyed birthday celebrations, and this one particularly delighted him. Norman Cousins, the editor of the *Saturday Review* and a close friend of the family, presided over the affair and read warm statements of tribute from Secretary of State John Foster Dulles, New York Senator Herbert Lehman, Dag Hammarskjöld, Secretary General of the United Nations, former Under Secretary of State Sumner Welles, and David Sarnoff, President of the Radio Corporation of America.

Some of those who wrote spoke of Shotwell's contribution as a scholar and historian. Others dwelt on his efforts on behalf of the peace movement. Still others talked about his dedication to the triumph of intelligence in human affairs. Norman Cousins said simply that he knew of no man in recent American history who had "done as much to insure the ideals of Woodrow Wilson as James T. Shotwell." David Sarnoff put it more generally when he wrote: "Your achievements as a scholar, a teacher, a historian, a humanitarian, mark you as a true benefactor of mankind."[1]

These tributes from such a diverse and prominent group touched Shotwell deeply. He had a sense of achievement, a feeling that he had come a long way from his rather humble beginnings. As a young boy living in a rural Canadian town, he had often thought of someday gaining wide recognition. He had never really sought wealth or personal power; he had been content working behind the scenes, convincing others that the ideas he presented were viable and worth putting into practice. He had not always reached his goals. In fact, he had probably failed more often than he had succeeded. Yet he remained optimistic, convinced that a new age was fast approaching, an age which in his own small way he had helped inaugurate. "We are at the beginning of things," he remarked to those who had come to Woodstock. "We are at the dawn of civilization—a red dawn as yet, but with the promise of a brighter day. . . . We have crossed the great divide. From now on, for all time, mankind will aways have to find its safety by intelligence and not by reverting to ancient saws but to solutions adaptable under different circumstances."[2]

He had indeed come a long way from his boyhood days in Ontario. He had traveled the world, been received by kings, prime ministers, and foreign secretaries, spoken before Congress, and written articles and books which were read by millions. Certainly his name was not a household word, but he had gained respect in many political and academic circles, and many others knew of him as an indefatigable fighter for international causes. He had not received all the recognition he thought he deserved. The decision of the Nobel Peace Prize Committee not to award him the Peace Prize in 1952 had been a great disappointment. Yet when he contemplated his boyhood dreams of

1. "Celebration in Honor of the 80th Birthday of James T. Shotwell, Woodstock, N.Y., August 6, 1954," Box 259, Shotwell Papers, Columbia University. (Shotwell hereafter referred to as J.T.S.)
2. Ibid.

honor and recognition, he realized that he had come closer to fulfilling those hopes than he had seriously believed was possible.

Strathroy, Ontario, where Shotwell was born and raised, closely resembled most rural Canadian and American communities. Founded in 1832 by John Stewart Buchanan, who settled with his family near the Sydenham River, the town developed slowly until 1856 when the Great Western Railway completed its Sarnia branch. After the coming of the railroad, Strathroy began to attract settlers from all parts of Canada. Its population multiplied rapidly; small businesses grew up; and the town became a central grain, wool, and horse market. By 1874, the year of Shotwell's birth, it had entered its "prosperous period." With a population of 4,000, it gained the attention of the entire province. The atlas of 1878 for Middlesex County declared that "very few of the towns of Ontario can boast of such rapid growth as Strathroy. A few years ago a dense forest covered the ground where now tasteful private dwellings, the many substantial business blocks and the workshops and factories of this progressive town have sprung up as if by magic."[3]

Looking back across the years, Shotwell remembered little of the growth and development of his native town. His life in Strathroy seemed like centuries gone by. More than anything else, the pioneer tradition stood out in his memory. It was a pleasant town, he recalled, and like much of the United States at that time, "still in touch with America's heroic age, that of the pioneers." This emphasis on his pioneer tradition stemmed not only from the fact that his ancestors had hewed their farms from the Ontario wilderness and had broken virgin soil in Kansas, but also from his belief that it provided the central theme of his own life. He, too, was a pioneer, "first in history and then in world affairs."[4]

3. Quoted in Jane Laughton, "Looking Over Strathroy in 1878," in Phyllis Mitchell, ed., *Strathroy Centennial, 1860–1960* (Marceline, Mo., 1960), p. 113. See also Phyllis Mitchell, "History of Strathroy: A Century of Progress," in ibid., pp. 11–18.
4. J.T.S., *The Autobiography of James T. Shotwell* (Indianapolis, 1961), Preface, p. 15.

His ancestors had come to America around 1665, shortly after the death of Oliver Cromwell and the restoration of Charles II to the throne of England. They settled in Elizabeth Town, New Jersey, along the upper reaches of a muddy little stream. Although he had little interest in genealogy, Shotwell found great pleasure in telling of the misfortunes of his first ancestor in America, Abraham Shotwell, who lost all his land because of his opposition to the "tyrannical and oppressive exactions" enforced by Governor Philip Carteret. It seems that Abraham took an outspoken position in the contentions between the people of Elizabeth Town and the proprietors over the question of quitrents. One day, upon meeting the governor on a bridge which crossed a shallow creek near the center of town, Abraham became embroiled in a heated argument and pitched the colony's leading citizen into the water. In return for the indignity, the governor confiscated all his holdings in New Jersey and forced him into exile.[5]

As a self-professed liberal, Shotwell delighted in the fact that his earliest ancestor had taken such a courageous stand. Other than his interest in Abraham, however, he showed little concern with his family's pedigree. His parents and grandparents provided some additional information about his more immediate family, but it was rather scanty, for they too had little interest in genealogy.[6] What fascinated him most as he listened to their tales, and what remained with him through the years, was not the story of any particular member of the family, but rather the epic of the pioneer as illustrated in their combined history. Early in the nineteenth century his ancestors, who by then had become Quakers, trekked across New York State in search for land. One branch of the family crossed over into Canada and settled in a Quaker community close to Niagara Falls, in Thorold, Ontario. Later they moved to another Quaker settlement in Lobo Township, just west of London, Ontario. Another branch of the

5. J.T.S., "The Reminiscences of James T. Shotwell" (Oral History Research Office, Columbia University, New York, 1964), pp. 2–3; J.T.S., "A Personal Note on the Theme of Canadian-American Relations," *The Canadian Historical Review* 27 (March, 1947): 32–35; Ambrose Shotwell, *Annals of our Colonial Ancestors and their Descendents: Or Our Quaker Forefathers and their Posterity . . .* (Lansing, Michigan, 1896–1897), p. 85.
6. J.T.S., "A Personal Note," p. 36.

family did not turn north at Buffalo, but continued west and settled in Indiana. His family's history, he believed, demonstrated above all else that the prime interest of the pioneers was land and a home, "and that nationalism played little if any part in deciding where that home should be."[7]

His great-grandfather, John Shotwell, found land in Lobo and remained there until after the Civil War when he moved along with his son's family to Garnet, Kansas. Here they all remained except for John Blansfield Shotwell, James' father. Before leaving Lobo he had met Anne Thomson, and as soon as he settled in the United States he asked her to be his wife. Although she had waited anxiously for his proposal and readily consented to marriage, she had heard too many stories about Kansas. She had heard of the pre-Civil War violence and the subsequent troubles with Indians. Nothing, not even the prospect of marriage, could persuade her to settle in that horrid state. A stubborn woman, she soon convinced John to return to Canada. In 1870 they married and settled in a small, comfortable house not far from Strathroy. Two years later Anne gave birth to their first child, William, and on August 6, 1874, James Thomson was born.[8]

About his mother's side of the family James knew very little other than they were of English and Irish descent. His maternal grandfather, after whom he was named, came from the family of Lord Kilvane in Ulster, in North Ireland. He was a sturdy pioneer and a devout Presbyterian. He believed so strongly in the truth of the orthodox Presbyterian creed, in fact, that when his church purchased an organ he left it and drove some six miles farther to have his Sunday worship with the Psalms "sung the way David wanted them sung."[9] As a boy James spent his best holidays at his grandfather's farm, fishing for bass and minnows in the Sydenham during the day and listening to stories of pioneer life by the fireplace at night. Despite his awareness of the hardships and toil which went with the settling of new areas, young James was fascinated with the heroism and romanticism of the age he had just missed. He was never quite able to give

7. Ibid., p. 35.
8. Interview with Helen Harvey Shotwell, New York City, December 20, 1966; J.T.S., "A Personal Note," p. 35; J.T.S., "Reminiscences," pp. 3–4.
9. J.T.S., "Reminiscences," p. 8.

up his boyhood conception of early life in America and Canada. Many years later, recalling an era gone by, he wrote: "In spite of all the books that have been written about pioneer days, it is impossible for us fully to appreciate the exploits of the heroic age of North American pioneering. It was only the sturdiest and strongest who could survive the rigours of primitive living."[10]

As in many other small towns, the church and the school played a central role in the social life of Strathroy. Despite his Quaker ancestry, John Shotwell joined the Methodist church and regularly attended Sunday service with his wife and their two sons. Once or twice a year, however, John took William and James to the monthly or quarterly meeting at the hamlet of Coldstream, some ten miles away. James later recalled that he was always "keen to go along." The Quakers' complete rejection of religious formalism impressed him, as did the fact that the "inner light" and the "still small voice" were all that were needed for "this religion without ceremony or creed."[11]

It is small wonder that the lack of formalism and ceremonial cults attached to Quakerism should have so impressed him. His own home life was extremely puritanical. Grace began every meal, and scripture reading and prayer followed breakfast and dinner. Sunday was not a day to be enjoyed beyond the reading of the Bible and *Pilgrim's Progress.* There were no Sunday papers, no games, "nothing but meditation on the world to come and talking among the farmers about their yearly crops."[12]

While life in Strathroy had its limitations, Shotwell never viewed it as superficial or frivolous. The scene was circumscribed and remote from the bustling activity of the great commercial centers, "but the doors were open to the great essentials of human experience." His father was a school teacher by profession and taught him to read at an early age. For this James was forever grateful. The relative isolation of nineteenth-century life in western Ontario, he soon discovered, had its compensations, not the least of these being that time moved slowly and there was leisure to read such masterpieces as the King

10. J.T.S., "A Personal Note," p.34. See also Shotwell's Centennial Address in the *Age Dispatch* (Strathroy, Ontario), July 7, 1960.
11. J.T.S., *Autobiography,* pp. 21–22; J.T.S., "Reminiscences," p. 6.
12. Ibid.

James version of the Bible, Shakespeare, Milton, and a "galaxy of classic English poets." Shotwell frequently took home from the town's lending library bound volumes of *Century, Scribner's,* and *Harper's* magazines. He also made good use of the libraries in the homes of Strathroy's well-to-do. Discovering the pleasures of reading at an early age, he rejected the idea that his boyhood life was trivial or overly restrictive.[13]

In his autobiographical accounts Shotwell mentioned his parents only briefly, but his recollections were vivid. Whenever he did talk about his father, he portrayed him as a quiet, gentle man, in sharp contrast to the rugged pioneers who were the objects of his hero worship. He probably had mixed feelings about his father's profession. As a country school teacher, his father gave the family a distinct place in the community, yet for a young boy growing up in an essentially rural area such a position might not be fully appreciated. The many tributes paid to his father as a teacher had little effect on him and were generally taken for granted. It was not as an adventurous pioneer who had fought the elements in Ontario and Kansas that he remembered his father, but rather as "a saintly character who was not practical in worldly affairs."[14] Later in life he would speak highly of country school teaching, calling it "a profession to which America owes a debt it can never repay," but there is little evidence that as a boy he understood or appreciated the importance of the part played by "the little red schoolhouse . . . in the American-Canadian epic."[15]

He remembered his mother as a small, but hard-working woman. Like most young pioneer daughters she lacked a formal education, but this only made her more determined that her own children would remain in school. She proclaimed, even before her sons had entered elementary school, that they would go to college, a privilege denied even their father.[16]

Anne Shotwell's ambition for her sons was admirable considering the family's economic condition. A teacher's salary of $300 to $400 a year allowed for little in the way of luxury. The Shotwells main-

13. J.T.S., *Autobiography,* pp. 18–20.
14. J.T.S., "Reminiscences," p. 7.
15. J.T.S., *Autobiography,* p. 22.
16. Ibid., 22–23.

tained their own garden, raised chickens, and kept a milk cow, which together with the most frugal household economy allowed them to make ends meet. The family purchased as little as possible from the local stores. Their mother made most of the boys' clothes, and when these wore out, she either cut them into little squares for bed covers or cut them into long strips, sewed end to end, and brought them to the local mill to be woven into rag carpets. The nearby maple trees provided more than half their sugar, and wild berries and apples furnished dessert. Young James spent long hours weeding the onions and hoeing the potatoes and corn on their five-acre garden. On Saturdays during the summer the boys took their surplus berries to the main street of Strathroy and sold them to the townspeople, and almost every morning they sold their surplus milk to the neighbors.[17]

Once through with the chores, James and his older brother found time for sports. During the spring and summer they played baseball, football, and occasionally lacrosse. Much more fun, however, were the winter sports: bobsleigh riding up and down the hills by their house, skating along the long stretches of ice in the river-flats, and the daring adventure of hitching their hand sleds to farmers' horse-drawn sleighs and riding far out into the country hoping to catch an incoming sleigh. Young James also found time for whittling and watercolor painting. Both brothers began writing poetry at an early age and James also became fairly proficient at playing the mouth organ.[18]

Boyhood for James consisted mainly of adventure and wonder. He must have had his share of frustration and anxiety, but nothing so traumatic as to linger with him into manhood. He recalled disagreements with his brother, but mainly his recollections were of friendship and companionship. While he did not see his father as a sturdy pioneer, he did respect him and felt particularly close to him. He fondly remembered his father reading newspaper editorials to the family by the fireside after supper and the lively discussions which followed. His father instilled in him a sense of wonder in learning and a respect for the intellect. From his mother he gained a stubborness

17. J.T.S., "Reminiscences," pp. 7–8. See also working manuscript for J.T.S. *Autobiography,* pp. 26–34, Box 268, J.T.S. Papers.
18. Working manuscript for *Autobiography,* pp. 34–39, Box 268, J.T.S. Papers.

of spirit and strong ambition. Despite his poverty, or perhaps because of it, he became convinced at a very early age that he would break out of the bounds of Strathroy and "make something of himself." His early successes in school both for his prose writing and poetry gave him added confidence. In fact, he later admitted that he was an "insufferable little conceited boy" in school. He had little idea what profession or even what direction he would ultimately take, but he was convinced that his own future was bright and that someday he would bring honor to the Shotwell name.[19]

Following his brother by two years, James went to the local Strathroy elementary schools and then on to the local high school, Collegiate Institute. The curriculum at Collegiate closely followed the English tradition with compulsory Latin, thorough drilling in grammar and literature, and mathematics. The only history course offered was English History, taught by a mathematics teacher who lacked enthusiasm and whose reading assignments were mostly dull and dry. Only the textbook, John Richard Green's *Short History of the English People,* saved the course from complete disaster. Young Shotwell found the book exciting. It was not a dull tale of dates or simple chronicle of kings, but a story of the people themselves, "a prose poem crowded with facts but shining with romance."[20]

Unlike most boys of his generation, James never regretted his classical education. He enjoyed the compulsory Latin in the curriculum and studied it eagerly. His mastery of the language proved a great advantage in college, for it allowed him to pay his way by earning money tutoring for the Latin prose examinations. Mathematics, on the other hand, he found distasteful and avoided it as much as possible. Whereas he did not mind the discipline involved in memorizing his Latin lessons, he found mathematics "a prosy world, where the imagination was held in check by rigid laws."[21]

Although he worked fairly hard at his studies at Collegiate, James found time to participate in the debates of the Literary Society where

19. J.T.S., "Reminiscences," p. 14; J.T.S. to Maurice Sherman, January 30, 1946, Box 237, J.T.S. Papers; Interview with Helen Harvey Shotwell and Mrs. Margaret Summers, Poughkeepsie, New York, July 26, 1971.
20. J.T.S., *Autobiography,* pp. 28–30; J.T.S., "A Personal Note," p. 37.
21. *Age Dispatch* (Strathroy), July 7, 1960.

he got his first taste of public speaking. He also played soccer and lawn tennis after school. The Shotwells had set up one of the few tennis courts in Strathroy and frequently his school friends would come to play. One of these was Margaret Harvey, the daughter of one of the leading physicians in western Ontario. Margaret was nine months older than James and lived in Strathroy only during the school year. Her father lived and practiced medicine in Wyoming, Ontario, a small town between Strathroy and Sarnia. Because of the school's fine reputation, her father sent her to live with an aunt in Strathroy and attend Collegiate Institute. Margaret was a pretty girl, slim and graceful, with beautiful large eyes and rosy cheeks. She was an excellent horsewoman, and Shotwell's earliest and most vivid recollections of her were on horseback riding through the open fields around Strathroy. They became good friends at Collegiate, for James was attracted not only to her beauty, but also to her quick mind, her sense of humor, and her strong will. Their friendship continued at the University of Toronto, which they both attended and where they first began to talk of marriage.[22]

While he attended Collegiate, Shotwell's fondness for poetry grew and developed. Wordsworth remained his favorite poet, but he began reading and memorizing more of Shelley and Keats. Both he and his brother wrote verse almost from the time they could put words on paper. Many of their poems appeared in the local Strathroy and Toronto newspapers, and both boys won several elementary and high school prizes. As Shotwell later recalled, he was writing "rather generally to young ladies at that time, but really to no particular young lady." He wrote to "the world in general," and filled his poems with "starlight and such, and also romantic things."[23]

Few doubted that the Shotwell boys would go to the University of Toronto. Despite the scarcity of money in the Shotwell household,

22. J.T.S., *Autobiography,* pp. 24, 29–30; J.T.S., "Through the Years," *Poems* (New York, 1953), pp. 37–38; Interview with Helen Harvey Shotwell and Mrs. Margaret Summers, Poughkeepsie, New York, May 27, 1971.
23. J.T.S., *Autobiography,* pp. 23–24; J.T.S., "Reminiscences," pp. 12–13. Shotwell continued to write poetry throughout his life. As one of his secretaries recalled, he wrote poems and jingles for almost every occasion, including birthdays, anniversaries, and holidays. (Interview with Mrs. Isadore Lubin, New York City, December 26, 1966).

their mother firmly rejected the idea of putting the boys to work. Although he was in the graduating class of 1893 from Collegiate Institute, James held back a year to earn enough money for his freshman year at college. He tutored, did odd jobs, and borrowed some money from his brother William, who had begun teaching school. In September, 1894, he enrolled in the Honour Course in the Department of Modern Languages and took a room with his brother, who had enrolled in the same course the year before. University life proved all that he hoped for. "Happily the spell continued," he later wrote. "Life at college was all that I had dreamed of and more."[24]

While life at the University of Toronto may have been exciting and enjoyable, it also had its moments of embarrassment. During his freshman year Shotwell was required to take trigonometry. His dislike for mathematics continued, however, and he rarely did the work. One morning the instructor surprised him by asking to borrow his textbook to put a theorem on the blackboard. Having given up with the subject entirely, Shotwell had not even bothered to cut open the leaves of the book. Finding most of the pages in that untouched condition, the instructor waited a moment as his young student blushed deeply and then loudly asked, "Don't you find it hard to study this way?" It was an incident Shotwell never forgot.[25]

His overall record at college was respectable, but not brilliant. In his freshman year he managed to pass both mathematics and biology, but ranked only eleventh out of the twelve students receiving First Class Honours in the Department of Modern Languages.[26] He did fairly well in English, but did not prove himself outstanding in either French, Italian, or German. Dropping mathematics and science in his sophomore year and adding Latin and history did not improve his standing. In fact, his rank in the department fell. He continued to receive First Class Honours in English, but dropped to Second Class

24. J.T.S., *Autobiography,* p. 31.
25. *Age Dispatch* (Strathroy), July 7, 1960.
26. The University of Toronto listed two types of courses—*honours* (used in computing a student's rank within his major department) and *pass courses* (where a mark rather than a rank was given). First Class Honours meant grades of 75% or better; Second Class Honours meant grades of 66% to 74.9%; Third Class Honours meant grades of 50% to 65%.

Honours in German and French and to Third Class Honours in Italian. His grades improved somewhat in his junior year and in June, 1898, he graduated first out of the seven students receiving Second Class Honours.[27]

Although Shotwell took some interest in university politics, his studies and tutoring jobs left him little time to become very active. In his freshman year, however, he did participate in a strike against the university administration and refused along with many other students to attend classes. The strike took place over the issue of faculty appointments and dismissals. The Chancellor had appointed his son-in-law, a clergyman, as a professor of history although he had no historical training. When one of the professors publicly protested the appointment, he lost his job. William Mackenzie King, later Prime Minister of Canada, led the student strike and although they did not win any major concessions, they did force the appointment of a Royal Commission of Investigation and had a chance to make their views known.[28]

Shotwell's social life at Toronto centered around the University Literary Society. He had come to enjoy public speaking at Collegiate Institute and had improved tremendously when he got to the University. While he did not cut a particularly impressive image while speaking—he measured only five feet, seven inches in height, had a very boyish face, a somewhat stocky frame, and tended to slouch—his bright blue eyes, which he used convincingly to convey his mood, and his deep resonant voice made him a very effective speaker. He took debating seriously and practiced various techniques whenever he had free time. In his junior year he led the battle against the incoming of the Greek letter societies, viewing them "both as an American intrusion and as snobs breaking up the student body from its democratic base." Other than his participation in the Literary Society, he found little time for extracurricular school activities and had neither the time nor the money for "riotous living of any sort."[29]

The problem of choosing a career did not seem to trouble him

27. Mrs. Mary Chipman, Statistician of the University of Toronto, to author, December 28, 1966.
28. J.T.S., "Reminiscences," pp. 21–22.
29. Ibid., p. 22.

greatly, nor did his decision result from any deep soul-searching or grave contemplative thought. Although desiring to "make something of himself," he entered the University of Toronto intending to follow his father and brother into a public school teaching career. Sometime in his senior year, however, this decision, so casually made, no longer seemed adequate. He could not see himself teaching French and German to high school students "who had no interest in them," nor did the alternative of teaching literature and correcting English compositions for the rest of his life seem any more satisfactory. Not entirely satisfied with his grades in modern languages, he decided to switch to history and apply to graduate school.[30]

To his great surprise no Canadian university offered a graduate degree in history. He was even more surprised when he began sending for applications to schools in the United States and found that most American universities required the submission of an original research paper as part of their admissions policy. Having never written such a paper before, he had no idea how to begin. The history courses he had taken at the University of Toronto were very thin in content and provided no training in historical research or writing. Professors in the Classical Department had taught the Greek and Roman history courses, and the one course in general European history had been very disappointing.[31]

Shotwell not only felt extremely handicapped, but could not even come up with a suitable topic. Then in the fall of 1897, Professor Morse Stephens of Cornell University gave a series of lectures in which he seriously questioned the accuracy of Thomas Carlyle's *French Revolution.* Up to this time Shotwell had greatly admired Carlyle and had viewed his work on the French Revolution as one of the "epoch-making books" in his life. Stephens' lectures aroused his curiosity and he decided to pursue the subject further. He spent the rest of the semester, including his Christmas vacation, doing research and produced a seventy-five page paper based primarily on the minutes of the Committees of the Convention during the Reign of Terror. James Harvey Robinson, then teaching European history at Co-

30. J.T.S., *Autobiography,* p. 38.
31. J.T.S., "A Personal Note," pp. 39–40.

lumbia, read the paper when it arrived with Shotwell's application and urged his admission. The Department of History, no doubt acting on Robinson's recommendation, awarded him a scholarship covering remission of fees. He happily accepted.[32]

His graduation from the University of Toronto caused a good deal of joy and excitment in the Shotwell household. It fulfilled a dream shared by both his parents. They viewed a university degree as "something like a patent of nobility." His own feelings about college were revealed several years later when he addressed a Phi Beta Kappa group at Columbia. He remembered the time spent as an undergraduate as "idyllic years . . . filled with companionship, a little work, a great deal of hope; and the certainty of life's realities just beyond." College life for him was "an interval of poetry in the prose of life."[33]

Although he might have remembered his college days as "idyllic," as an undergraduate he constantly had to think of the mundane. Throughout his four years at the University of Toronto he worked just to keep himself in school. During the academic year he tutored in Latin and during the summers he took any job he could get. One summer he worked for a fire insurance company and another he tutored the sons of several lumber company executives in Muskoka, Ontario.[34]

In the spring of his senior year, James Brebner, the registrar of the University and the unofficial supervisor of the tutoring program, asked Shotwell to drop his other students and concentrate on the son of William Mackenzie, president of the Canadian Northern Railway and owner of several utility companies in both Canada and Latin America. Shotwell tutored Alec Mackenzie throughout the rest of the semester and the two of them became very close friends. As the semester came to an end, Alec, still unsure of his Latin prose, asked him to accompany his family to their summer home in Muskoka in order to continue the lessons. Needing the money to pay several debts

32. J.T.S., "The Achievements and Possibilities of History," *Indiana Magazine of History* 9 (June, 1913): 67; J.T.S., *Autobiography,* pp. 38–40.
33. J.T.S., "The Student and the Citizen, Phi Beta Kappa Address at Columbia University, March 16, 1922," *International Conciliation* 175 (June, 1922): 215.
34. J.T.S., "Reminiscences," p. 20.

he had gathered while attending college and with the prospect of earning it in a fairly enjoyable way, Shotwell accepted.

The summer proved even more pleasant than he had anticipated. His fondness for Alec grew as did his respect for the elder Mackenzie. The three of them spent many evenings together discussing business propositions, Shotwell's future career, and a wide range of academic subjects. One evening Mackenzie asked him if he would be willing to forego graduate school and take an executive position with his utility company in Sao Paulo, Brazil. It was an excellent opportunity and demanded serious consideration. Shotwell finally came to the conclusion, however, that he had very little aptitude for the business world and would probably make a poor executive. He carefully explained his decision to Mackenzie, who accepted it with understanding and even loaned him two hundred dollars to make ends meet in New York.[35]

At the end of the summer Shotwell returned to Strathroy to spend a few short weeks with his parents. He carefully packed his belongings and made plans for his first year of graduate study. As he made his way around the town saying goodbye to friends and neighbors, he became saddened by the receding signs of pioneer life. Farms, no longer covering the countryside helter-skelter, were now meticulously blocked out in square or oblong form. The orchards, gardens, and fields surrounding the town were also assiduously planned and set primly side by side for miles on end. The layout had become too clearly symmetrical with all farms alike. Progress had "made prose instead of poetry of the countryside."[36] A much beloved world was quietly coming to an end, but he had little time to contemplate its demise. A new life awaited him in New York and he was eager to meet it.

35. Ibid., p. 19; J.T.S., *Autobiography,* pp. 32–37.
36. J.T.S., *Autobiography,* p. 16.

2
The New Historian

New York City teemed with excitement, romance, and adventure, or so it seemed to the young Canadian who stepped off the railroad train on October 1, 1898 and made his way to the Grand Central Hotel on Forty-second Street. His arrival in the city seemed like a dramatic step out of the old world and into the new modern age. In a geographical and cultural sense Shotwell was much less an alien than those immigrants who had crossed the Atlantic from Eastern and Southern Europe. Yet the shift from Strathroy and Toronto to New York City was in many ways a journey between two worlds—from the relative security and tranquility of home and school to the bustling, bawling urban America of the late 1890s.

New York was indeed an exciting city. Immigrants poured in at a fantastic rate making it one of the largest and most cosmopolitan cities in the world. The very year of Shotwell's arrival the four boroughs of Brooklyn, Queens, Richmond, and the Bronx joined Manhattan to form Greater New York. The city, of course, had its problems. The slums contained as many as six hundred people living on an acre. The filthy streets of sections like Hell's Kitchen were edged with grimy-windowed stores and endless rows of five and six-story "walk-ups." But there was also the skyline, with its tall slender shafts rising out of the sea to pierce the sky on the southern tip of the island. One could also walk in envy along magnificent "millionaires' row" on Fifth Avenue between 50th and 80th Streets where each mansion seemed more enormous, expensive, and lavish than the next.[1]

Culturally, as well as physically, New York seemed worlds apart from Strathroy and Toronto. In 1898 New Yorkers fondly talked about the new free Public Library which the city fathers promised to build at 42nd and 5th. Music in the city was superb. Emil Paur, who had been with the Boston Symphony, had just started to direct the Philharmonic Orchestra and the expected rivalry between the Philharmonic and the Symphony Society promised exciting results. Maurice Grau sought out the world's most famous singers and brought them to the city, making the Metropolitan one of the centers for opera in the world. The Metropolitan Museum of Art was also thriving and rounded out New York's cultural attractions.[2]

Not only the city, but Columbia University itself had undergone great change and development during the last decade of the nineteenth century. It was during these years that the real transition from the College of Frederick Barnard's administration to the University of Seth Low's regime took place. The year before Shotwell arrived the university moved into its new buildings on West 116th Street. As Shotwell remembered it, Columbia "stood on Morningside Heights in almost solitary splendor." Besides the few building that the school had erected and one or two private dwellings, the hilltop was bare except for several "huts . . . put together by clapboards and tin cans in which there were families living with goats feeding around outside."[3]

The Faculty of Political Science, particularly, experienced considerable growth and expansion under the leadership of such men as John W. Burgess, Samuel B. Ruggles, Richmond Mayo-Smith,

1. Margaret Clapp, "The Social and Cultural Scene," in Allan Nevins and John A. Krout, eds., *The Greater City of New York, 1898–1948* (New York, 1948), pp. 187–96.
2. Ibid., pp. 205–6.
3. J.T.S., "Reminiscences," p. 28.

Munroe Smith, and Clifford Rush Bateman. The various departments within the Faculty not only doubled and tripled in size, but acquired some of the most noted men in their respective fields. In 1885, Edwin R. A. Seligman became the second member of the Department of Economics headed by Richmond Mayo-Smith. Within the next ten years he was joined by Franklin H. Giddings, who accepted a newly created professorship in sociology, and John Bates Clark, one of the foremost economic theorists of the time. In 1891, John Bassett Moore joined John W. Burgess, Munroe Smith, and Frank Johnson Goodnow to make the Department of Public Law and Jurisprudence one of the finest in the country. By the late 1890s, the Department of Anthropology could boast of a faculty consisting of Franz Boas, Livingston Farrand, and William Z. Ripley, and the Department of History, which had not formally come into existence until 1896, could offer courses by such eminent scholars as William Archibald Dunning, John W. Burgess, Herbert L. Osgood, James Harvey Robinson, William Milligan Sloane, and William R. Shepherd.[4]

With only slightly less than the two hundred dollars he had borrowed from Mackenzie, Shotwell's first major problem was finding a place to live. The Grand Central Hotel where he spent his first night in New York offered rooms at reasonable rates, but for someone hoping to stretch two hundred dollars over a seven- or eight-month period they seemed exorbitant. Taking the elevated railway from 42nd Street to the Harlem station at 110th Street, and then walking up the long hill of Morningside Drive, Shotwell made his way to the Bursar's Office of Columbia University. After making several inquiries, he found an unheated room on 124th Street in Harlem which he rented for $1.35 a week. Although often teased about his cramped and humble student quarters, he rationalized that it had the great advantage of forcing him to live in the heated library of the University which

4. Ralph Gordon Hoxie, et al., *A History of the Faculty of Political Science: Columbia University* (New York, 1955) contains several articles on each of the departments within the Faculty: see Joseph Dorfman, "The Department of Economics," pp. 161–84; Sally Falk Moore, "The Department of Anthropology," pp. 147–53; John D. Millet, "The Department of Public Law and Government," pp. 256–59; and Richard Hofstadter, "The Department of History," pp. 207–29.

remained open from 8:30 in the morning until 11:00 at night. The choice between returning to his freezing little room or sticking to his work in the library was not a difficult one to make, and he found himself reading more in that one year than in any other of his life.[5]

Having experienced frugal living as a young boy, Shotwell had little trouble during the next seven months and even had enough money left for a railroad ticket back to Toronto at Easter. Columbia agreed to give him full credit for the second semester and a fellowship for the following year. Once back in Canada he obtained a substitute position at the Harboard Street Collegiate Institute in Toronto teaching modern languages for the rest of the school year. He wrote to Mackenzie and offered to tutor Alec in the evenings so that he could pay back most of the loan. Mackenzie not only agreed, but invited Shotwell to live with them in Toronto. The Mackenzies saw in Shotwell's arrival a way out of a difficult family problem. They had decided to vacation that summer in Europe and everyone wanted Alec to go along. Alec, however, had fallen behind in his studies and unless he could pass the supplemental Latin examination in September he would not be able to continue with his class. Mr. Mackenzie asked Shotwell to go with them to Europe, both to watch over his younger son, Joe, and to continue working with Alec. Without any hesitation Shotwell accepted.[6]

He traveled through Europe with the Mackenzies during the first half of the summer and during August lived in Paris with Alec in a quiet boarding house studying Latin prose. Not only did his friendship with Alec revive, but he also renewed his friendship with Margaret Harvey, who having graduated from the University of Toronto had gone to Europe to study painting and to take several post-graduate courses in Modern Languages. The young couple spent as much of their free time together as possible, and although Margaret remained in Europe after Shotwell left, she eventually took a teaching job in Paterson, New Jersey. In the summer of 1902 they both returned to Canada and in August had a small, quiet wedding in Wyo-

5. J.T.S., "Reminiscences," p. 20; J.T.S., "A Personal Note," pp. 40–41; Harry Elmer Barnes to author, February 14, 1967.
6. J.T.S., *Autobiography*, p. 34.

ming, Ontario. By September they had returned to New York City and rented a small, but comfortable, apartment near Columbia University.[7]

As a graduate student Shotwell took many courses and studied with some of the most brilliant academic minds in the country. He studied Comparative Constitutional Law under Dean Burgess, American Diplomatic History under John Bassett Moore, Political Theory under William A. Dunning, Economic Theory under John Bates Clark, Napoleonic History under William Milligan Sloane, General Economics under Richmond Mayo-Smith, Economic History under R. A. Seligman, and Roman Law under Munroe Smith. No one at Columbia, however, impressed or influenced him more than James Harvey Robinson, Professor of Medieval and Modern European History.[8]

Robinson had come to Columbia just three years before Shotwell. Prior to his appointment he had taught at the University of Pennsylvania, where he had achieved a reputation for excellence in historical scholarship. Although he was soon expounding the tenets of his "New History," Robinson, during his early career, took a great interest in source material and in fulfilling completely Leopold von Ranke's prescription to tell "precisely what happened." In his *Introduction to the History of Western Europe,* first published in 1902, he maintained that the major aim of the historian was "not to prove that a particular way of doing a thing is right or wrong," but "to show as well as he can how a certain system came to be introduced, what was thought of it, how it worked and how another plan gradually supplanted it."[9] Many of his students remembered his strict discipline in class more clearly than his broad interpretations of history. Although he offered a wide range of courses, including lectures on the Middle Ages and the Renaissance, the Reformation, and the French Revolution, his mastery of the relevant source material always seemed astonishing.

7. *Ibid.,* pp. 34–37; Interview with Helen Harvey Shotwell and Mrs. Margaret Summers, May 27, 1971; *Age Dispatch* (Strathroy), July 15, 1965.
8. J.T.S., "Casual Notes of Imperfect Memories of the Faculty of Political Science," June 27, 1930, pp. 1–10, Special Collections, Columbia University Library.
9. Hofstadter, "Department of History," in Hoxie, et al., *History of the Faculty of Political Science,* pp. 221–22; James Harvey Robinson, *An Introduction to the History of Western Europe* (Boston, 1902), p. 3.

Alexander Flick, one of Robinson's better students, recalled that "as part of his work, he was constantly quoting the sources and urging students to read more widely in them."[10]

Shotwell, who attended both his seminars and lectures, was particularly impressed with Robinson's ability to make a situation live again from an interpretation of the sources. Robinson never permitted any fumbling in either translation or interpretation, and always urged his students to find out not merely the literal meaning of the words, but what the text had actually meant to the writer in his own time and place.[11] In 1926 Shotwell wrote to Harry Elmer Barnes, who had attended Columbia during the First World War, about the tight discipline maintained in Robinson's seminars:

> I recall the classroom of more than thirty years ago when the Seminar of Mediaeval History met under his direction. Whether it was the structure of the Mediaeval Church or the growth of the monarchy of France in the Thirteenth Century, the subject was never permitted the easy path of a mere restatement of the narrative of manuals or non-contemporary documents. One had always the sense of working directly with the sources themselves. The closest application of the historical discipline controlled the imagination, while stimulating it by this contact with the genuine records of events or institutions.[12]

Shotwell's relations with Robinson extended beyond the classroom. Despite their difference in age, they became quite close friends and spent many hours together. He later recalled that he was "completely carried away" by Robinson's generosity of spirit and his highly critical mind.[13] Shotwell, for his part, earned Robinson's respect by his academic standing and intellectual ability. In fact, he impressed most of those at Columbia. Guy Stanton Ford, who entered the University

10. Quoted in Harry Elmer Barnes, "James Harvey Robinson," in Howard W. Odum, ed., *American Masters of Social Science: An Approach to the Study of the Social Sciences Through a Neglected Field of Biography* (New York, 1927), p. 383.
11. J.T.S., "Casual Notes of Imperfect Memories," p. 3.
12. Quoted in Barnes, "James Harvey Robinson," pp. 348–49.
13. J.T.S., "Reminiscences," p. 54.

shortly after him, recalled that he was one of the outstanding students on campus, one of "the white hopes of that time."[14]

At the end of his second year, Robinson urged him to take his Ph.D. examination. Having had only a few undergraduate courses in history, and having taken mostly research courses and seminars at Columbia, he felt extremely unprepared. His ignorance of American history, he later admitted, was "colossal." But somehow he managed to get by and was given a teaching position at Barnard even though he had not yet received his degree. This special appointment of "assistant" was the first awarded by the Department of History.[15]

Besides preparing lectures for his World History course, Shotwell spent most of his time doing research on the Middle Ages. His first published work appeared as the introduction to the volume on the Middle Ages in Henry Smith Williams' *The Historians' History of the World,* which he also helped to edit. The short essay attempted to appraise the development of the medieval mind and to distinguish the major influences on medieval man. He maintained that a close examination of the documents revealed that medieval society was quite different from the picture painted in most historical accounts and that the idea of humanity being in "a comatose condition for a thousand years, to wake up one fine day and discover itself again in a Renaissance" was totally false.[16]

Like so many other historians of the Middle Ages, Shotwell's attention soon centered on the Church. His research convinced him that the central doctrine of the medieval church had been the Eucharist, and so he decided to make a study of its early history for his Ph.D. dissertation. Because Robinson had urged his seminar students to concern themselves with the evolution of institutions and the commonplace, rather than with the dramatic and the spectacular, Shotwell decided to narrow his topic down to the growth and development

14. Guy Stanton Ford, "The Reminiscences of Guy Stanton Ford" (Oral History Research Office, Columbia University, 1956), p. 193.
15. J.T.S., *Autobiography,* p. 46; Hofstadter, "Department of History," pp. 229–30.
16. J.T.S., "A Survey of the History of the Middle Ages," in William Henry Smith, ed., *The Historians' History of the World* (New York and London, 1904), 7: xvii, xx.

of the Eucharistic ceremony and its influence on the political, economic, and social life of the early Christians. He carefully avoided theological speculation. His major aim was to "explain the rise of an institution which has had an influence upon the history of Europe hardly less vast than that of those greatest products of the antique world, Greek art or Roman law." The sacrament of the Lord's supper, he believed, had not only determined the constitution of the Christian Church, but had for over a thousand years deeply affected the art, literature, philosophy, economics, and politics of western civilization.[17]

His dissertation was of particular interest not so much for its contribution to church history, but because it contained the early seeds of what James Harvey Robinson later called the "New History." Although Robinson eventually gained a reputation as one of the leading critics of the Rankian school of scientific history, the New History, in its early stages, grew directly out of the older school.[18] While he taught at Columbia, Robinson never rejected the historical method of the nineteenth-century historians. He firmly held to the idea that the historian had a responsibility to be as objective and detached as possible. He also felt that the historian should avoid making judgments about the subjects of his study and should take particular care to avoid making moral judgments. As was noted by many of his students, he put a great deal of emphasis on historical preparation and the need to develop a working familiarity with the primary sources in the field.

Where he did depart from the nineteenth-century historians was over the consequences of their rigid form and over their conception of the nature and scope of history. He believed that they had placed too much emphasis on past politics and diplomatic history and not enough on the history of the common man—his customs, thought, environment, and basic interests. Their failure to deal with economic, social, and intellectual problems had made their historical writing dull and sterile. The main task of the historian, he argued, was to explain

17. J.T.S., *A Study of the History of the Eucharist* (London, 1905), p. 1.
18. John Higham with Leonard Krieger and Felix Gilbert, *History* (Englewood Cliffs, N.J., 1965), pp. 92–116, argues that the New History not only contained many of the elements of the older scientific approach, but also suffered from some of the same weaknesses in methodology.

how civilization had developed into its present state, for an understanding of the evolution of contemporary society would enable mankind to better deal with its everyday problems. History should be used as a tool for progress and reform, not as a tool for conservatism. Finally, he maintained that history could achieve these goals only by divesting itself of the notion that it was a completely separate discipline which had little to do with other social sciences. The historian could only understand the past and its relation to the present by using the tools of the economist, the anthropologist, the archaeologist, as well as those of any other relevant discipline. He denounced the individualistic aspirations of past historians as having led to a very narrow conception of history and the task of the historian. Instead he called for cooperation between overlapping disciplines as the only means for bringing about progress in the field of knowledge.[19]

The concepts incorporated into the New History were neither original with Robinson nor held by him alone. The writings of Karl Lamprecht, Germany's leading cultural historian, certainly influenced him and helped him to formulate his attack on Ranke's overemphasis on national political history. He also read many of the other leading European historians, such as Ernst Bernheim, Charles Langlois, and Charles Seignobos, and adopted aspects of their work on historiography into his New History idea.[20] Even in America both the titular phrase and the major tenets of the New History were used before Robinson began to popularize them. In 1898, Earl Dow of the University of Michigan touched on aspects of it in his review of the writings of Karl Lamprecht in the *American Historical Review,* and in 1900, Edward Eggleston spoke of the "New History," as he also called it, in an address to the American Historical Association.[21] Yet Robinson must be given credit for effectively advancing and promot-

19. Robinson's most complete statement of the New History approach appears in his *The New History* (New York, 1912). He elaborated on many of its aspects in *The Mind in the Making: The Relation of Intelligence to Social Reform* (New York, 1921) and in *The Humanizing of Knowledge* (New York, 1923).
20. Barnes, "James Harvey Robinson," pp. 360–61; Harvey Wish, *The American Historian: A Social-Intellectual History of the Writing of the American Past* (New York, 1960), p. 147.
21. Higham, *History,* p. iii.

ing the concepts of this new approach to history among educators, textbook writers, and the general reading public.

Shotwell, of course, was deeply impressed with the work of his major professor. He, too, believed that the study of the past could help explain why certain institutions arose and why they declined. He, too, maintained that history could help free the human mind from superstition and taboo. He certainly had this in mind when he wrote his dissertation. "We have explored the secret springs of Christian practices," he declared, "mainly in order that we may place them properly with more assurance when in the religious systems of mankind we find them made imperative for salvation of the individual and essential for the divine prerogatives of the church."[22] By showing that the early Christians did not consider the sacrament of the Lord's Supper necessary for salvation, that it was simply "a meal with religious association" and had served economic and social functions as well as religious, he believed that he had disproved the divine nature and absolute necessity which had been accorded the sacrament by the Church since the time of Paul. He found the Eucharist similar to all other institutions in that it had evolved and developed gradually. It was, therefore, incorrect to view it as a prerequisite for salvation or incapable of further change and interpretation.[23]

While Robinson had a good deal of influence over his young graduate student, Shotwell's conception of history was not derived from him alone. In 1903, after completing his dissertation and receiving his degree, he was quietly informed that unless he spent some time studying in Europe he could not expect to receive a professorship at Columbia.[24] Believing that the experience would do him good, Robinson urged him to go. Shotwell agreed, and the following year along with Margaret and their six-week-old daughter he left for London. He hoped to pay his way in Europe by writing a few articles for the new eleventh edition of the *Encyclopaedia Britannica,* which had been purchased by the publishers of *The Historians' History of the World.* Because of a managerial dispute and because they liked his previous

22. J.T.S., *A Study of the History of the Eucharist,* p. 51.
23. Ibid., pp. 33–50.
24. J.T.S., *Autobiography,* p. 58.

work, the publishers not only allowed him to write a few articles, but offered him the position of managing editor at a salary of several thousand dollars.[25] His new-found wealth allowed him to travel extensively and study in many European universities. He spent several months in Paris, Rome, and Heidelberg attending the lectures of such eminent scholars as Gabriel Monod, Alphonse Aulard, and Charles Seignobos. In addition, he attended Achille Luchaire's course on the Middle Ages, Maurice Prou's course in medieval paleography, and Charles Bémont's course in the sources of English history.[26]

Although he considered his work on the *Britannica* secondary to his education, it proved an extremely satisfying experience. It not only provided him with a substantial salary, but allowed him to meet some of the leading European scholars. Moreover, the editors and publishers of the eleventh edition were determined to make it the authoritative record of modern scholarship—"a real mirror of the best intellectual life of the present," as Shotwell explained to R. A. Seligman.[27] Besides his duties as managing editor, he wrote over one hundred articles for the eleventh edition and helped make it one of the most successful scholarly enterprises of its time.

Upon his return to the United States in 1905, Shotwell accepted the post of Adjunct Professor in the Department of History at Columbia and began his career as teacher and historian in earnest. Whereas Robinson became the major advocate and publicist of the New History idea, urging historians and educators to adopt it, Shotwell became one of its best known practitioners. He demonstrated more clearly than any of the other Columbia historians the importance of interpretation and conceived of his field even more broadly than his mentor. In one of his best essays published during his early career, he denied that history was simply a museum for dead things of the past. It was much more than that. It was "the laboratory where may be studied those phenomenon which Time cannot destroy, those forces which find immortality in change, which express themselves in the life of nations or of society at large." History, he added, included all those

25. Ibid., pp. 60–65.
26. Ibid., pp. 65–66.
27. J.T.S. to R. A. Seligman, May 8, 1905, Seligman Papers, Columbia University.

things that can be distinguished "in the tumultuous currents of that river of oblivion we call Time."[28]

By 1908 Shotwell had become a full professor and had begun to gain a national reputation for his historical writing. His reputation at Columbia, however, had already become well established. On the lecture platform he now cut quite an impressive figure. Although he remained short and somewhat stout, he had ceased slouching and had become impeccable in his dress. Believing that he looked too young, he grew a mustache, which contrasted nicely with his bright, boyish eyes and gave his face a degree of maturity. As a teacher few were more popular or stimulating. Whether it was his course on the "Epochs of History," or on the "Primitive Institutions of Europe," or on "Social History," his lectures were always filled to capacity. His deep resonant voice, his wit, his ability to break down the most complex problems, and his willingness to experiment with new teaching techniques gained him a large following among undergraduates and graduates alike. Harry Elmer Barnes, who later became a bitter critic of his non-academic activities, remembered him as the best teacher he had at Columbia and as a "better master of the various phases of the New History, by far, than Robinson and Beard."[29]

In his historical writing, as in most of his courses, Shotwell focused on three special interests—the persistence of superstition and magic in the thought of man, the influence of science and technology, and the growth of critical thought in western civilization. Like Robinson, he had a deep interest in the persistence of outmoded ideas and attitudes. He was particularly concerned with the persistence of religious superstition and taboo and the way in which these forces continued to play an important role in the thinking and actions of western society. He viewed magic as one of the oldest and most important subjects in the human past. It had not only served as both science and religion in prehistoric times, but had remained "the most important basis of action and of belief for millions of human beings." It so profoundly affected European history that it modified the structure of

28. J.T.S., "Social History and the Industrial Revolution," *Proceedings of the Association of History Teachers of the Middle States and Maryland* 9 (1911): 15–17.
29. Harry Elmer Barnes to author, November 19, 1965.

both church and state, dominated a large part of the philosophy, and influenced the very progress of science.[30]

Despite its long history and great impact, Shotwell believed that superstition was gradually losing its force over the minds of men. Whereas Robinson insisted that men must strive to overcome their anachronistic beliefs if they were to make progress, Shotwell went a step further and argued that the process had already begun and that it was irrevocable. The scientific method, which originated in the physical sciences, had spread to other disciplines and had slowly begun to eat away at the strength of the mysterious. In the competition between science and religion for the minds of men, the former had gained the upper hand. He proclaimed that one of the most important revolutions in history had commenced—a revolution which would emancipate the minds of men and allow them to deal with the major ills of society in an intelligent manner.[31]

Although he warned against making judgments about the desirability of the revolution and simply to accept it as fact, Shotwell himself clearly believed that the change was for the better. Not only would increased secularization free men's minds from the burden of past superstitions and taboos, but it would lead toward the growth of republican government and the rule of law. The growing importance of science and the application of the scientific method to other disciplines could only bring progress, for progress, according to Shotwell, was the product of the critical mind. Only by questioning authority and testing accepted practices could man cope with his changing environment. He urged his generation not to shrink from the conclusions of the new scientific age:

> The hope must lie in following reason, not in thwarting it. To turn back from it is not mysticism; it is superstition. No; we must be prepared to see the higher criticism destroy the historicity of the most sacred texts of the Bible, psychology analyze the phenomena of conversion on the basis of adolescent passion,

30. J.T.S., "The Role of Magic," *The American Journal of Sociology* 15 (May 1910): 781.
31. J.T.S., *The Religious Revolution of To-Day* (Boston and New York, 1913), pp. 1–2.

> anthropology explain the genesis of the very idea of God. And where we *can* understand, it is a moral crime to cherish the un-understood.[32]

Much more than any of the other New Historians, with the possible exception of Charles Beard, Shotwell emphasized science and technology as determining factors in history. As early as 1905 he began offering an undergraduate course in "Social History." Despite its title, the main theme of the course was economic development, especially the impact of the industrial and transportation revolutions on modern society. The course, as he explained it, did not "run along from king's court to king's court, from politics to politics," but attempted "to get at the life of the common people, the work of the world, the history that has never been written yet, the things we do, that we spend the most of our lives at, but which have never been recorded."[33]

He often brought models of steam engines and other inventions to his classes in order to give his students a clearer understanding of just what had occurred to usher in the modern world. He stressed the fact that while repetition had been the keynote for most of man's existence, science had now made change the dominant note in society. He even went so far as to argue that the Industrial Revolution was "the greatest single event in the world's history."[34]

The importance of science and technology remained his major theme throughout his early career at Columbia. Harry Elmer Barnes, who attended his lectures just prior to America's intervention in World War I, recalled that his course on the evolution of European civilization centered largely around the progress of pure and applied science and its impact upon civilization, particularly its effect upon economic life and activities.[35] Unlike Henry Adams, who also recognized the vast importance of the Industrial Revolution but preferred to move back to the world of Mont-Saint-Michel and Chartres, Shotwell found intellectual peace in the dynamic world of the twentieth century. He had a truly cosmic conception of the world and main-

32. Ibid., pp. 51–65, 151.
33. J.T.S., "The Achievements and Possibilities of History," pp. 69–70.
34. J.T.S., *Autobiography,* pp. 69–70; Shotwell, "Social History and the Industrial Revolution," pp. 6, 11–14.
35. Harry Elmer Barnes, *The New History and the Social Studies* (New York, 1925), p. 416.

tained a wonder in the common things of life, which Plato said was the beginning of philosophy. "How many of us in New York," he once asked, "have ever thought . . . of the historic setting of the subway train? And yet that is as significant a fact in our civilization as the newspapers, the theatres or colleges along its route, or the election that takes place once a year in the street above. In that chasm in the rock of Manhattan Island, more electric horse-power flashes along the rails than all the cavalry of Tamurlaine. Go down to the cathedral-like power-house . . . and see its power loosened from the coals of Pennsylvania, a process which links our era with the geologic ages."[36]

Although he showed no real interest in political problems during his early years at Columbia and rarely discussed the questions of war and peace, his study of the Industrial Revolution gave him insight into the vastly changed nature of international conflict. He realized that the course of military events could no longer be determined by the General Staff or the fighting men in the field; it would now be determined in the factories and on the farms of the home front. That nation which could best mobilize its economy for the crisis would have the greatest advantage. Napoleon, he suggested, was not defeated at Waterloo so decisively as he was at Manchester and Birmingham. Though this was a theme he would not fully develop until after World War I, he had come to understand the implications of science and technology on the waging of war long before its outbreak.[37]

It was not Shotwell's economic interpretations alone, however, which brought him the recognition of his profession, but also his work on historiography. Because he believed that the study of the past encouraged critical thinking and analysis, and because he also believed that progress depended upon the development of these qualities, he concluded that the study of past historians might provide a key to understanding the progress of civilization. Using the development of critical thinking as his unifying theme, he examined the historical writing of past civilizations in several articles and one major book.[38]

36. J.T.S., "Social History and the Industrial Revolution," pp. 16–17.
37. Ibid., pp. 15–16.
38. See J.T.S., "History," in *Encyclopaedia Britannica* (11th ed., 1910–1911), 13: 527–33; J.T.S., *An Introduction to the History of History* (*Records of Civilization: Sources and Studies,* New York, 1922).

He concluded that all the written records kept prior to the sixth century were unhistorical in the true sense of the word, for they merely recorded past myth and legend without any attempt to judge the validity of the fact. The first "real" historian according to Shotwell was Hecataeus of Miletus. He was the first to question the traditions of the Greeks and was the first to approach history in a "scientific" manner. Shotwell also classified Herodotus and Thucydides as major historians. They, too, had adopted a critical approach to Greek myth and legend. Thucydides, in fact, he judged the "greatest historian of antiquity" not only because he combined a higher art and a higher science than all past historians, but because he was the first to take an interest in his own contemporary history.[39]

Going back to his earlier theme of the similarity between myth and religion, Shotwell proclaimed it a great calamity for historiography when the new standards of Christianity won the day. The small gains which had been made by the Greeks and the Romans in the development of the critical and scientific approach were entirely lost by the recorders of the growth of the early Christian church. Since the Church had emphasized faith, and Shotwell saw a basic contradiction between faith and history, he argued that the rise of Christianity had no genuine historian to record it. As theology replaced the secularism of the ancients, history lost out. "The authority of revealed religion," he declared, "sanctioned but one scheme of history through the vast and intricate evolution of the antique world. A well-nigh insurmountable obstacle was erected to scientific inquiry, one which has at least taken almost nineteen centuries to surmount."[40]

The greatest crime of Christianity was that it turned away from criticism and placed major importance on the supernatural and the dominance of authority. Christianity "saturated philosophy with dogma and turned speculation from nature to the supernatural." In its rise "the story of nations, of politics, economics, art, war, law—in short of civilization—culminated and ceased."[41] Not until the Age of Enlightenment did the authority of the Church seriously come into question. While Shotwell admitted that the eighteenth-century em-

39. J.T.S., *Introduction to the History of History,* pp. 51–177.
40. Ibid., p. 286.
41. J.T.S., *The Faith of an Historian and Other Essays* (New York, 1964), pp. 86–87.

phasis on natural law did little to advance historical interpretations, he did feel that it disputed the old authority and by so doing began the emancipation of the human intellect.[42]

Shotwell never wrote the second volume of his history of history, which would have continued his study from the early Christian writers to his own age. But on numerous occasions he implied that he considered the New History approach far more fruitful than any that had preceded it. He admitted that each age interpreted history from its own particular perspective and point of view, but did not feel that this meant that "interpretations of history are nothing more than the injection into it of successive prejudices." New interpretations, he claimed, meant progressive clarification. Each new theory which forced itself upon the attention of historians brought up new data for their consideration and so widened the field of investigation. Interpretations should not assume the position of a final judge of conduct or an absolute law, they were merely "the suggestive stimulus for further research."[43]

Despite his relativistic position, Shotwell felt that the New History was not only the most fruitful approach to historical interpretations, but also the most progressive. Its scope being much broader than all past interpretations, it could incorporate into its general framework that which was best in all of them and at the same time avoid their limitations. The emphasis on intellectual and cultural history added a new and vital dimension to historical scholarship. The willingness to break away from the individualistic tendencies of past historians and to accept the findings of other relevant disciplines allowed students of the past to use material not available in traditional historical sources. The emphasis on the present made history a much more vital and relevant discipline. New interpretations and other perspectives might present themselves in the future, but Shotwell believed that for his own age the concepts of the New History would prove the most productive.

Shotwell's contribution to the development of the New History stemmed from his ability to synthesize rather than from his original-

42. Ibid., pp. 78–79.
43. Ibid., p. 87.

ity. Aside from his work in historiography, he did not present anything significantly new or original. But he did go further than most of his colleagues in linking up history with the other social sciences, in placing history against the background of cosmic and natural forces, and in stressing the importance of the interpretation of history as the final and most important stage in historical work. According to Harry Elmer Barnes, who studied with most of the Columbia New Historians, Shotwell surpassed them all in his knowledge of the social sciences, in his capacity to size up the nature and totality of human development, in his understanding of social development, intellectual history, and comparative religion, and in his ability to write history in the grand manner.[44]

Along with Robinson and Beard (with whom he also became very friendly during his early years at Columbia), Shotwell became one of the best known and widely read of the New Historians. By 1917 his scholarly reputation was well established. His presence at Columbia was viewed as such an asset that a minor crisis developed when the Carnegie Endowment for International Peace invited him to become its director of research. The heads of various departments along with the Committee on Instruction of the Faculty of Political Science sent a memorandum to President Nicholas Murray Butler strongly urging him to discourage Shotwell from leaving. The loss of several other members of the faculty had created an element of bitterness, and those remaining did not wish to lose one of the University's most talented teachers and investigators.[45]

The protest flattered Shotwell and he politely turned down the Carnegie offer. He did not remain at Columbia, however, for very long. America's entry into World War I sent him off to Washington where he found an exciting new career and a new purpose in life. The pen he had used so well to promote the concepts of the New History was now turned toward the important task of winning the war and establishing a "lasting peace."

44. Harry Elmer Barnes to author, March 27, 1966.
45. Hofstadter, "Department of History," p. 230.

3
The Historians Mobilize

In the sense in which we have been wont to think of armies there are no armies in this struggle. There are entire nations armed. . . . The whole Nation must be a team in which each man shall play the part for which he is best fitted.

—Woodrow Wilson, May 18, 1917

President Woodrow Wilson's call to make the world "safe for democracy" brought an energetic response from historians throughout the nation. Many college and university scholars honestly desired to contribute to the war effort and began searching for avenues of service. Some were able to take up arms and enlist, but many others were beyond the fighting age. It was clear, however, even before the United States entered the war, that this was to be a battle not only of armed men, but of mobilized intelligence and material resources. The need for total mobilization in Great Britain, France, and Germany demonstrated that this was a new and different type of war. Those with a keen eye could see that behind the men and the guns, behind the great armies and navies, behind the munition storehouses and factories, there would be waged another and equally important battle—the battle for men's opinions and for the conquest of their convictions. As historians, this was the battle they could wage best; this was the part for which they were best fitted.

While President Wilson's call to arms brought American historians out of the libraries and classrooms, it also presented them with a fundamental problem. Many wondered if they would be able to maintain their professional integrity and historical "neutrality," and yet impel men to victory both on the battlefield and on the home front. Some scholars, such as Professors Ferdinand Schevill and James W. Thompson of Chicago, Professor William R. Shepherd of Columbia, and Professor Preserved Smith, then unattached, did not feel that supporting the war was necessarily their responsibility as historians. Refusing to join the wartime effort, they cautioned others to be aware of the consequences.[1]

But their warnings had little effect. A large and significant group of historians believed that they could participate in the war of words without giving up the standards of scholarship they had emphasized on the college campus. Most of them were well aware of the difficulties involved in maintaining this dual position. The example of the German scholars, who had abandoned *en masse* their long cherished standards of "objectivity" when their country went to war, stood as a grim warning of possible things to come. Yet American scholars continued to believe that by restraining their emotional tendencies they could remain true to their academic values while fulfilling their duty and obligation to the nation.[2]

James Thomson Shotwell disliked the idea of leaving Columbia. He had turned down the Carnegie Endowment offer because he enjoyed academic life. He was content. His work in history had brought him status and recognition in his chosen profession. Yet he strongly supported President Wilson and had been greatly inspired by his address

1. C. Hartley Grattan, "The Historians Cut Loose," *American Mercury* 11 (August 1927): 415.
2. William T. Hutchinson, "The American Historian in War Time," *Mississippi Valley Historical Review* 29 (September 1942): 164–68. See also J. F. Jameson, "Historical Scholars in War Time," *American Historical Review* 22 (July 1917): 831–34.

to Congress. He understood,.moreover, the necessity of entering the war. Even before the President had come out for intervention, Shotwell had taken sides with Great Britain and France, and had advocated more direct American aid to the Allies.[3]

He did not, however, support an interventionist policy from the start. One of his students recalled that he displayed almost no interest in world affairs during the first two years of the war. His major interests remained in European and medieval history.[4] In May, 1915, a few days after the sinking of the *Lusitania,* he had even opposed the interventionist arguments of Charles Beard and Franklin H. Giddings at a meeting held by the Faculty of Political Science to determine what stand, if any, it should take on the question of American entry into the war. Not until December, 1916, when the Allies were in deep trouble and their front began weakening, did he come to the conclusion "that the United States for its own sake, not just as an ally for the sake of the others, should enter the war to cast the balance against Germany." Having reached this decision, he became one of the most vocal interventionists on the Columbia campus.[5]

After studying the wartime situation in Europe, he concluded that American historians would have a vital role to play in the war effort. On April 15, 1917, he wrote to his good friend Claude H. Van Tyne of the University of Michigan asking if he would help organize a committee of historians to study wartime problems.[6] By the time he made his inquiry, he had already begun a vigorous campaign to mobilize the Columbia faculty for the war effort. He set up a "department of intelligence" which served as a reference service for inquiries about the war and organized the library to collect and preserve wartime material more efficiently.[7]

Shotwell was not alone in urging some sort of unity in the historical profession. The members of the Mississippi Valley Historical Associa-

3. John Bassett Moore, "Memorandum," June 28, 1917, Box 206, folder IV B, Moore Papers, Library of Congress.
4. Harry Elmer Barnes to author, December 15, 1965.
5. J.T.S., "Reminiscences," pp. 65–67.
6. J.T.S. to Claude H. Van Tyne, April 5, 1917, Box 26, Papers of the National Board for Historical Service, Library of Congress. (Hereafter referred to as NBHS.)
7. J.T.S. to Claude H. Van Tyne, April 15, 1917, Box 26, NBHS.

tion at their April meeting adopted a resolution recommending that "means be taken by the Government of the United States to facilitate the sound historical instruction of the people of the United States to the end that a correct public opinion with full knowledge of the facts that have made for our freedom and democracy in the past may stand stubbornly in our struggle for the maintenance of those principles in the future." Frederic L. Paxson, a prominent member of the History Department at the University of Wisconsin, went so far as to draw up a memorandum outlining the organization and function of a "bureau of historical information." The bureau, as he conceived it, would be under the Committee on Public Information and would aid in the formation of public opinion, advise governmental departments needing historical data, provide accurate information for writers and journalists, and coordinate existing historical agencies.[8] In Washington, J. Franklin Jameson, in his capacity as head of the Carnegie Institution's Department of Historical Research, also set in motion the initial moves to organize the historians of the country for the war effort. He contacted scholars from numerous colleges, emphasizing the important role they had to play in the coming struggle.[9]

The result of all this activity was that in mid-April Shotwell, Jameson, Frederick Jackson Turner, and Waldo Leland, the secretary of the American Historical Association, met in Washington and made the necessary arrangements for a conference of historians to meet in the capital on April 28 and 29.[10] In addition to these four, those present at the first meeting of the National Board for Historical Service, as they eventually decided to call the new agency, included Guy Stanton Ford of the University of Minnesota, Charles D. Hazen of Columbia, Henry E. Bourne of Western Reserve, Charles Hull of Cornell, Andrew McLaughlin of the University of Chicago, and Frederic L. Paxson of the University of Wisconsin. After nearly two days

8. See folder marked "Minutes of the Board," Box 25, NBHS. See also Waldo G. Leland, "The National Board for Historical Service," in Newton D. Mereness, ed., "American Historical Activities During the World War," in *Annual Report of the American Historical Association for the Year 1919,* vol. 1 (Washington, 1923): 162.
9. Frederick J. Turner to Charles Haskins, May 2, 1917, Box 3, NBHS.
10. "Circular letter from J. Franklin Jameson," April 20, 1917, Box 25, NBHS.

of discussion the conference agreed that the new agency should aid the war effort by placing the historical scholarship of the country at the service of the government and by using it for "patriotic and educational ends." The assembled historians also expressed the hope that the new organization would facilitate and promote the intelligent collection and preservation of historical material dealing with the war.[11]

Nowhere in the discussion did the specific topic of maintaining "scientific objectivity" come up. Each participant seemed to take for granted that high standards of scholarship would be maintained by the National Board as a whole. Although they were vague as to what specifically their organization would do, they discussed several possibilities including the publication of historical information for the press, lectures, aid to education through the revision of textbooks and public school curriculums, the compilation of bibliographies and guides to war material, and work for the government both in terms of research for governmental agencies and in the formation of public support for governmental policies.[12]

As a temporary measure, until the election of officers could be held, the conference appointed a committee of nine to serve as an organizing and executive body. Included among the nine were Shotwell, Turner, Leland, Carl Russell Fish of the University of Wisconsin, Charles D. Hazen of Columbia, Charles Hull of Cornell, Victor Clark, a staff member with the Carnegie Institute, Robert Connor, Secretary of the North Carolina Historical Commission, and Gaillard Hunt, Chief of the Division of Manuscripts of the Library of Congress. The committee, in turn, chose Shotwell as its first chairman and Leland as its secretary-treasurer. It also decided that its first order of business was to advise other historians of the National Board's creation. On May 1, Leland sent out a letter to one hundred and fifty historians throughout the country explaining the Board's organization, its purposes, and inquiring if those receiving the letter had any advice or suggestions which they cared to contribute. He emphasized the fact

11. "Minutes," April 28–29, 1917, Box 25, NBHS; Docket, April 28–29, 1917, Box 25, NBHS; "Circular letter #2," Box 25, NBHS.
12. "Minutes," April 28–29, 1917, Box 25, NBHS.

that the Board was a voluntary and unofficial organization of individuals, "spontaneously formed in the hope that through it the store of competence and patriotic good-will possessed by the history men of the country instead of running in part to waste or even lying untouched, may eventually be drawn upon to meet the needs of the public or of the government." The National Board, he added, would not set up any state or local chapters, but would serve as a coordinating body between "voluntary workers in the common cause."[13]

In order to establish a definite program of activities, Shotwell conferred with several government officials. He established contacts with the Council of National Defense, the Advisory Commission, the National Research Council, the Committee on Public Information, and the Departments of State, Navy, and Interior. The consensus of these official sources was that the National Board could most effectively serve the government and the war effort by establishing a close tie with the Committee on Public Information and the Bureau of Education. After several meetings with George Creel, the head of the Committee on Public Information, Shotwell helped set up a Division of Civic and Educational Cooperation, with Guy Stanton Ford as chairman. Ford's agency, which was actually part of the Creel Committee, acted as a liaison between the government and the historians of the country. To further strengthen this tie, Creel appointed Shotwell to his committee as an adviser on historical matters.[14]

The response to the Board's circular letter of May 1 was generally favorable. Most of those replying believed that the American people needed enlightenment regarding the issues involved in the conflict, but few could make any specific suggestions as to the proper course to follow. Carl Becker's response was typical and illustrated the ambiguity of those responding. He declared that he sympathized strongly with the "ideas" of the Board and would be glad "to do anything to help the committee that either occurred to me or that might be pointed out to me."[15]

There were a few, however, who expressed great skepticism about

13. "Circular letter from Waldo G. Leland," May 1, 1917, Box 1, NBHS.
14. Waldo G. Leland to J. Franklin Jameson, June 1, 1917, Box 4, NBHS.
15. Carl Becker to Frederick J. Turner, May 14, 1917, Box 1, NBHS.

the new organization and its possibilities. One of these was E. D. Adams of Stanford University. He felt that the Board was little more than the creation of a group of historians in Washington, "very anxious to do something for their country and plunging, without sufficient consideration in this movement, which may perhaps embarrass more than it will help our national cause." He pointed out that the Board's program as stated in the May 1 letter was very vague. From his own point of view he could see only one legitimate purpose for the new organization. Only if it put itself under the government's direction and assumed the duties of censoring historical writers could it serve the national interest. "In every other respect," he concluded, "it seems to me that your program and queries indicate a desire to 'get into the game' as historians, just to show that historians can be really useful human beings, and that there is nothing much else in your program."[16] While Adams did not represent the majority of historians responding to the Board's intial letter, at least one other agreed that the only legitimate function for a wartime organization of history men was to act as censors. Although much less critical of the National Board than the Stanford professor, E. E. Sperry of Syracuse University wrote to Shotwell that the Board could provide a useful service only if it adopted some of the German techniques of historical propaganda.[17]

The executive committee consistently, at the outset, frowned upon suggestions such as those put forward by Adams and Sperry. It urged historians to maintain their prewar standards and avoid distorting the past in order to explain the war to the American people. On May 3, 1917, Waldo Leland wrote to William G. Standard of the Virginia Historical Society that the purpose of the Board was "not to carry on any propaganda nor to try to direct public opinion in any given direction, but to endeavor to supply the general public with that information of an historical nature which is the essential basis of intelligent opinion upon the various issues that present themselves at this time."[18] Three weeks later, Leland again emphasized, on behalf

16. E. D. Adams to Waldo Leland, May 16, 1917, Box 1, NBHS.
17. E. E. Sperry to J.T.S., May 29, 1917, Box 6, NBHS.
18. Waldo Leland to William G. Standard, May 3, 1917, Box 6, NBHS.

of the executive committee, that the Board's object was not to give public opinion any shape or direction, "but to supply it with a basis of sound information, so that it itself may be intelligent." The horrible example of the German professors furnished a warning and a lesson from which historians in the United States might profit. "It has been our unanimous opinion," he added, "that no anti-German propaganda was necessary, because the Germans have so completely occupied that field themselves."[19]

Shotwell, too, found it necessary to emphasize that the National Board did not intend to succumb to wartime emotions. Although historians had very important work to do for the war effort, the most important thing to consider was what permanent lines of work could be taken up. "We must think in terms of constructive statesmanship," he declared, "rather than the mere question of fighting the war through, although that is before us as a primary object." From the beginning, then, it seems that his main interest was in the making of the eventual peace, rather than in the promotion of the war.[20]

On June 8, 1917, in his capacity as chairman of the National Board for Historical Service, Shotwell formally announced the Board's creation in an article in the *History Teacher's Magazine.* He discussed the purposes for which the organization had been created, emphasizing the collection and preservation of war documents as one of its primary aims. He urged both teachers and students alike to aid more directly in the determination of the historical outlook of the American people by writing articles, pamphlets, and books on topics related to the war. "Upon the whole," he declared, "it should be emphasized that in the opinion of the Board, historians can continue to serve the country best at this time, as in the past, as historians." He concluded by asking his professional colleagues to strive to meet the wartime demands without giving up the standards of their profession: "To serve the time without yielding to it, to boldly confront new facts without losing our historical point of view, will require all our wisdom and all our talent."[21] It

19. Waldo Leland to W. S. Ferguson, May 26, 1917, Box 2, NBHS.
20. J.T.S. to F. C. Ensign, June 4, 1917, Box 2, NBHS.
21. J.T.S., "The National Board for Historical Service," *History Teacher's Magazine* 8 (June 8, 1917): 199–200.

was by no means certain, however, that American historians possessed the "wisdom" and "talent" of which Shotwell spoke.

Because of the Board's limited funds,[22] the executive committee decided against publishing anything itself. Instead it encouraged historians to write articles on their own initiative, while they restricted the Board's work in this area to finding suitable publishers for its members. One of the most important functions that Shotwell performed as chairman was getting space for historical articles in the various educational magazines. He had many contacts with publishing companies and proved very successful in convincing several of them to accept material submitted by Board members. Immediately after the creation of the Board, he began negotiating with Albert E. McKinley, the editor of *History Teacher's Magazine,* and quickly persuaded him to accept material dealing with the war. He also succeeded in getting *Century Magazine* to put aside thirty-two pages in each month's edition for material submitted by the executive committee of the Board.[23]

Besides the *History Teacher's Magazine* and *Century Magazine,* George Creel's Committee on Public Information became the Board's chief means of publication. This association, however, was hardly one to keep the Board's publications judicious and in conformity with the "scientific spirit" of historical scholarship. Creel, a Denver journalist and an original Wilson man, hoped to "sell the war to America" and justify the American cause abroad. He endeavored on the one hand to picture the American cause as just, democratic, and eminently Christian, and on the other to picture the Germans as depraved, bloodthirsty, and cruel. When Shotwell offered the services of the National Board, Creel readily accepted, for he saw in this connection an excellent opportunity to get the nation's leading historians behind his propaganda machine. His decision proved extremely wise, at least from his own point of view, for Guy Stanton Ford's Division of Civic

22. Support for the National Board came almost entirely from the Carnegie Institution of Washington. The Board received an initial grant of $600 in April, 1917 and then beginning in June received $450 monthly. J. Franklin Jameson to Waldo Leland, August 16, 1917, Box 4, NBHS.
23. J.T.S. to Waldo Leland, May 29, 1917, Box 6, NBHS; "History Teacher's Magazine folder," Box 10, NBHS.

and Educational Cooperation issued nearly fifty pamphlets with a total circulation of some seventy-five million copies.[24]

One of the most successful pamphlets produced under the direction of Shotwell and Ford was *The War Message and the Facts Behind It,* written by Professor William Stearns Davis of the University of Minnesota. Davis dissected Wilson's war message to Congress and tried to show historical justification for most of the President's arguments and statements. The clear intent throughout was to demonstrate the peaceful designs of the United States and the brutality and disregard for international law on the part of Germany. In general, the pamphlet met all of Creel's demands and suited his purposes extremely well, but it was by no means a sound or an accurate historical statement such as Shotwell and the Board's executive committee intended to put out. Besides its very biased slant, it violated numerous scholarly rules. Quotations were often incorrect, sentences were changed and shifted to convey meanings other than those intended in the original documents, and points of history and international law were often misstated and incorrect.[25]

Not all historians were as willing as Shotwell to let these errors go by without protest. John H. Latané of Johns Hopkins University became extremely annoyed when he read it. His criticisms were particularly significant because he had orignally supported the creation of the Board. Only a few weeks before the release of *The War Message,* he had written Frederick Jackson Turner expressing the belief that the new organization had a vital role to play in moderating those historians who, under the pressures of the war, seemed to be losing their historical perspective and taking untenable positions. "What we need to do most," he argued, "is to give the American people a clear perception of the grounds on which we have entered this war and our relation to the issues at stake."[26] Both Turner and Waldo Leland

24. George Creel, *How We Advertised America: The First Telling of the Amazing Story of the Committee on Public Information that Carried the Gospel of Americanism to Every Corner of the Globe* (New York, 1920), pp. 113–14.
25. Committee on Public Information, *The War Message and the Facts Behind It* (Washington, 1917).
26. John H. Latané to Frederick J. Turner, June 15, 1917, Box 4, NBHS.

assured the Johns Hopkins professor that the Board had no intention of promoting propaganda of any sort.[27]

Latané was therefore quite upset when he read the analysis of Wilson's war message. He went over the pamphlet carefully, checking quotations and points of international law. He then sent off a letter to the *American Historical Review* denouncing the entire effort as a hack job, carelessly and irresponsibly written. The errors in the quotations cited seemed to annoy him most. "I was under the impression," he declared, "that the methods of Jared Sparks had long ago been repudiated and abandoned by historical scholars, but in the remarkable document before us they are not only applied to Washington but extended to Lincoln whose English has usually been considered good."

Because he greatly respected the honesty and academic ability of many of his colleagues on the National Board, he found it difficult to explain the inaccuracies in *The War Message* pamphlet. The only explanation he could come up with was that these scholars had delegated the editorial work to incompetent associates or subordinates. "As soon as a man finds himself installed in a Washington office," he observed, "he appears to find it difficult not to adopt the pernicious practice of getting other people to do his work and putting it over his name." If these men were prepared to appropriate all the credit for such work, they should "not be permitted to avoid the blame."[28]

In normal times Latané's letter of protest, so clearly argued and so carefully documented, would have been published in the *American Historical Review.* But these were not normal times, and J. F. Jameson, in his capacity as managing editor of the *Review,* refused to print the letter. In responding, he completely dodged the issue by charging Latané with seeking publicity for his own anti-Board sentiments.[29] He failed to see, or at least admit, the truth of many of Latané's observations. Latané was probably correct in his accusation that Shotwell and the other members of the executive committee had become so preoccupied with their work for the Creel Committee and their task of

27. Waldo Leland to John H. Latané, June 26, 1917, Box 4, NBHS.
28. John H. Latané to the Managing Editor of the *American Historical Review,* August 15, 1917, Box 4, NBHS.
29. J. Franklin Jameson to John H. Latané, August 25, 1917, Box 4, NBHS.

selling the war to America that they found little time for checking the accuracy of the pamphlets produced under their direction. Some of the leading Board members, in fact, even began to weaken in their opposition to outright propaganda attempts. When E. E. Sperry suggested to Shotwell that the Board follow the German example and produce "genuine historical propaganda," the chairman replied that the suggestion was "certainly a thoroughly justifiable one" and suggested that Sperry "work up something along that line."[30]

Even Frederick Jackson Turner, one of the first to demand that the Board maintain a high level of scholarship, reversed his position once he became caught up in the work. On June 19, 1917, he wrote that historians should begin "applying history to the statement of those American ideals and aspirations which justify this war, and which alone can make it the war of a united people, a people willing to sacrifice personal and class selfish interests for a lofty purpose and the good of the coming American generations." "No efficiency of a scientific sort," he added, "can prevent us from failing in this task; it is a matter of American ideals. Mr Wilson should not be expected to do this single-handed."[31]

With the blessing of such well known and respected scholars as Shotwell and Turner, the other Board members fell more and more in line with the policies of the Creel Committee. It was only with the help of these historians that the Committee on Public Information was able to publish two of its most successful ventures—the "Red, White, and Blue" series and the "War Information" series. In fact, by lending their names to these publications, the members of the National Board gave the Creel Committee an air of authenticity which it might never have achieved with the help of men less distinguished.

Although only a few historians openly objected to the Board's connection with the Creel Committee, several voiced their opposition to the establishment of committees on the "adjustment" of history teaching in the public schools. These committees planned to survey the content of textbooks generally used in elementary and secondary

30. J.T.S. to E. E. Sperry, June 4, 1917, Box 6, NBHS.
31. Frederick J. Turner to Waldo Leland, June 17, 1917, Box 7, NBHS.

school history courses and to recommend possible ways of making these courses more relevant to the war conditions.[32] Few historians disagreed that the majority of textbooks in use needed revision, but many questioned the idea that emphasizing the war would improve history teaching in the lower grades. The committees on the "adjustment" of history teaching, they argued, would only add to the general impulse among elementary and secondary school teachers to bring the various fields of history under tribute to the rousing interests of the war. They believed that it would be much better if the Board moderated this tendency instead of encouraging it. William S. Ferguson of Harvard complained that all too often he had to sit and listen to the "ancient times exploited by ignorant politicians, clergymen, and journalists." He wished to have no part in urging "half trained teachers and immature pupils" to follow in this tradition.[33] William L. Westermann of the University of Wisconsin fully backed Ferguson's position and even resigned from the Committee on Ancient History in protest. He declared that the Board's efforts to help elementary and secondary school teachers make analogies and draw lessons from the past to stimulate patriotism or to explain the war was a "serious wrong." Such an effort would simply play into the "hands of the pseudo-historians of the ultra modern tendency," and would give "responsible sanction to a thing which the teachers are prone to do too much anyway."[34]

Shotwell, who helped initiate the program of historical revision, became very concerned about these criticisms. He agreed that the Board should take all necessary measures to insure that its members maintained a judicial attitude toward the facts of history, but felt that historians could not avoid their responsibility. They had a vital function to perform in keeping the American people informed. If historians failed to take up the work, the information would either be supplied by "those of a purely journalist cast of mind upon the basis of inadequate preparation and research" or it would not be forthcoming at all "with the result that those who demand light upon questions

32. Carl Russell Fish to Albert E. McKinley, May 17, 1917, Box 5, NBHS.
33. William S. Ferguson to R. V. D. Magoffin, July 17, 1917, Box 5, NBHS. For other criticism see Boxes 5–7.
34. W. L. Westermann to R. V. D. Magoffin, July 10, 1917, Box 5, NBHS.

affecting us will be left in ignorance or forced to accept the prejudicial statements of the various European belligerents." His defense of the Board's efforts at readjusting history stemmed as much from his acceptance of the New History and its emphasis on "presentism" as from his wartime fervor. The Board, he argued, was not distorting history by quickening the student's interest in past events, but reminding him of its lasting influence and thus getting him to see the past in the light of long historical perspectives. He agreed, however, that this should be done with "moderation" and "common sense."[35]

Shotwell spent most of the spring and summer of 1917 in the Washington office of the National Board. The work, especially during the scorching month of July, proved arduous and fatiguing. Lack of sleep and lack of adequate food finally caught up with him and caused a nearly total collapse, the first of several complete physical breakdowns he would suffer during crisis periods. Forced to return home to New York in early August, he was still unable to do any work by the end of the month. Uncertain how long his condition would continue, he decided to resign as chairman of the Board. Explaining the situation to Waldo Leland, who in addition to his own work as secretary-treasurer had taken over Shotwell's tasks as well, he wrote:

> This is the first day I've been able to write letters. Nothing left of the bugs but an apologetic cough and nothing left of me but a memory. I'm almost as strong as I was at the age of say 2½ years. I write this lying on the bed—like R.L.S. writing *Treasure Island.*[36]

Leland, himself, had come to the conclusion that the National Board could not continue along its current lines and recommended its complete reorganization or else its dissolution. He pointed out that the Board had either carried out or was in the process of carrying out most of the initial proposals. Evarts Greene of the University of

35. J.T.S. to W. L. Westermann, July 21, 1917, Box 7, NBHS. For a more detailed description of this controversy, as well as for a more detailed study of the National Board as a whole, see Harold Josephson, "History for Victory: The National Board for Historical Service," *Mid-America* 52 (July 1970): 205–24.
36. J.T.S. to Waldo Leland, August 28, 1917, Box 6, NBHS.

Illinois had taken over the work of the revision of history teaching and the Board decided to leave that area up to him. The prize essay contests, which the Board had initiated in June, had become "largely a matter of routine." The bibliography of war material had been completed and was awaiting publication, while the syllabus of lectures for reading courses on the war had already been turned over to Guy Stanton Ford for publication by the Creel Committee. The only really important project left was the collection and preservation of war materials, but as Leland pointed out, this work could go forward with or without the formal organization of the National Board.[37] Despite these arguments most of the executive committee believed that the Board should continue with only slight modifications. Before resigning, Shotwell appointed a reorganizing committee which chose Evarts Greene as the new chairman and Dana C. Munro as the new vice-chairman. Leland continued as secretary-treasurer. Although Shotwell refused to serve on the reorganized executive committee, he did accept the chairmanship of the newly formed Research Committee.[38]

While Shotwell strongly supported the work of the National Board, he never looked with much favor upon the other super-patriotic groups which organized after America's entry into the war. He had some contact with a fanatically pro-British group known as the History Circle, but quickly disassociated himself from the organization when its intentions became clear.[39] As chairman of the National Board he also kept in touch with the National Security League, whose membership included William Roscoe Thayer and Albert Bushnell Hart of Harvard, Robert McNutt McElroy of Princeton, and E. E. Sperry of Syracuse. His close association with the League, however, did nothing to alter his initial impression. The more closely he followed its activities and the more he heard from its members, the more dubious he became about its value.[40]

If Shotwell had any complaints about the work of the National Board, he never revealed them in any of his public statements or in

37. Waldo Leland to Evarts Greene, September 5, 1917, Box 3, NBHS.
38. Waldo Leland to Evarts Greene, September 14, 1917, Box 3; "Minutes of November 9, 1917," Box 5, NBHS.
39. Grattan, "Historians Cut Loose," p. 27.
40. J.T.S. to Waldo Leland, July 12, 1917, Box 6, NBHS.

his personal correspondence. As late as November, 1918, he urged Leland not to let the Board dissolve, for he believed that it had a vital role to play in the work of reconstruction.[41] Although he realized the danger of the intense anti-German sentiment which had developed in the country, he never viewed the National Board as a direct contributing factor to the wartime hysteria. His failure to see the true effects of the Board's publications stemmed mainly from his conception of the historian's task in wartime and his strong commitment to the tenets of the New History.

Along with other members of the executive committee, he believed that historians had a vital role to play in explaining the war to the American people. He also felt that students of history could render the government an important service by providing historical data. On both counts the National Board seemed to be successful. Shotwell was not blind to the chauvinism of the Board's publications, but he seemed to feel obligated to tolerate it as a wartime necessity. He often used the argument that if the National Board did not take up the task of supplying information to the public, some less responsible and more extreme organization would have to provide it. Despite his frequent statements on the importance of maintaining a "scientific spirit" in historical scholarship, he never made any direct attempt to restrain the jingoism of the Board members, and once even went so far as to encourage it.[42]

Shotwell's complete acceptance of the New History approach also led him to support the work of the Board. He believed, as did the other New Historians, that history should be viewed pragmatically, as a study which could and should contribute directly to the understanding and explanation of current affairs. In other words, he accepted the legitimacy of subordinating the past to the present.[43] He sympathized with those who tried to use the past to explain the war, and while he remained a cautious scholar, refusing to pervert the past in order to promote patriotism, once he had sanctioned the concept of "presentism" in history, he could not easily restrain others less moderate than

41. J.T.S. to Waldo Leland, November 19, 1918, Box 13, NBHS.
42. J.T.S. to E. E. Sperry, June 4, 1917, Box 6, NBHS.
43. Morton White, *Social Thought in America: The Revolt Against Formalism* (Beacon Press ed., Boston, 1957), pp. 48–49.

himself. He may not have signed his name to any of the articles or pamphlets put out by the National Board, and he may have even regretted their publication, but his silence and his acquiescence did little to improve the quality of scholarship of the Board's work.

Shortly after the war ended, Harold Stearns offered another explanation for the attitude and actions of scholars like Shotwell. Noting how many intellectuals had become involved in the war effort and had succumbed to wartime pressures, Stearns suggested that there must have been a certain charm in "being important" and in being "on the inside." College professors by the dozens had busied themselves with the numerous administrative needs created by the war and had turned away from criticism and analysis. The psychological attraction of keeping in touch with the main current of events had seduced many of America's leading intellectuals, and historians had been no exception.[44]

Given his background, his desire to overcome his humble beginnings and achieve recognition, it was not surprising that Shotwell enjoyed his new position. He quickly discovered that the wartime opportunities offered him something that college teaching could never duplicate. They put him in the center of things and near the sources of power. He enjoyed feeling that his efforts counted and that he could directly help in the control of things. He soon came to see that the making of peace and the problems of reconstruction offered even more possibilities for the active intellectual than the waging of war, and it was to this new and vastly more complex problem which he next turned.

44. Harold Stearns, *Liberalism in America* (New York, 1919), pp. 102–6.

4
Peace Preparations

Shotwell's success in setting up and guiding the policy of the National Board for Historical Service soon brought him to the attention of Colonel Edward M. House, who, in September, 1917, was busy organizing a committee to deal with postwar peace problems. President Wilson had asked House to establish the committee in order to examine potential Allied demands at the end of the war and help the President decide which of these demands he should support and which he should oppose. Wilson hoped that the committee would not only evaluate Allied peace plans, but would also act as a research staff, gathering and evaluating facts dealing with the world settlement, digesting them for prompt and handy use, and making preparations to deal with the many technical problems which would inevitably come up at a future peace conference.[1]

1. Woodrow Wilson to Colonel Edward M. House, September 2, 1917, in Ray Stannard Baker, *Woodrow Wilson, Life and Letters,* 8 vols. (Garden City, 1927–1939), 7: 254; Sidney E. Mezes, "Preparation for Peace," in Edward M. House and Charles Seymour, eds., *What Really Happened at Paris: The Story of the Peace Conference, 1918–1919* (New York, 1921), p. 6.

The President emphasized that the committee would not concern itself with overall policy, for he had already established basic guidelines several months before the United States entered the war. By February, 1917, in fact, Wilson had committed the United States to a broad policy of liberal internationalism. On January 22, he told the Senate that "there must be not a balance of power, but a community of power; not organized rivalries, but an organized peace." He envisioned a peace with no victors nor any vanquished; it would be a "peace without victory." He went on to say that if the United States was going to assume its rightful place in the postwar world, it would have to support and participate in a world organization to maintain peace. Such a concert of power, he believed, did not involve entangling alliances, for "when all unite to act in the same sense and the same purpose, all act in the common interest and are free to live their own lives under common protection." America had to support the principles of a liberal peace, for they were the "principles of mankind and must prevail."[2]

The President did not originate the tenets of his liberal peace program, but he did become their most articulate and influential advocate. The origins of internationalism and world organization went back many centuries before the outbreak of the world war, as far back as ancient times. The idea of world organization was implicit in suggestions for a league of Greek city-states and in the term "Pax Romana," which envisioned a world where all countries were organized under Roman rule. Specific plans for a European association of nations were formulated as far back as the fourteenth century, and almost every major war since the fifteenth century had produced some proposal to substitute such plans for armed conflict. Such noted figures as Henry IV, Émeric Crucé, William Penn, Jean Jacques Rousseau, Immanuel Kant, and Jeremy Bentham, among others, sponsored projects for an association of nations to maintain peace. The formation of the United States in 1789 gave additional impetus to the idea of world federa-

2. Ray Stannard Baker and William E. Dodd, eds., *The Public Papers of Woodrow Wilson, The New Democracy,* 2 vols. (New York, 1926), 2: 407–14; Arthur S. Link, *Wilson the Diplomatist: A Look at his Major Foreign Policies* (Baltimore, Md., 1957), pp. 96–97.

tion, for it proved that the concept of federalism could work.[3]

During the nineteenth century internationalism gained momentum as scientific advances in transportation, communications, and production drew the economic life of nations closer together. As the century came to an end, many Americans and Europeans talked of arbitration, international law, and conferences to solve specific international problems. Some even expressed support for the creation of a general international organization to preserve peace. Although the first Hague Peace Conference of 1899 avoided the question of world organization, it did establish a permanent court of arbitration and was viewed by many internationalists as a major step in the right direction.

By the turn of the century the United States had come to dominate the movement for world organization. Internationalist thought in America, however, lacked any unified set of beliefs or program of action. Some individuals like Josiah Royce, the philosopher, Thorstein Veblen, the political economist, and Jane Addams, the social reformer, viewed international life organically and tended to focus their attention upon social and economic changes which would increase the sense of human unity.[4] Others championed more specific schemes of arbitration, codification of international law, the establishment of a world court, the creation of a federalist-designed world organization, or the building of a unitary world government. Even those who agreed upon a specific program often disagreed over details. Those who advocated world organization might also support the idea of an international army and navy. More cautious advocates might limit the role of sanctions to economic pressures alone. Between these two extremes there existed a wide variety of sanctionists, who agreed that some force might be necessary, but who could not agree on the degree of power needed or what form that force should take. Internationalism, in other words, meant many things to many people, and the

3. Sandra R. Herman, *Eleven Against War: Studies in American Internationalist Thought, 1898–1921* (Stanford, Calif., 1969), pp. 55–56; Warren F. Kuehl, *Hamilton Holt: Journalist, Internationalist, Educator* (Gainesville, Fla., 1960), p. 66; Warren F. Kuehl, *Seeking World Order: The United States and International Organization to 1920* (Nashville, Tenn., 1969), pp. 3–21.
4. Herman, *Eleven Against War,* pp. viii–ix.

schemes to promote international organization were almost as numerous as their promoters.[5]

Theodore Roosevelt gave the movement for world organization a big boost when in 1910 he urged the great powers to form a League of Peace, "not only to keep the peace among themselves, but to prevent, by force if necessary, its being broken by others." The coming of the World War served only to intensify the efforts of both Americans and Europeans to develop a viable scheme for world organization. The Central Organization for a Durable Peace, started at the Hague in April, 1915, served as a focal point for the movement in the neutral countries and won the cooperation of representatives from nearly all the belligerent nations. In England, the League of Nations Society and the Fabian Society Research Department promoted widely discussed schemes. In 1916, Lord Robert Cecil persuaded the British cabinet to set up a special committee on international organization which ultimately produced a draft treaty that had a major impact on the delegates to the Paris Peace Conference.[6]

In the United States many of the internationalists rallied around the League to Enforce Peace, publicly launched at an impressive meeting in Independence Hall, Philadelphia in June, 1915. The League supported the creation of a world organization of all the great nations in which the member-states agreed to submit all justiciable questions not settled by negotiation to a judicial tribunal and all nonjusticiable disputes to a Council of Conciliation. The League's program also provided that the member-states use their joint military power to prevent any one of their number from going to war or committing acts of hostility before submitting their disputes to the judicial tribunal or Council of Conciliation, and that they meet in periodic conferences to formulate and codify international law. Although the program of the League to Enforce Peace was not new, it quickly gained widespread support partially because the world was at war and partially because of the skillful and diligent labors of such supporters as Hamilton Holt, editor of *The Independent,* Theodore Marburg, a wealthy Baltimore publicist and founder of the American Society for the

5. Kuehl, *Seeking World Order,* pp. viii, 145–49, 200–203.
6. Ibid., pp. 236–37; Denna F. Fleming, *The United States and World Organization, 1920–1933* (New York, 1938), p. 14.

Judicial Settlement of International Disputes, and William Howard Taft, the former President of the United States.[7]

Woodrow Wilson, who had shown little interest in the internationalist movement prior to the outbreak of war, could not long ignore the effective campaign of the League to Enforce Peace. He gradually came to see the idea of a league of nations as crucial to his broader conception of the future world order. Wilson held that it was America's historic mission to bring Europe into a peaceful international order based on world law. A league of nations would not only secure the peace with Germany and provide an ongoing structure capable of handling all future imperialist threats to world order, but would also provide the crucial ingredient in transforming the world from a warlike state of nature to an orderly global society governed by liberal norms. It offered the perfect compromise between traditional imperialism which had taken the international community into innumerable wars over the centuries and revolutionary-socialism which threatened to destroy all that was good and progressive in the existing system. Wilson's vision was of an association of nations which would guarantee a liberal-capitalist world order in which America could exert her moral, economic, and political leadership while moving the world toward universal peace and prosperity.[8]

On May 27, 1916, Wilson spoke before the League to Enforce Peace and publicly committed the United States to an international organization. His position, however, involved more than just joining a league of nations, although this had become the "central pillar" of his peace program. He now articulated a set of ideas about the world and the future peace which closely paralleled the thinking of international liberals throughout America and Europe. Fundamentally the basic orientation of liberal-internationalism was to make more rational and orderly the existing world system of competing nation-states while avoiding the extreme solution of socialist revolution. International liberals proposed to end the system of entangling alliances, balances

7. Kuehl, *Seeking World Order,* pp. 190–92; Ruhl J. Bartlett, *The League to Enforce Peace* (Chapel Hill, N.C., 1944), pp. 25–47.
8. N. Gordon Levin, Jr., *Woodrow Wilson and World Politics: America's Response to War and Revolution* (New York, 1968), pp. 4–10, 126; Carl Parrini, *Heir to Empire: United States Economic Diplomacy, 1916–1923* (Pittsburgh, 1969), p. 14.

of power, and secret diplomacy which they believed had helped make war inevitable. In the place of the old methods they proposed to substitute open diplomacy, sweeping reductions in armaments, self-determination, the internationalization of waterways like the Panama, Suez, and Kiel canals and strategic points like Gibralta and the Bosporus, and the elimination of obstacles to international trade. European liberals such as Joseph Schumpeter and Karl Kautsky, as well as Wilson, believed that the international-capitalist system could still put behind it the militant imperialism of the past and stabilize itself through peaceful trade and through economic development of the backward areas of the world.[9]

Once Congress declared war on Germany in April, 1917, Wilson's interest in the future peace settlement became more immediate and direct. He realized that to achieve the type of peace he desired he would have to do more than just mediate at the conference table. Besides establishing the general principles for a peace arrangement, he would have to solve the difficult technical problems which were sure to come up. Only five months after the United States entered the war, therefore, he called upon Colonel House to begin peace preparations. Both Wilson and his top adviser felt that the State Department did not have the competence to handle the detailed research required and decided to set up an independent committee made up mostly of university and college scholars.[10]

Colonel House began by selecting a group of qualified men to staff the new committee. This proved more difficult than he expected, for there were very few men schooled in modern history or contemporary world affairs. Very few historians regarded themselves as primarily concerned with twentieth-century problems, and scholars in international law, political science, and economics were as little prepared to face the problems of peacemaking as were their colleagues in history.[11] House had to begin somewhere, however, and decided to appoint Sidney E. Mezes, his brother-in-law and President of the College of the City of New York, to head the new organization. President Wilson

9. Levin, *Woodrow Wilson,* pp. 4–5; Link, *Wilson the Diplomatist,* pp. 92–94.
10. Lawrence E. Gelfand, *The Inquiry: American Preparations for Peace, 1917–1918* (New Haven, 1963), pp. 28–31; J.T.S., *At the Paris Peace Conference* (New York, 1937), p. 3.
11. Gelfand, *Inquiry,* pp. 34–37.

suggested that Walter Lippmann, then assistant to Secretary of War Newton D. Baker, be appointed to the committee, and Felix Frankfurter pushed Walcott H. Pitkin, the American political adviser to the Siamese government. Herbert Croly, editor of the *New Republic,* urged that Shotwell be considered on the grounds that he had taught a few courses on modern European history at Columbia before the war and had been largely responsible for the successful mobilization of historians in the National Board for Historical Service.[12]

Shotwell had no knowledge of the administration's plan to create a postwar planning commission until he received a telephone call from Croly late in September. Croly did not provide much information over the phone, but suggested that Shotwell see Colonel House as soon as possible. Arriving at the Colonel's office the next day, Shotwell was greeted by Mezes, who informed him that the President wanted to organize a group of students of international affairs "whose duty it would be to study the political, economic, legal, and historical elements of the problems which would have to be faced in the treaty of peace." Mezes made it quite clear that although the group was technically attached to the Department of State, it would be autonomous and responsible directly to Colonel House.[13]

Besides Mezes and Shotwell, the other "original" members of the committee were Walter Lippmann and David Hunter Miller, a New York law partner of Colonel House's son-in-law, Gordon Auchincloss. Of the four, Shotwell alone had any real background in modern European history, although Lippmann probably had a better understanding of contemporary politics and international affairs. To this core group—affectionately known as "The Inquiry" by its members —Colonel House left the work of soliciting the services of other scholars and the planning of a specific program of research. As soon as they got down to serious work, it became obvious that a substantially larger organization was needed. Shotwell at once suggested that they ask his friend Isaiah Bowman, then Director of the American Geographical Society, to join. Bowman not only agreed to help, but offered to let the Inquiry move into the Society's building on Broadway and West 115th Street in New York City. The building had the

12. Ibid., pp. 38–39, 51.
13. J.T.S., *At Paris,* p. 3.

perfect equipment for the making of maps and was located in a quiet part of the city where the activities of the group would not attract attention.[14]

Because of the diversity of the problems with which they had to deal, Mezes and his associates decided to seek the aid of "experts" in many fields. Fortunately, some unsolicited and unwanted publicity given the peace preparations resulted in scores of letters being sent to Colonel House offering the services of individuals and groups. Although many of the letters were from "good Democrats" seeking a political job, several came from serious and able scholars such as George Louis Beer, Manley O. Hudson, Sidney Fay, and Stanley Hornbeck.[15] Other "experts" were directly solicited by one or another of the original Inquiry staff and were asked to take on specific geographical or topical problems. Archibald Coolidge of Harvard was brought in as an Eastern European authority. Allyn A. Young of Cornell took over the economic studies of the group, while Charles Haskins and Robert Lord of Harvard and Charles Seymour of Yale were asked to study the questions of the French frontiers, Poland, and Austria-Hungary respectively.

Among the other scholars who eventually did research for the Inquiry were William L. Westermann of Wisconsin, Dana C. Munro of Princeton, Douglas Johnson and Preston W. Slosson of Columbia, Samuel E. Morison of Harvard, and Clive Day of Yale. By January, 1918, thirty-five persons were drawing salaries from the Inquiry, and by October of that same year, when the organization reached its maximum growth, there were some one hundred and twenty-six "executives and research collaborators."[16] Shotwell's monthly salary of $541.66 was the highest paid to any Inquiry member. Except for Lippmann and Robert Lord, no other staff member received half that amount.[17]

14. Ibid., pp. 6–8; J.T.S., "Reminiscences," pp. 78–80.
15. Gelfand, *Inquiry,* pp. 42–44.
16. Ibid., pp. 45–78; J.T.S., *At Paris,* pp. 6–9.
17. "Administrative Matters," Box 17, Inquiry Archives, National Archives, Washington D.C. It should be pointed out that several members of the Inquiry staff such as Mezes, Bowman, and Miller continued to receive outside incomes and, therefore, took no salary from the government.

Shotwell helped the Inquiry by getting materials and documents from both the Carnegie Endowment for International Peace and the League to Enforce Peace.[18] Much more important, however, was his success in getting historians, both on an individual basis and through the National Board for Historical Service, to aid in the work. Besides organizing a special Research Committee within the National Board, he also arranged for individual members to set up committees at their respective universities to help with general projects related to the peace settlement. These committees consisted not only of historians, "but any in the political and social sciences who could conceivably bring special qualifications to bear upon the solution of the problems of peace." Charles Haskins and Frederick J. Turner organized a group at Harvard, while William E. Dodd, Dana C. Munro, and Max Farrand set up committees at Chicago, Princeton, and Yale respectively.[19]

Although the recruitment of men did not prove very difficult, the organization and function of the Inquiry remained hazy. One of the first things done was to divide the labor among the leading members. David Hunter Miller took over the field of international law, Lippmann the field of politics, Bowman the field of geography, and Allyn Young the field of economics. Shotwell took charge of European History questions and accepted the crucial position of editor, through which all Inquiry reports had to pass before being placed in the files.[20]

During the first few months the members of the Inquiry restricted themselves to the collection of data and to the making of maps. The Executive Committee, composed of Mezes, Shotwell, Lippmann, Bowman, and Miller, felt that the accumulation of factual information would avoid the many dangers of subjective impressions, interpretations, and judgments. They believed that the American peace delegation would probably be more interested in facts than in particular impressions or recommendations of Inquiry members. In March, 1918, Mezes announced that the paramount responsibility of the organization was to gather material and arrange it in such flexible form

18. J.T.S. to Sidney E. Mezes, December 7, 1917, Box 12, J.T.S. Papers.
19. J.T.S. to Max Farrand, December 4, 1917, Max Farrand to J.T.S., December 8, 1917, "General Correspondence," Box 5, Inquiry Archives.
20. J.T.S., "Reminiscences," p. 81.

that its utility would be assured regardless of how or in what order the questions were introduced at the peace conference.[21] Since the executive committee was not certain what issues would actually come up at the conference, it decided to make studies of all related geographical, economic, and political problems. Most of the work, however, centered on questions involving Central Europe and the Near East.[22]

Throughout the winter and spring of 1918 the work of the Inquiry moved along slowly. Reports on a vast number of problems were drawn up, together with statistical tables and maps. Despite the slow, but steady progress of the work, dissatisfaction and resentment built up toward the director of the Inquiry. Bowman, Miller, Shotwell, and many other scholars engaged in research felt that Mezes was on the one hand attempting to control their efforts too much and on the other hand failing to unify and coordinate the work as a whole. Bowman, especially, felt strongly that the research lacked direction and was inefficiently administered. He also accused Mezes of acting independently of the Executive Committee and arrogating its authority for himself. Shotwell, for his part, resented the degree of power which the youthful Lippmann had acquired. He felt that the editor of the *New Republic* acted in too high-handed a manner and without consulting his other colleagues. He was particularly irked by the fact that Lippmann had been able to oust him from the crucial job as editor of the Inquiry, taking the work on for himself.[23]

The dissatisfaction with Mezes' leadership finally came to a head in July, when several members of the Inquiry threatened to resign. Bowman, backed by Shotwell, took his case directly to Colonel House. Fearing that the work of the Inquiry would come to an abrupt halt, House agreed to put the operation in the hands of Bowman and an executive committee of his choosing. Mezes remained the nominal head of the group, but lost all effective authority. During the turmoil, Lippmann resigned to accept a commission as captain in Military Intelligence.[24]

21. Gelfand, *Inquiry,* pp. 89–93.
22. Mezes, "Preparations for Peace," pp. 4–6.
23. J.T.S., "Reminiscences," pp. 81–83.
24. Isaiah Bowman, "Notes on the Inquiry," November 30, 1918, in Box 13, J.T.S. Papers. See also Gelfand, *Inquiry,* pp. 94–97.

Bowman's first step was to appoint a "Research Committee" composed of himself, Charles Haskins, Allyn Young, and Shotwell. This committee served as the Inquiry's executive body in charge of "men, money, and plans."[25] Next, Bowman appointed Shotwell editor of the Research Committee. As before, all reports and memorandums drawn up by Inquiry members were to pass through his hands. In order to make the editorial work more efficient, Shotwell appointed an editorial board composed of George Louis Beer, William A. Dunning, James Harvey Robinson, Vladimir Simkhovitch, Allyn Young, and W. P. Willcox. He established a basic set of editorial rules and divided the editorial work regionally among the committee members.[26]

From the outset, the distribution of assignments had been a major stumbling block. Mezes had not worked out a suitable plan, and Bowman proved no more successful. Basically, the problem lay in the fact that the American peace planners did not have the background nor the experience to deal with the many complex technical questions certain to come up at the conference table. Whenever possible a person familiar with a particular geographical area or issue drew up a report related to his field of interest or edited a report on that field. But the studies needed were so numerous and diverse that assignments often had no correlation to the scholar's particular knowledge or experience. Besides reviewing reports on western Europe, Shotwell found himself dealing with questions concerning Russia, the Balkans, colonial expansion, and western Asia.[27]

Most Inquiry members recognized the weakness of this procedure, but surprisingly few seriously objected. They seemed to feel that by applying intelligence and the "scientific method" to research, they could handle all problems involved in the world settlement. Few seemed to realize that even those with an academic knowledge of a particular area would not necessarily have the proficiency to deal

25. Isaiah Bowman to Colonel Edward M. House, August 17, 1918, "General Correspondence," Box 7, Inquiry Archives.
26. "Editorial Committee Minutes," September 11, 1918, October 19, 1918, Box 10, J.T.S. Papers.
27. For various reports and critiques written by Shotwell see Entries 3, 4, 27, 152, 156, 321, 421, 478, 517, 526, 559, 585, 633, 634, 870, and 871, Inquiry Archives.

adequately with the complex political questions involved in peacemaking. They worked under the misguided assumption that their approach was far superior to that of the professional diplomats. Like President Wilson, many of them blamed power-politics for most of the world's ills, and they eagerly began building a model for a new world order which would be both "rational" and "just."

Shotwell's approach to the world settlement closely resembled that of President Wilson and the international liberals. He, too, believed that the United States had a definite responsibility throughout the world not only to maintain peace, but to promote justice and national self-determination. America could no longer accept isolationism as the fundamental principle of its foreign policy. In an interdependent world, the United States was affected by the actions of every other nation, and, as a major world power, had to take the lead in guaranteeing a just and equitable international settlement.

In general, his reports and critiques were blunt, concise, and illuminating. He had an extensive knowledge of European history, and when he found himself working on unfamiliar problems, he often spent days reading background material on the particular question at hand. His devotion to the Inquiry's work won him the respect of most of his colleagues. Bowman probably expressed the feeling of many when he wrote to Colonel House that Shotwell was "a brilliant scholar whose wide experience and knowledge make him an indispensable critic of research plans and results."[28]

Although Shotwell was certainly an able scholar and dedicated worker, nothing in his reports or critiques indicated that he clearly understood the vast complexities involved in the making of a new world order. Like most of his colleagues, he worked in a vacuum, dealing with his own specific issues and rarely seeing the picture as a whole. Perhaps this was the greatest weakness of America's peace preparations: each of the "experts" worked on his own particular problems, never seeing how his proposals would fit into the general context of the world settlement. The various proposals might have stood on their own, but it did not necessarily follow that when taken

28. Isaiah Bowman to Colonel Edward M. House, August 17, 1918, "General Correspondence," Box 7, Inquiry Archives.

together the overall plan would meet the Inquiry's demand for "rationality" or "justice." The work of the Inquiry, from the start, lacked coordination and integration. This was true not only when Mezes and Lippmann had control of the organization, but also when Bowman and Shotwell became responsible for "men, money, and plans."

In October, 1918, when it became clear that the war would end shortly, the Inquiry staff shifted into high gear. With the signing of the armistice on November 11, they began making frantic efforts to complete their research before the assembling of the peace conference. Shotwell turned over most of the remaining editorial work to his committee and began devoting most of his time and energy to the gathering of a suitable reference library for use by the American peace commissioners. He completed the task just before the American delegation sailed for Paris.

Shotwell's contributions to the peace preparations of the United States consisted mainly of administrative organization and research. Unlike Walter Lippmann, David Hunter Miller, or George Louis Beer, he contributed little to the making of general policy. Nor did he contribute very much to the articulation of the fundamental principles which were to guide the American delegation at the conference table. Basically, he accepted the Wilsonian conception of the interdependence of the world and the need for a liberal peace program. He did, however, make contributions in other ways. His many contacts with historians, his success in getting them, as well as other scholars, to give their time and energy to the work of the Inquiry, his many suggestions for research projects, and his blunt and often well-informed critiques all proved invaluable to America's efforts at drawing up a blueprint for a new world order.

In general, Shotwell's approach to the problems of peace planning reflected many of his prewar assumptions about the nature of progress in the modern world. Like his teacher and friend, James Harvey Robinson, he believed that problems could be solved and advances made by the application of the "scientific method" to human thinking. As a New Historian, he had urged his colleagues to abandon the study of the past for itself alone. The historian's major purpose, he had often argued, was to help man understand his present situation and provide him with the past experience necessary to meet his most pressing problems. As a corollary to this view, he believed that man was basically rational and could be swayed by intelligent arguments and reasoned conclusions. It is understandable, therefore, that he should have viewed the war as a fundamental test for his philosophical conceptions. Historians could fulfill a vital function by helping to explain the war to the American people. Because of this emphasis on service, the National Board for Historical Service seemed extremely important and he gave it his full support even after it had deviated from its original purposes.

It was logical for him next to accept a position on the Inquiry and undertake the task of peace planning. Here was a chance for historians and other scholars to apply the "scientific method" to the most difficult and important problems facing mankind. His great faith in the ability of academicians to handle these complex political and geographical problems was shared by almost every other member of the peace-planning group. Through scholarly research and the application of human intelligence, they hoped to remake the world and usher in a new age.

The task was challenging and inspiring. As social engineers, they would draw up a blueprint for the entire world based upon objective reasoning and fundamental truths. Since mankind was rational, the blueprint would necessarily win favor with the peoples of the world. They in turn would demand its implementation. Shotwell never seemed to consider seriously the possibility that the Inquiry's well-reasoned plan might be rejected. The fact that the "experts" often disagreed among themselves over the solution to some of the more complex problems did not seem to weaken his faith. Nor did it weaken the faith of the other Inquiry members. With their numerous books and maps giving them strength, they looked toward the Paris Peace Conference with great optimism. They viewed it as a magnificent laboratory where they would rearrange the world according to the rational model they had so painstakingly created. They would soon find out, however, that it was one thing to draw up a plan for a new world order, but it was quite another thing to win its acceptance.

5
A Peace with Social Justice

December 4, 1918 was an extraordinary day in the life of James Thomson Shotwell. For on that day, along with President Woodrow Wilson, Secretary of State Robert Lansing, and the rest of the American Commission to Negotiate Peace, he boarded the *George Washington* to begin the momentous journey to France and the Paris Peace Conference. The citizens of New York and New Jersey gave the President and his entourage a tumultuous send off. With airplanes droning overhead, guns booming, tugboats shrieking, and the masses on the shore shouting enthusiastically, the ex-German liner slowly made its way out of Hoboken harbor, past the Statue of Liberty, through the Narrows into the open sea. It was the beginning of a great adventure, the importance of which escaped few of those on board.

Along with Shotwell were twenty-two other members of the Inquiry, with their maps, reports, statistical tables, and other "peace conference munitions." Although they were only one of several advisory groups to the American plenipotentiaries, they were the most widely known and typified what many Americans viewed as the President's "academic" approach to peacemaking. One New York journalist irreverently referred to them as "Colonel House's troupe of performing professors," while William Allen White captured the boarding of the *George Washington* in his well-known style: "Down the gangplank walked this Yankee knight errant followed by a desperate crew of college professors, in horn-rimmed glasses carrying textbooks, encyclopaedias, maps, charts, graphs, statistics, and all sorts of literary crowbars with which to pry up the boundaries of Europe and move them around in the interests of justice, as seen through the Fourteen Points."[1]

Although White's description reflected the suspicions held by many Americans toward the academicians on the American delegation, it did not give credit to the long months of research and careful selection of a reference library which made the Inquiry not only the most prepared group of advisers that Wilson had to rely upon, but probably the most knowledgeable group at the Paris Peace Conference.[2]

The voyage proved quite uneventful for Shotwell and the other Inquiry members. There was some discussion of possible topics which might come up at the conference, and the President met briefly with a select group of Inquiry leaders, but for the most part they were not informed of Wilson's overall program or of their own relation to the rest of the American Commission to Negotiate Peace. As Shotwell wrote in his diary, most were "all perfectly in the dark" as to how useful they might be when they got across.[3] The President's inaccessibility on board ship caused resentment not only among his advisers, but also among the other American negotiators. Even Secretary of State Lansing complained that the President never really informed him or the other delegates what overall policy they were to follow at Paris. Lack of communication between the "experts" and the American peace commissioners, and the lack of coordination in general, remained a problem throughout the conference.[4]

1. Quoted in Thomas A. Bailey, *Woodrow Wilson and the Lost Peace* (New York, 1944), pp. 108–9.
2. Harold Nicolson, *Peacemaking 1919* (Universal Library ed., New York, 1965), pp. 27–28.
3. J.T.S., *At Paris,* p. 70.
4. Robert Lansing, *The Peace Negotiations: A Personal Narrative* (Boston and New York, 1921), p. 202.

Shortly after their arrival in Paris, Isaiah Bowman called a meeting of the Inquiry staff (now officially known as the "Division of Territorial, Economic, and Political Intelligence") and announced the reorganization of the entire American delegation. He informed his colleagues that according to the new scheme they would advise the peace commissioners directly instead of through the State Department as originally planned. He also announced the creation of a new "History Division," of which Shotwell was to take charge along with his duties as Librarian.[5]

The responsibilities of this new division remained unclear. Most of the problems on which Shotwell had worked before the armistice were now under the purview of other divisions within the structure of the American delegation. After several discussions with Bowman and Allyn Young, Shotwell decided that the one field not delegated to other experts was the field of "social justice," or more specifically, the demands of labor. Like many other intellectuals of a liberal persuasion, Shotwell was both confused and disturbed by the Bolshevik takeover in Russia. Believing that the "ominous threat of revolution . . . hung over Europe," he saw a great need for the conference to consider international labor legislation. Failure to take action, he warned, would result in widespread uprising throughout western Europe.[6]

Surprisingly, the Inquiry had almost totally neglected the question of international labor legislation. A few superficial studies were made, but no serious attention had been given to the problem.[7] Even after they arrived at Paris none of the other advisers viewed the demands of labor as a vital issue or as one that might come up at the conference. The entire field, therefore, fell to Shotwell through default.

During the last half of December, while President Wilson triumphantly toured Europe, Shotwell carefully went over material related to the international labor question and early in January submitted a

5. J.T.S., *At Paris,* pp. 16–17, 85–90.
6. Ibid., p. 98. For a general discussion of liberal reaction to the events in Russia see Christopher Lasch, *The American Liberals and the Russian Revolution* (New York, 1962).
7. Liefur Magnusson, "American Preparations," in J.T.S., ed., *The Origins of the International Labor Organization,* 2 vols. (New York, 1934), 1: 97–102.

memorandum to the American peace commissioners urging them to back various demands of labor, especially a child labor law. Humanitarian concerns aside, he felt that the threat of labor unrest was sufficient reason for the peace negotiators to take up the subject. Since the socialist program was far too radical and impractical to serve as the basis for international labor legislation, he suggested that the conference adopt specific legislation which had little to do with the economic system in general, but which would appease the discontented elements in society and put an end to the increasing revolutionary fervor.[8]

Shotwell's recommendation reflected the predominant approach to social reform in the United States. He was clearly aware of the many evils in the industrial system and desired to see them removed. Yet he also strongly believed in capitalism and did not wish to see it destroyed. Through the adoption of social legislation, such as child labor laws and restrictions on the work of women, he hoped to remove the more glaring evils of the system, appease the discontented elements in society, and save capitalism in its basic form. His emphasis on the dangers of inaction demonstrated his overwhelming concern with protecting the free enterprise economy of Europe. As in the case of many other experts and political leaders at the Paris Peace Conference, the "unbelievable Bolshevist revolution" was very much on his mind. In the increasing labor unrest, he saw a dangerous trend toward socialism, or, even worse, anarchism. He felt obliged, therefore, to counsel the Allied and Associated governments to offer labor some definite and formal recognition at the opening of the conference. Such an action, he believed, would hold forth the hope of further international agreements and would give aid to the more moderate elements in the labor movement.[9]

Although his memorandum circulated only among the members of the American delegation, Edward J. Phelan of the British Labour

8. J.T.S., "Memorandum on Labor Legislation," January 3, 1919, Box 9, J.T.S. Papers.
9. For Shotwell's views on the need for international labor legislation as an alternative to revolution and socialism see: J.T.S., "The International Labor Organization as an Alternative to Violent Revolution," in *The Annals of the American Academy of Political and Social Science* 166 (March 1933): 18–25; and J.T.S., "Origins of the ILO," in Spencer Miller, Jr., ed., *What the International Labor Organization Means to America* (New York, 1936), pp. 1–7.

Ministry heard of it and approached him shortly before the conference officially convened. Phelan informed him that the British had gone much farther in their planning for international labor legislation than the American delegation and had come to the conclusion that the problem could not be settled at any single conference. Instead they desired the creation of an international organization capable of carrying on the work from year to year. Shotwell had long seen the advantage of this proposition, but had not proposed anything more than having the League of Nations assume the continuing responsibility. Phelan quickly attacked this position arguing that the League could not possibly secure social legislation as effectively as an organization specifically appointed for that purpose. He informed Shotwell that the British delegation intended to propose the creation of an international labor organization as soon as the opportunity arose and offered to give the American advisers open access to all its labor material.[10] Shotwell accepted the offer and for the next few days worked closely with the British labor experts. In his second memorandum, dated January 11, he again urged the conference to deal with specific labor problems, but also suggested that the League of Nations establish a special bureau to study labor problems exclusively.[11]

On January 18, Georges Clemenceau, the French premier, convened the first plenary session of the peace conference and startled the American delegation by announcing that labor legislation would be one of the three main items on the agenda. While the American commissioners were prepared to deal with the other two questions concerning war guilt and war crimes, they had given no serious thought to international labor problems. They were at a loss, moreover, to explain to American newspapermen in Paris precisely what the French premier had in mind by "legislation in regard to international labor." Immediately after the session, therefore, Ray Stannard Baker, who was in charge of American publicity, asked Shotwell to prepare a memorandum for the press.

The statement, released that very day, proclaimed that no real political peace could exist under the "threat of an economic competition which might destroy the safeguards of labor." It emphasized that

10. J.T.S., *At Paris,* pp. 106–10.
11. "Memorandum" of January 11, 1919, printed in ibid., pp. 113–14.

the demands for labor legislation were not new and that substantial gains had been made during the war. Shotwell hoped that by stressing the nonrevolutionary character of international labor legislation, he could win support from the more conservative elements in Europe and the United States. He made it quite clear that the actions contemplated by the British and French delegations had nothing at all to do with socialism. They were concerned only with specific labor problems, "without regard to the existing social and economic order."[12]

Two weeks after Clemenceau called the first plenary session to order, he appointed a Commission on International Labor Legislation. Two representatives from each of the five Great Powers—the United States, Great Britain, France, Italy, and Japan—were appointed to the Commission, as were representatives from Belgium, Cuba, Poland, and Czechoslovakia. President Wilson sent for Samuel Gompers and appointed him to the Commission along with Edward N. Hurley, the head of the United States Shipping Board. Hurley, however, could not remain in Paris and Wilson replaced him with Henry M. Robinson, a California banker. Among the other key figures on the Commission were George N. Barnes and Malcolm Delevingne of Great Britain, Arthur Fontaine of France, A. Cabrini of Italy, Minoru Oka of Japan, and Ernest Mahaim of Belgium.

A dispute immediately arose between the French and British over the exact nature of the recommendations they should submit. The French insisted upon the inclusion of specific reforms in the treaty, while the British opposed this approach and favored the establishment of a separate organization to deal with labor problems in general.[13] A compromise was finally worked out by Fontaine and Delevingne. The Commission would "inquire into the conditions of employment from the international aspect," "consider the international means necessary to secure common action on matters affecting conditions of employment," and "recommend the form of a permanent agency to continue such inquiry and consideration in co-operation with and under the direction of the League of Nations." In order to facilitate their work, they agreed to take up the British scheme as their starting point, but

12. J.T.S., "Memorandum on International Labor Legislation," January 18, 1919, Box 115, J.T.S. Papers; J.T.S., *At Paris,* p. 123.
13. Charles Picquenard, "The Preliminaries of the Peace Conference: French Preparation," in J.T.S., ed., *Origins,* 1: 91–92.

each delegation reserved the right to make additional proposals.[14]

As a reward for his work on the labor question, Shotwell became an adviser to the American representatives on the Commission. Gompers and Robinson, however, rarely consulted him and did not ask him to attend any of the committee sessions. Most of his information regarding the progress of the work came from the British delegates who viewed him as more sympathetic to their point of view than either of the appointed American representatives.[15] His work on international labor seeming to have ended with the creation of the Peace Conference Commission, Shotwell began studying other questions. As head of the History Division, he considered himself as having a "roving commission" which could "touch on any frontier."[16] In truth, however, besides his work in the Library, he had no specific assignments and simply took up problems which either personally interested him or were casually suggested by other members of the Inquiry. Although he often volunteered his views on many geographical and economic issues, they rarely received major consideration. Besides serving as an adviser to the Labor Commission, he did not participate in the work of any of the other technical committees. Gradually his failure to receive a specific assignment caused him to grow pessimistic about the conference in general and about his own usefulness in particular. On February 7, he wrote in his diary:

> Of course there is a great deal of wasted time in such a conference, and some of the most important results come from casual talks with people who haven't their minds quite made up. I sometimes wonder whether we of the Inquiry, or rather, whether I am doing any good at all here; there are so many blocks on the wheels we try to turn.[17]

Shotwell, however, was not a man to sit idly by at such a momentous event as the Paris Peace Conference. The war had demonstrated that scholars could provide useful services to society outside the college classrooms, and he believed they had even more to contribute to

14. "Report of the Commission on International Labor Legislation," March 24, 1919, Box 41, J.T.S. Papers.
15. J.T.S., *At Paris,* pp. 168–69.
16. J.T.S. to Isaiah Bowman, December 2, 1919, Box 9, J.T.S. Papers.
17. J.T.S., *At Paris,* p. 168.

the making of peace. With the same energy he had shown in establishing the National Board for Historical Service and in organizing America's peace preparations, he now undertook any assignments suggested to him, no matter how inconsequential, and enthusiastically studied many problems on his own initiative. Among other things he drew up a memorandum on Spitzbergen in which he recommended that it be entrusted to Norway as a mandate of the League of Nations. He also worked on the Manchurian problem, coming to the conclusion that peace would come to this area only if the southeastern section of Manchuria, between Port Arthur and Korea, were ceded to Japan.[18]

It was not until early March, however, that he again found himself working on something "important." On February 28, the work of the Commission on International Labor Legislation reached an impasse and the delegates found themselves at a point of giving up the whole idea. Although most of the British plan was accepted, the question of the authority of the new international labor organization to make treaties and its relation to the participating governments remained in contention.

The article creating the greatest amount of difficulty was that giving authority to the labor conference to draw up international conventions. It provided that if these treaties received a two-thirds vote of the conference, they would be transmitted to each of the member-states for ratification, and unless specifically rejected by that state's lawmaking body would be put into operation. Basically the scheme represented a compromise between the idea of a conference with mandatory powers and one with merely consultive powers, for while each of the participating governments had the option of accepting or rejecting the treaty, they had to consider it within a year after the conference ended. In other words, no member could simply ignore the treaties framed by the International Labor Organization; they would have to be considered and voted upon. Hopefully this would allow public opinion to organize and develop, thereby giving added strength to the work of the new agency.[19]

18. Ibid., pp. 181, 195–96.
19. Edward J. Phelan, "The Commission on International Labor Legislation," in J.T.S., ed., *Origins,* 1: 145–46.

Although a few of the European delegates criticized the plan as too weak, the American representatives raised the most serious questions. Both Gompers and Robinson argued that the article violated the United States Constitution. According to American law, the authority over labor legislation rested in the hands of the various states and not with the Federal Government. Since the British plan insisted that the international labor treaties be considered by the national lawmaking body in each country, and since the states themselves were forbidden by the Constitution from making international agreements, there was no way the scheme could be applied in the United States.[20]

Both sides in the debate took such absolute positions that no agreement seemed possible. The British and French delegations argued that to give the new organization any less authority was to give it no authority at all, while Gompers and Robinson held fast to their position that the United States could never participate in an organization which violated one of the basic principles of its Constitution. On February 28, with the outlook for success very bleak, the Commission adjourned for two weeks. During the interim Edward J. Phelan and Felix Frankfurter, who had come to Paris as an observer, approached Shotwell and asked him to attempt to work out some compromise solution. Although he had no official authorization, Shotwell eagerly took up the task.[21] Here was his chance to make a mark at the Paris Peace Conference. Believing that failure to deal with labor questions would result in revolution throughout Europe, he saw in the breakdown of negotiations a chance for himself not only to contribute to the making of needed reforms, but also a chance to make a substantial contribution to the peace settlement in general.

On March 9, he approached Colonel House and tried to convince him that a compromise was indeed possible. House was extremely skeptical, but permitted him to take a seat on the Commission as a "technical adviser." Shotwell's task was not an easy one. First, he had to find some way to get around the purely legal and constitutional problem raised by the American delegation. Second, his solution had to avoid raising the jealousies of the state governments in the United

20. Ibid., 1: 147–48; J.T.S., *At Paris,* pp. 56–57.
21. J.T.S., *At Paris,* pp. 199–200.

States which were very protective of their political prerogatives regardless of the constitutional powers of the national government in Washington. Third, he had to find some way to win over Gompers and Robinson, who had become disillusioned with the whole idea of an International Labor Organization. And lastly, he had to find a solution acceptable to the British delegates who were strongly committed to an "effective" ILO and not one relegated to the mere making of "pious resolutions."[22]

It was a delicate situation, but Shotwell proved up to it. By sounding out the various delegations, by convincing Gompers and Robinson to negotiate privately with Malcolm Delevingne, George Barnes, and Edward J. Phelan, and by using various forms of pressure, he finally arrived at a solution. Briefly, he suggested that instead of the ILO's proposals taking the form of draft treaties, they should take the form of "recommendations" for legislation. By a two-thirds vote the labor conference might embody these recommendations into draft conventions, which if passed by the same majority would be transmitted to the governments concerned. "In the case of a federal state," however, "the draft convention would be viewed as only a recommendation." In other words, according to Shotwell's proposal the ILO would have the option of incorporating its proposals into either simple recommendations or draft treaties. In the case of recommendations, the various governments would decide for themselves if any action should be taken. In the case of draft conventions, those states capable of acting upon them would do so, while federal states would simply view them as recommendations and take action accordingly.[23]

On March 18, Shotwell presented his compromise plan to the Commission on International Labor Legislation. Having won the support of Gompers and Robinson by giving special recognition to the peculiarities of the American federal system, he sought to win over the other delegations by arguing that the compromise far from lessen-

22. Phelan, "Commission on International Labor Legislation," 1: 155–56; J.T.S., *At Paris,* pp. 207–9.
23. J.T.S., *At Paris,* p. 215; See Part XIII, Article 405 of the Treaty of Versailles in United States, Department of State, *Papers Relating to the Foreign Policy of the United States, Paris Peace Conference 1919,* 13 vols. (Washington, 1942–47), 13: 706–7.

ing the scope of the new organization would actually enlarge its sphere of action. He pointed out that by having the power to make recommendations in addition to drafting treaties, the labor conference could deal with questions other than those absolutely ripe for legislation. By influencing public opinion through its proposals, the conference could act as a stimulant to the enactment of reform instead of merely registering contemporary political possibilities. Instead of restricting the work of the ILO, Shotwell maintained that the compromise actually made it more flexible and consequently more important. He believed that the revised plan would transform the organization from a somewhat narrow and legalistic body "into an adjustable instrument for world legislation."[24]

While he convinced the British and French to accept the compromise, several representatives of American labor visiting Paris expressed their determined opposition. Andrew Furuseth of the Seamen's Union, particularly, opposed the establishment of an International Labor Organization on the grounds that it might force the United States Senate to relax the protection given seamen in the LaFollette Seaman's Act. Furuseth maintained that American labor would make more substantial progress without the proposed ILO than with it. Believing that the whole scheme would go down to defeat in America if Furuseth and other labor leaders were not won over, Shotwell suggested the insertion of a clause into the ILO Constitution to remove their fears. He proposed that "in no case shall any Member be asked or required, as a result of the adoption of any recommendation or draft convention by the Conference, to lessen the protection afforded by its existing legislation to the workers concerned." The British and French delegations saw little need for the clause, but agreed to include it as a concession to Furuseth and Gompers. Although at first appeased, the head of the Seaman's Union soon resumed his attacks on the ILO and returned to the United States to warn American labor of its dangers.[25]

When the Commission on International Labor Legislation decided to take the British scheme as the basis for discussion, several delegates

24. J.T.S., *At Paris,* pp. 62–63, 215.
25. Ibid., pp. 212–23.

reserved the right to put forward other proposals. One of the things most often demanded was the inclusion of a Labor Charter or statement of principles. Once a compromise on the British plan seemed in sight, the Italian delegation began to push for consideration of such a charter. Samuel Gompers strongly favored the idea and as chairman of the Commission appointed a subcommittee composed of Shotwell, Malcolm Delevingne, Minoru Oka, A. Cabrini, Ernest Mahaim, and Léon Jouhaux to prepare the document. Eventually nine principles were agreed upon. They ranged from the declaration that "the labor of a human being should not be treated as merchandise or an article of commerce," to guidelines for specific legislation such as the prohibition of child labor and the limitation of hours in industry.[26]

With the acceptance of the Labor Charter, the work of the Commission on International Labor Legislation came to an end. On March 24, it met for the last time and adopted a report outlining its accomplishments. Very shortly thereafter, Gompers and his associates departed for the United States leaving Shotwell and the members of the other delegations to push their work through the Paris Peace Conference in plenary session.

Shotwell's work on the Commission changed his entire outlook toward the peace conference. His early pessimism faded and was replaced by a strong belief that the conference had made substantial progress toward the establishment of a just and fair settlement. His optimism was somewhat odd, because at that very time many of the other Inquiry members were losing faith. On March 21, George Louis Beer, Shotwell's close friend and constant companion at Paris, wrote: "I am becoming more and more convinced that a real peace is impossible and that virtually all the work that is being done is ephemeral." Four days later he added: "Pessimism is still rampant in all quarters and the illusion of a new world order is vanishing."[27] Yet Shotwell, who was certainly aware of his colleague's feelings, believed that the conference had done "much better than even its friends are likely to be aware of, for the initial difficulties of pulling together so many

26. "Draft Articles for Insertion in the Treaty of Peace," April 28, 1919, in J.T.S., ed., *Origins,* 2: 412. See also Phelan, "Commission on International Labor Legislation," pp. 185–96.
27. George Louis Beer, "Diary," 42, 49, in Box 22, J.T.S. Papers.

different people and getting them to understand and compromise when they were in a spirit to neither understand nor make compromise has been a tremendous task."[28]

His optimism most likely reflected the success of the International Labor Commission rather than a close analysis of the work of the peace conference in general. This failure to see the peacemaking process in perspective was, perhaps, the greatest weakness in the Allied attempt to draw up a treaty of peace with Germany. Each of the experts worked in a vacuum, seeking solutions to their own particular problems and never knowing precisely what their colleagues were doing or how their own suggestions would fit into the general settlement. Lack of communication between the various experts and the failure to coordinate their work created the same problems at Paris as it had during the preparatory stages in New York and Washington. While each of the experts viewed their proposals as necessary or fair taken by themselves, they had no idea how they would affect the peace treaty as a whole. For the most part the advisers had little idea of what was going on in other delegations or in the other sections of their own delegation. It became a standard joke to answer inquiries about the conference after it was over by declaring: "I don't know anything about it, I was only there."[29]

Shotwell's general pessimism of February reflected not the actual conditions at the conference, but rather his own frustration over his limited assignments. Consequently, his success with the Labor Commission, which actually constituted a very minute part of the work at Paris, led him to believe that all was going well. This vacuum in which each of the various parts of the Treaty of Versailles was framed accounted for many of its shortcomings.

By the end of March, numerous reports came to Paris describing strong opposition to the League of Nations in the United States. Criticism came not only from opponents of international organization in general, but also from internationalists who believed that the Covenant neglected the legal and procedural ideas which they had come

28. J.T.S. to Munroe Smith, March 17, 1918, Smith Papers, Columbia University.
29. Bailey, *Woodrow Wilson and the Lost Peace,* pp. 135–36.

to accept as necessary. The structure of the League of Nations as established at Paris had little relationship to the structure envisioned by most American internationalists. During their long campaign prior to the calling of the Paris Peace Conference, they had emphasized the creation of a court to hear justiciable disputes as an integral part of the League. They also wanted the establishment of separate and clearly defined bodies to hear different types of controversies. Finally, they conceived of a league with the power to formulate and codify international law, but with only limited powers to employ sanctions. The Covenant drawn up by the delegates at Paris did not reflect these views, for it reversed priorities and subordinated law to sanctions. While few American internationalists rejected the Covenant completely, they did qualify their support and suggested numerous changes which eventually strengthened the hands of the irreconcilable opponents of international organization.[30]

The doubts and misgivings of American internationalists disturbed Shotwell greatly, and he began to brood over the possibility that the United States might refuse membership in the League of Nations. His fears led him to draft a memorandum on the need for a special status for those countries which refused to ratify the peace treaty. Basically, he suggested that nations rejecting membership in the League might still wish to participate in the various international conferences on specific problems such as labor legislation, disarmament, and trade. He therefore proposed an amendment to the Covenant declaring that "States not Members may become Associates of the League through membership of the periodic conferences held under the auspices of the League. Such Associates assume no further responsibilities than arise from the action of the conference in which they participate."[31] By the adoption of such a clause, countries not willing to accept the internationalism involved in the League of Nations, might take a smaller step by participating in international conferences and working with other nations to solve common problems. Shotwell believed that a return to isolationism had to be avoided, and unlike President Wilson, he was

30. Kuehl, *Seeking World Order,* pp. 285–88, 307–12.
31. J.T.S., "Suggestion for an Amendment of the Covenant Making Provision for Association with the League," n.d., Box 114, J.T.S. Papers. See also J.T.S., *At Paris,* pp. 230–33, 240–45.

willing to see the structure of the League weakened rather than force the various governments to decide between a full commitment to internationalism or a return to blatant nationalism.

The International Labor Organization, alone of the League agencies, incorporated the idea of "association" status, for although it was technically connected to the world organization through its budget, it remained largely autonomous and had its own membership. The general principle as advocated by Shotwell, however, was never seriously considered at the Paris Peace Conference and was nowhere included in the Treaty of Versailles.

On April 11, the Fourth Plenary Session took up the report of the Labor Commission. The peace commissioners unanimously accepted the Constitution of the International Labor Organization, but refused even to discuss the Labor Charter. While Shotwell was pleased over the success of the ILO, he believed that inclusion of the Labor Charter was an absolute necessity for gaining the support of American labor. He contacted George Barnes of the British Labor Delegation and began to map out strategy for getting the Charter accepted. Both men spent several days rewriting the various clauses and altered the preamble to meet the criticisms leveled at it by the peace negotiators. They revised every one of the nine articles and on April 28 again presented it to the plenary session. After a brief debate it was accepted.[32]

Shotwell's work, however, did not come to an end. He took an active part in the making of preparations for the first session of the International Labor Organization scheduled to meet in Washington in October, 1919. Secretary of State Lansing appointed him to the Organizing Committee, and he was largely responsible for framing the rules of procedure adopted by the ILO for their annual conferences.[33] He also received an appointment to a special committee to answer German grievances on the labor provisions in the peace treaty. Although opposed to most of the German suggestions, he did convince the Supreme Allied Council that Germany should be permitted to partici-

32. Ibid., pp. 255–69; "Draft Article for Insertion in the Treaty of Peace," April 28, 1919, in J.T.S., ed., *Origins*, 2: 412–13.
33. Robert Lansing to J.T.S., May 5, 1919, Papers of the American Commission to Negotiate Peace, #185.161/55, National Archives (hereafter cited ACNP); J.T.S., *Autobiography*, pp. 134–35.

pate in the ILO even if not a member of the League of Nations. He was also responsible for the inclusion in the Treaty of Versailles of a special provision declaring that the social insurance funds belonging to workers in ceded German territory be used specifically for their original purpose.[34]

With the financial aid of Great Britain, the labor conference met as scheduled and the International Labor Organization formally came into existence. Shotwell's enormous contribution to the establishment of the new organization was recognized by almost everyone who had worked on the labor sections of the treaty. His counsel, his ability to find compromise solutions to diametrically opposed points of view, and his talent for soothing ruffled feelings proved vital in getting the blueprint for the ILO off the drawing board.[35]

Shotwell was quite pleased with his efforts on behalf of labor. While he realized that the ILO was not the most crucial piece of work carried on at Paris, he felt that the labor section of the treaty contained far-reaching possibilities. On June 13, he wrote to his Columbia colleague, Joseph P. Chamberlain, stating that there was "nothing more interesting in the whole field of political theory at present than this proposed mechanism for International Labor Legislation half-way along the line of mere informal agreements, and half-way reaching toward the crystallization of principles into treaties with an international sanction." He believed that the ILO was an important starting point—"indeed, the most definite starting point that the Peace Conference has brought for experimentation along the lines of both social legislation and international cooperation."[36]

Despite his enthusiasm for the International Labor Organization, Shotwell tired of his work at Paris. By the end of the Conference he desperately wanted to return to Columbia and wrote to his friend William A. Dunning:

34. Joseph Grew to J.T.S., May 13, 1919, #181.255/3, ACNP; "Letter of Labor Committee to Secretary-General of the Peace Conference," May 15, 1919, #180.03402/1, ACNP; J.T.S. to Joseph Grew, n.d., #185.16/119, ACNP; J.T.S., "Memorandum for the President," June 6, 1919, Box 118, J.T.S. Papers. See also Edward J. Phelan, "The Admission of the Central Powers in the ILO," in J.T.S., ed., *Origins,* 1:256–80.
35. Phelan, "Admission of the Central Powers," 1: 281.
36. J.T.S. to Joseph P. Chamberlain, June 13, 1919, Box 113, J.T.S. Papers.

> My career as a diplomat is, I suppose, approaching a conclusion and I assure you that I have no desire to keep it going any longer than there is need. It is a wearisome and thankless task with every chance to make blunders if one takes the job seriously, and every temptation to let things slide if one is simply intent upon avoiding trouble.[37]

To return to teaching was his "hope, dream, and ambition."

Germany's reluctance to sign the Treaty of Versailles unless substantially revised caused much anxiety and speculation at Paris. Renewed war seemed unlikely, yet on June 20, the Allies instructed Marshall Foch to march into Germany if the treaty was not signed by 7:00 P.M. on June 23. The suspense ended only a few hours before the deadline with a new German government agreeing to sign unconditionally. Shotwell reacted to the Versailles settlement with mixed emotions. Like most of the other delegates he did not have a chance to see the treaty as a whole until it was presented to the Germans on May 7. His reaction, while not completely favorable, was not as severe as that of George Louis Beer or Robert Lansing, who viewed the settlement with complete "disappointment, depression, and regret."[38] He had favored the giving of Fiume to Italy and felt that the final solution to this question was a poor one. He seriously questioned the idea of the Polish Corridor, believing that it was neither politically wise nor "in Poland's own interest." He was disappointed that the League Covenant did not recognize the principle of periodic recurring conferences on political and economic problems. And finally, he strongly regretted that his proposal for "association with the League" was not given formal recognition.[39]

He did not, however, condemn the entire settlement. Like Wilson he felt that the League of Nations could iron out the major inequities in the treaty at a later date and under less emotional conditions. He hoped that the United States would turn from its traditional isolation and take a more internationalist approach to world affairs. America,

37. J.T.S. to William A. Dunning, June 10, 1919, Dunning Papers, Columbia University.
38. Beer, "Diary," p. 81; Lansing, *Peace Negotiations,* pp. 272–74.
39. J.T.S., *At Paris,* pp. 190, 301–6; J.T.S. to Isaiah Bowman, December 2, 1919, Box 9, J.T.S. Papers.

he believed, could no more step out of the League of Nations than it could step out of international law, for it was now "the basis of the international law of the future." For the United States to denounce its share in the new organization "would be regarded by large and small nations alike as a sign that through all our idealism we have been essentially hypocrites."[40] While he did not view the new world organization as ideal, Shotwell did believe that it would facilitate international cooperation and was, therefore, a worthwhile experiment.[41]

If Shotwell took the time to analyze the various sections of the treaty or if he had any theory as to the cause of its many inequities, he did not publicize them. In fact, he refrained from making any general analysis of the Versailles settlement until he published his diary some eighteen years later. Unlike many of his contemporaries, he did not place the major blame on Wilson or on the other negotiators. He believed, rather, that the great weaknesses in the treaty were due to the organization of the conference and the failure of the Allies to negotiate with the ex-enemy states. He felt that Wilson's original plan to have two treaties—a preliminary one dealing with the most urgent military and economic problems and then a more comprehensive one worked out through negotiations by both sides—was the proper approach. Yet the very organization of the conference precluded the possibility of two treaties. Once launched upon the study of detail, it was unreasonable to expect that all the labor would be spent on a preliminary document which might be completely changed during subsequent talks. "The preparation of a detailed provisional text," Shotwell declared, "created a situation which could not easily be changed and a text which could not readily be done over again. In my opinion this was hardly less decisive for the making of the treaty than the strategy of its leaders."[42]

The real difficulty in Wilson's decision to have just one treaty—a

40. J.T.S. to William H. Carpenter, February 26, 1919, Carpenter Papers, Columbia University.
41. J.T.S. to Munroe Smith, March 17, 1919, Smith Papers.
42. J.T.S., *At Paris,* pp. 38–39. Secretary of State Lansing also felt that Wilson's decision not to first negotiate a preliminary treaty was a bad mistake. See Lansing, *Peace Negotiations,* pp. 206–8.

difficulty which Shotwell only indirectly touched upon—was that the delegates, believing that their work would be subject to negotiations with the ex-enemy states, included a series of maximum demands which they fully expected would be whittled down by the Germans. Once it was agreed to forego the preliminary treaty, however, many of these demands remained and accounted for the severity of the final draft.[43]

Another cause for the inequities in the treaty, according to Shotwell, was the fact that each of the experts worked on their own specific problems without seeing how their suggestions or proposals would fit into the general peace settlement. The fault did not lie in any single section of the treaty, "for in most cases these sections contained provisions that were not without justification and were not merely the embodiment of vindictive and arbitrary power over a helpless victim." The major wrong was that "when all the sacrifices were added together, the whole was greater than the sum of the parts." He believed that the Treaty of Versailles was impossible to accept because it was impossible to fulfill on the part of the citizens of the conquered nations and still maintain a decent standard of living.[44]

Although Shotwell's analysis of the Paris Peace Conference was quite perceptive, it came many years after the event. In 1919 he refrained from making any overall evaluation and seemed quite content to accept the Treaty of Versailles as an accomplished fact. His experience as a diplomat proved both satisfying and frustrating. He enjoyed working on the labor sections of the treaty and believed that the ILO would develop into an important international agency. Yet his hope for a great liberal peace settlement did not come to fruition. Compromises were made which seemed to destroy the very basis of the Fourteen Points upon which he had placed so much faith. His counsel on political and territorial matters was rarely sought nor accepted when freely given.

Despite the success of the Washington Conference and the creation of the ILO, the Senate rejected the Treaty of Versailles and refused membership in either the League of Nations or the new labor organi-

43. Bailey, *Woodrow Wilson and the Lost Peace,* pp. 213–14.
44. J.T.S., *At Paris,* pp. 43–45.

zation. As he told his friend William A. Dunning at the close of the conference, he was not entirely unhappy to see his career as a diplomat end. Yet when it finally came to a close, he again postponed his much desired return to Columbia. Before he could return to teaching, he felt obliged to undertake the important task of explaining the Great War and its possible consequences to the peoples and governments of the world.

At Columbia University, 1915.

At Woodstock with family.

At Inauguration of Joseph E. Johnson as President of Carnegie Endowment for International Peace, 1950. John Foster Dulles is seated.
Courtesy the Carnegie Endowment for International Peace

6
Entrepreneur of Scholarship

With the Paris Peace Conference over and the International Labor Organization established, Shotwell returned to the study of history. But it was not as a lone scholar combing the stacks of the Columbia University Library in search for a book on medieval universities or spending long, tedious hours in his office translating early Christian church records that he devoted himself to the Muse of Clio. Nor did he return as a dedicated teacher, preaching the tenets of the New History and instilling in undergraduates and graduates alike the need for adopting the scientific method to human thinking. Instead he chose a relatively new approach to history and became one of the first great entrepreneurs of scholarship. Appointed general editor of the Carnegie Endowment's *Economic and Social History of the World War,* he organized an international cooperative effort in behalf of scholarship on a scale never before attempted. Setting up editorial committees, submitting progress reports, scrutinizing manuscripts, lobbying for appropriations, pleading with reluctant bureaucrats to open classified information, and soliciting the aid and support of scores of ex-cabinet members and government officials became his chief occupation for the next seven years and remained a major obligation for eleven more years after that.

Shotwell's interest in twentieth-century problems developed slowly. His first courses at Columbia dealt exclusively with the Middle Ages, but eventually he began offering courses on various aspects of eighteenth- and nineteenth-century history. Just before the outbreak of World War I his courses tended to concentrate almost entirely on modern history. His work on the Inquiry and his participation at the Paris Peace Conference directed his attention to the field of foreign relations. While in Europe for the conference, he participated in several academic discussions on the nature of foreign affairs which eventually led to the founding of the Royal Institute of International Affairs in London and the Council on Foreign Relations in the United States.[1]

Like his teacher and friend, James Harvey Robinson, Shotwell turned away from history as a purely academic subject and became increasingly concerned with its didactic aspects. In many ways this trend away from academic scholarship for its own sake was the logical result of the New History and the prominent position given to the concept of "presentism" by the Columbia group of historians.[2] The war and its aftermath made Shotwell particularly aware of the problems of his own time and dramatically broke his ties with the medieval world. Contemporary problems not only seemed more important than the academic questions which had concerned him at Columbia, but they also contained a certain sense of urgency which demanded attention. Most likely the same type of reasoning which led him to reject the idea of teaching high school while an undergraduate at the University of Toronto, forced him now to turn away from purely academic pursuits and concentrate on the practical application of intelligence. College teaching no longer seemed sufficient as a career goal. For

1. Malcolm Davis, "The Reminiscences of Malcolm Davis" (Oral History Research Office, Columbia University, 1950), p. 90.
2. This emphasis on the didactic value of history not only predominated the post-World War I work of Robinson and Shotwell, but also became a major aspect of the writings of Charles Beard and Harry Elmer Barnes, two other prominent Columbia New Historians. See Warren I. Cohen, *The American Revisionists: The Lessons of Intervention in World War I* (Chicago, 1967), pp. 235–37.

many years, along with Robinson, John Dewey, and many other Columbia professors, he had advocated a more active role for academicians. The war had allowed scholars to apply their knowledge to social and economic problems, and Shotwell believed that these efforts should continue in the postwar period.

In July, 1918, he published an article in the *Columbia University Quarterly* seriously questioning the educational and teaching system at Columbia. He conceived of the university not merely as an institution of learning, but also as a laboratory where the intellectual forces of the nation could work on the numerous problems confronting society. He called upon the Columbia adminstration to "make scientific research careers possible for young men, instead of throwing upon them a crushing burden of instructional work." Scholars had a responsibility to take a greater interest in applied knowledge, and Shotwell believed that Columbia should encourage such interests. "Perhaps," he declared, "we are teaching too much. In any case, if the resources of the University do not permit of extreme drill work in classes except at the cost of the creative or scientific productivity of instructors, we must lessen instruction, or our University can never perform its true function in either city or nation."[3]

Like John Dewey, Shotwell saw no conflict between thought and action—between the role of a scholar in the traditional sense and his role as activist. In fact, he believed that only by applying intelligence to the problems of society could democracy survive. The war had released discontent among the masses throughout the world, and unless the state offered some outlet for these grievances, disorder and rebellion were bound to break out. No group, according to Shotwell, was better prepared to take up the problems of society than the academic community.[4]

To prevent another holocaust, to heal the major social and economic ills of society—these were the issues which scholars had to face. Only by the development of an "applied social science" could they be solved, and Shotwell urged his colleagues to accept the challenge.[5] But

3. J.T.S., "University War Problems," *Columbia University Quarterly* 20 (July 1918): 230–33.
4. J.T.S., *Intelligence and Politics* (New York, 1921), pp. 19–20.
5. Ibid., p. 20.

how best could scholars make meaningful contributions to the solution of social and economic problems? This was the question which disturbed him most. It was one thing to apply the scientific method to "practical" questions, but it was quite another to get "rational" solutions accepted by those in power or by the public in general.

Several alternatives presented themselves to Shotwell. He might enter politics; but the necessity of compromise involved in a political career and the effort expended in soliciting votes and running campaigns made such a decision unacceptable. He might enter government service as he had in 1917; but now that the crisis was over and the American people demanded a return to normalcy, there seemed little likelihood that university scholars would be given policy-making positions. He might return to Columbia to study the problems of society in a clinical manner; but this too seemed unacceptable. Although the academic approach might have appealed to him before the war, it was no longer satisfactory. During the conflict he had come close to the sources of power and had become involved directly in decision-making. He found it enjoyable and invigorating. He liked being in the center of controversy and on top of problems as they arose. He seemed to flourish in the give and take of debate and had come to believe that political considerations were of major importance in the successful solution of social problems.

Given the limitations of these other alternatives, the one which seemed to offer the best opportunity for a man with his background and interests was acceptance of a position with one of the major American foundations. By working through a respectable reform organization he could devote all his time to the consideration of contemporary problems, avoid undesirable compromises, maintain a degree of intellectual freedom, have access to those in power, and be assured that his proposals would get maximum national circulation.

Although Shotwell probably did not systematically study the various alternatives and calculate the possibilities of each, he saw in the prospect of joining the Carnegie Endowment for International Peace and in editing a massive history of the First World War a logical beginning for a man trained as an historian to influence public opinion and win recognition for his ideas. The war history was a good starting point, he believed, for if all the facts involved in the war were carefully analyzed, the cause of peace would gain immeasurably. In addition, it would enable the general editor to make worldwide contacts which might prove useful in promoting specific reforms and peace proposals.

Shotwell's desire to render more "useful" service to society was not the only reason for postponing his return to Columbia and a teaching career. A more subtle influence, and one which he never seemed to recognize, was the enormous personal satisfaction he received by associating with people in power. His fascination with power and with those who wielded it was understandable given his rather humble beginnings, but at times it seemed excessive. He filled his diary with descriptions of dinners with European diplomats and foreign dignitaries. Just the fact that he ate in the same room with them seemed sufficient reason to jot down their names. Often he mentioned a conversation with an important official, neglecting to say what the discussion had been about, but carefully describing the man and his rank in government as if that was important in itself.[6]

As part of the American Commission to Negotiate Peace he fully realized that he was now making history instead of writing about it. On December 9, 1918, just five days after the *George Washington* left New York Harbor on its way to France, he wrote:

> I nearly forgot to say that the Military Intelligence took our pictures this morning—not merely as a group, but individually, and then took films of us for a movie! The Committee on Public Information plans to give them out some day, when they get back to America. They will be preserved in the records in Washington as part of the history of the war.[7]

Here was excitment and a new sense of importance. To return to Columbia after months of taking part in discussions affecting the fate of millions of people seemed intolerable. The Carnegie Endowment's project, on the other hand, would enable him to continue working within the framework of his profession and at the same time allow him to make a substantial contribution to the cause of peace. Moreover, it would keep him in Europe, close to the drama and excitement of the new experiment in international organization.

The idea for a history of the World War was not originally Shot-

6. J.T.S., *At Paris,* pp. 121–22, 129–34, 140–43, et passim.
7. Ibid., p. 71.

well's, but he had much to do with its initial planning. The suggestion was first made by John Bates Clark in his capacity as Director of the Division of Economics and History of the Carnegie Endowment. Clark believed that a study of the economic effects of war would reveal the economic interdependence of nations and the consequences of this interdependence in wartime. Such a recognition by the governments of the world, he claimed, would lead to policies which would contribute to their mutual welfare and might, therefore, lessen the danger of armed conflict in the future.[8]

After discussing his project with William A. Dunning, then head of the Department of History at Columbia, Clark asked Shotwell to draw up a memorandum and outline for the proposed war history. The memorandum, completed in time for the Trustees' meeting in November, 1914, called for an objective and scientific study of the war. Employing the concepts of the New History, Shotwell suggested that the study should not restrict itself to diplomacy, military history, and economics, but should include all the social and political sciences in an interdisciplinary attempt to explain the meaning and consequences of the war. He envisaged in addition to a preparatory series of volumes dealing with Europe prior to the war and the actual history of the economic effects of the conflict, a group of studies on the way the war affected the "common outlook" and "common activities" of the world.[9]

The Trustees approved the project and instructed Clark to begin preparations. At Clark's suggestion, the Executive Committee appointed Shotwell Associate Director of the Division of Economics and History in charge of the war history at an annual salary of $6,000 a year. The appointment, to take effect on July 1, 1917, required Shotwell to resign from Columbia in order to devote his full-time to the Endowment.[10]

8. Carnegie Endowment for International Peace, *Year Book,* 1915, pp. 92–99. (Hereafter cited CEIP.)

9. J.T.S., "Memorandum on the History of the War, 1914," Division of Economics and History, 1914, #1175–89, CEIP Archives, Columbia University.

10. CEIP, *Year Book,* 1915, p. 23; CEIP, *Minutes of the Meetings of the Board of Trustees and Executive Committee* (Carnegie Endowment Library), 6: 91–92. (Hereafter cited as *Minutes.*) See also George A. Finch, "History of

To the Executive Committee's great surprise, Shotwell turned down their offer. Instead he accepted the general editorship of a "semi-official" history of the Great War sponsored by the *Encyclopaedia Britannica.* In a letter to Elihu Root, president of the Endowment, he indicated that his interest in the *Britannica* project stemmed mainly from its possible effect on public opinion. He assured Root that it was "not the offer of larger financial rewards, nor the specious attraction of the mere greatness of the new enterprise" that determined his choice, but rather "the possibility of contributing to a survey which will bear the outward mark of authority and which—sold widely throughout the world—will have much to do in directing the public opinion of the future, the justification of scientific scholarship and of historical insight."[11]

The letter revealed a major change in Shotwell's philosophy of history. He was no longer interested in historical scholarship for its own sake. In fact, he seemed to imply that research had no value other than its application in the contemporary world. The change in outlook had taken place gradually. By the time he had moved from the concept of "presentism," which held that historical research and understanding of the past might be of benefit in explaining the present, to the conclusion that the major justification for historical scholarship was its power to influence public opinion and national action, his career goals and aspirations had also changed. No longer could he find satisfaction in fighting historiographical battles or in training novice historians. All his ideas and proposals would now have to be judged by their "usefulness" to society and their ability to move people to action.

When the *Britannica* project fell through, the Carnegie Endowment renewed its offer and Shotwell accepted. On July 1, 1919, he resigned from the American Commission to Negotiate Peace and established an office at the London School of Economics. Margaret and his two children joined him in England, where they lived intermit-

---

the Carnegie Endowment for International Peace: 1910–1946" (unpublished manuscript in the Carnegie Endowment Library, New York City, 1950), 1: 170–71.

11. J.T.S. to Elihu Root, April 18, 1917, Division of Economics and History, 1917, #228–30, CEIP Archives; CEIP, *Minutes,* 7: 36–37.

tently for the next several years. They frequently accompanied him on his travels through western and central Europe, and the entire family returned to the United States periodically. His eldest daughter remained in America in 1923 when she entered Vassar College, but rejoined the family during the summers.[12]

Gaining access to the various national archives so that an accurate history of the war could be written was one of the first and most difficult problems for Shotwell to solve. The question of collecting and preserving war material had disturbed him throughout the war. As chairman of the National Board for Historical Service he had emphasized the archival problem above all others and even suggested to a *New York Times* correspondent that "unless a systematic effort is made to deal with the problem of preserving the records of the present, our age will leave no more record than that which saw the fall of Rome."[13] As a member of the American Commission to Negotiate Peace he tried unsuccessfully to get the archives of the Central Powers opened to "qualified" researchers. Although his efforts failed in this regard, he achieved partial success once he took over his editorial duties by convincing the Austrian government to open all its archives to Endowment-sponsored scholars. In addition, the British Academy, at his request, called a conference on local war records in order to coordinate the collection and cataloging of war documents in Great Britain.[14]

Despite his efforts to get the governments of Europe to open their archives, much material remained classified and inaccessible. As an alternative he decided to solicit the aid of "those who had played some part in the conduct of affairs during the war, or who, as close observers in privileged positions, were able to record from first or at best second-hand knowledge the history of different phases of the great economic war and of its effect upon society."[15] Aspects of the war for

12. Interview with Helen Harvey Shotwell and Mrs. Margaret Summers, May 27, 1971; CEIP, *Minutes,* 8: 96; CEIP, *Year Book,* 1920, p. 20.
13. *New York Times,* June 29, 1918, p. 7.
14. CEIP, *Year Book,* 1921, p. 78; *Year Book,* 1932, pp. 151–52; J.T.S., "Report on the Years' Work: September 30, 1920—October, 1921," Division of Economics and History, 1921, #553–77, CEIP Archives.
15. CEIP, *Year Book,* 1923, p. 80.

which the source material was not available were to be covered by volumes consisting for the most part of unofficial yet authoritative statements. Eventually some thirty-five wartime cabinet ministers worked on the war history and contributed volumes.

Rejecting the original plan of organizing the history around a series of comparative and topical studies covering the effects of the war on various countries, Shotwell decided to organize it on a national basis. Such a plan would simplify the international aspects of the history as well as the editorial work. By creating editorial boards in each of the contributing countries, he hoped to delegate a good deal of the editorial responsibility and have access to the advice of national representatives on topics and possible choice of authors.

Having set up his central office in London, Shotwell organized the British editorial board first. He chose Sir William Beveridge as chairman of the group. Beveridge not only served in the Ministry of Food and in the Ministry of Munitions during the war, but was also director of the London School of Economics. Other members of the British board included H. W. C. Davis, adviser to the War Trade Intelligence Department and a professional historian, Professor E. C. K. Gonner, Director of Statistics, Ministry of Food and professor of economic science at the University of Liverpool, Thomas Jones, Acting Secretary of the War Cabinet, John M. Keynes, Adviser to the Treasury during the war and editor of the *Economic Journal,* F. W. Hirst, a member of the Carnegie Endowment's Committee of Research, and W. R. Scott, a member of the British Academy.[16]

He chose men of a similar type and reputation for the editorial boards in France, Belgium, Italy, Czechoslovakia, the Netherlands, Switzerland, Portugal, and the Balkan countries. Since the volumes contemplated for the Central Powers presented some of the most difficult and complex problems, Shotwell himself took personal charge of the editorial work. In Germany, he worked closely with Max Sering of the University of Berlin, Carl Joseph Melchior, a member of the German delegation at the Paris Peace Conference, and Professor Albrecht Mendelssohn-Bartholdy, who served as executive secretary in charge of research. His closest advisers for the volumes

16. Ibid., 1921, pp. 81–82.

composing the Austro-Hungarian series were Professor Friedrich von Wieser, of the University of Vienna, Dr. Gustav Gratz, Minister of Foreign Affairs for Hungary, and Dr. Richard Schüller, Chief of the Economic Section of the Austrian Foreign Service.[17]

The Russian series presented unique problems. The Bolshevik government showed no interest in the Endowment's project and absolutely refused to open its archives to historians. Shotwell therefore decided to restrict the series to the period before the Bolshevik Revolution and appointed exiled Czarist scholars to the task. He later justified the decision on the grounds that "they alone knew what had taken place during the war."[18] In reality, however, Shotwell simply wanted a few volumes on Russia for the series and had no alternative but to appoint those available for the work. He chose Paul Vinogradoff, then teaching at Oxford, as head of the Russian series and asked Michael Florinsky, a student at the London School of Economics and later a graduate student at Columbia, to serve as his assistant.

Although the proposed scope and cost of the war history was enormous, Shotwell felt that the project would justify itself in the end. In his report to the Endowment's Executive Committee in 1921, he declared that if the study of the World War were "undertaken by men of judicial temper and adequate training," it would "ultimately by reason of its scientific obligations to truth of fact, furnish a basis for the forming of sound public opinion, and thus contribute fundamentally toward the aims of an institution dedicated to the cause of international peace."[19] When critics questioned the usefulness of the Endowment's project and argued that a mere academic enterprise could do little to relieve the chaotic situation of Europe following the war, he replied:

> In the long years to come, if our work is done properly we may contribute a body of fact for students of history and politicians as well as economists which may help to guide the intelligence

17. Ibid., pp. 87–102; J.T.S. to George A. Finch, August 29, 1921, Division of Economics and History, Economic and Social History of the War, 1922, #722, CEIP Archives; J.T.S., *Autobiography*, pp. 137–53.
18. J.T.S. to Alger Hiss, June 24, 1947, I.F.3. #43285, CEIP Archives.
19. CEIP, *Year Book*, 1921, p. 75.

of the world from such catastrophes as have befallen Europe in our time; and that is perhaps as important work as we can do in the grip of the forces of today.[20]

Like most reform-minded intellectuals of his generation, Shotwell had an indomitable faith in the potency of data and facts. By merely presenting the "facts" concerning the recent holocaust to the public, he believed that the evils of war in general would become clear. Once people understood the true nature of war they would support a movement to abolish it. This was the assumption with which he began the war history. He soon realized, however, that facts can be interpreted in many ways and objective studies alone cannot secure peace.

The first volumes of the war history appeared in the summer and fall of 1921. Arthur L. Bowley's book on *Prices and Wages in the United Kingdom, 1914–1920* was the first to go to press, followed by Arthur B. Keith's *War Government of the British Dominions,* and J. A. Salter's *Allied Shipping Control: An Experiment in Industrial Administration.* The reviews of the three volumes were excellent and Salter's book was acclaimed as a major accomplishment. While Shotwell was quite pleased with the initial volumes, he was very disappointed when Sigmund Freud, who had agreed to write a volume on the "Psychological Aspects of War Reactions," asked to be released from his contract. Shotwell had hoped that this would be one of the highlights of the history, but Freud stated that after working on the volume for several months he was unable to make any progress and could not continue.[21]

The generous acclaim accorded the first volumes of the war history did not prevent several Endowment trustees from criticizing the entire project. Andrew J. Montague, a member of the House of Representatives from Virginia and former governor of the state, not only disapproved of the enormous cost, but questioned whether the history as outlined by Shotwell was really within the scope of the Endowment's Charter. He had serious doubts as to the general editor's "sense of

20. J.T.S. to Carl Melchior, July 27, 1933, Box 75, J.T.S. Papers.
21. Pauline Stearns to George A. Finch, December 12, 1921, Division of Economics and History, Economic and Social History of the War, 1921, #309, CEIP Archives.

proportion" and "his ability to visualize the true line of his tremendous undertaking."[22] Frederic A. Delano, a former member and vice-governor of the Federal Reserve Board, also questioned the possible cost of the enterprise, but more important he feared that many of the proposed volumes would prove more useful to military men as manuals for conducting future wars than to the opponents of militarism who hoped to use the study in behalf of peace. By pointing out the economic errors made during the First World War and by illustrating the necessity of commandeering the economic and industrial strength of a country in order to wage a successful war in the future, the *Economic and Social History of the World War,* he argued, might aid the militarists rather than discredit them.[23]

James Brown Scott, Secretary of the Endowment and Director of the Division of International Law, supported Delano's argument.[24] He too believed the project might prove a great value to militarists by helping them deduce "from the World War methods of conducting more efficiently wars in the future." In addition, he questioned the advisability of using ex-cabinet members to fill in the gaps where the sources were inadequate. He believed that nothing more would come of these contemplated monographs than a mere justification for the author's personal conduct in the war and a denunciation of his opponents. He did not see how the purposes of the Endowment would be served through such an approach.[25]

22. Andrew J. Montague to John Bates Clark, November 15, 1922, Division of Economics and History, Economic and Social History of the War, 1922, #82, CEIP Archives.
23. CEIP, *Minutes,* 12: 63–67.
24. James Brown Scott to Elihu Root, January 27, 1923, Division of Economics and History, Economic and Social History of the War, 1923, #115–19, CEIP Archives.
25. The fears of Delano and Scott were partially confirmed during the 1930s. In 1930, Colonel Irving J. Carr asked the Endowment to send free copies of the war history to the Army Industrial College in Washington D.C. (See J.T.S. to George A. Finch, April 16, 1930, Secretary's Office and Administration, 1930, #1814, CEIP Archives.) In the mid-thirties officials in the Italian government requested permission from the Endowment to publish an Italian translation of J. A. Salter's book on shipping control. The request, which was granted, made it very clear that the translation was intended for the professional use of military officers in Italy. (See CEIP, *Minutes,* 27: 53.) Mrs. Isadore Lubin, one of Shotwell's secretaries during the thirties, adds that the

The debate among the Trustees resulted in a clear division of opinion regarding the publication of the war history. Shotwell with the support of John Bates Clark and Elihu Root prevented the scrapping of the entire series, but had to postpone contracting for any new volumes. The most significant result of the debate was that it made Shotwell much more conscious of the possibility of military uses of his history and caused him to scrutinize each of the manuscripts more carefully. After reading the French volume on the war blockade, for example, he decided that the Endowment could not publish it because it was more a contribution to the "method of carrying on a blockade" than a study of the effects of the blockade during World War I.[26]

In 1924 the *Economic and Social History of the War* received a large boost. In January, Shotwell took over as Director of the Division of Economics and History replacing Clark, who had resigned the previous July. In November, he became a Trustee and gained a much larger say in policy decisions. More important in terms of the war history than Shotwell's advancement within the Endowment, however, was the Carnegie Corporation's decision to help finance the project. Beginning in 1924 with a grant of $350,000, it eventually appropriated more than $505,000 for the war history. The added appropriations enabled Shotwell to complete the volumes originally planned and contract for several additional ones.[27]

Shotwell's duties as general editor were by no means over after he had secured access to archival material, organized editorial boards, and secured the cooperation and support of some of the most renowned scholars and politicians in Europe. His major task began when the various manuscripts were submitted for publication. Although he viewed himself only as the "director" of the project and hoped to leave the writing to the authors and the editorial work to the

---

Japanese government requested her to send it a set of the war history. (Interview with Mrs. Isadore Lubin, December 26, 1966.)

26. J.T.S. to James Brown Scott, January 11, 1924, Box 66, J.T.S. Papers; J.T.S. to ? Peylade, February 18, 1925, Box 66, J.T.S. Papers.

27. The Endowment itself spent $344,134.36 on the war history. Added to the Carnegie Corporation's $505,557.96, it brought the total cost of the project to a phenominal $849,692.32. See "Appendix 2, Classification of Receipts and Expenditures from Organization to June 30, 1946," in Finch, "History of the Carnegie Endowment," 2: 13.

European boards, his influence was felt at every level of preparation. He usually went along with the recommendations of the national boards, yet he scrutinized every volume himself in order to make certain that it achieved a high level of objectivity and did not appeal to or affront nationalistic sentiment. He not only rejected the French volume on the blockade, but turned down two volumes in the Austrian series, forced major revisions on numerous other volumes, and demanded minor changes in almost all the studies.[28] In the long run, it was probably his very vigilance in keeping the volumes free from political controversy that prevented the war history from attracting wide popular approval. He missed an excellent opportunity, moreover, to take up the "revisionist" debate and shed light on some of the more controversial issues such as war guilt and the effects of the Treaty of Versailles. The Endowment researchers had greater access to war material than any other group of historians, but by carefully restricting their studies they evaded the major historical questions of the day.

Shotwell personally disdained the "revisionist" techniques of scholars like Sidney Fay of Harvard and Bernadotte Schmitt of the University of Chicago who, while coming to different conclusions, had reexamined the diplomatic notes and the timing of the international moves in an effort to determine the relative blame for the war. He objected even more to the polemics of those who, like his former student, Harry Elmer Barnes, had shifted the blame for the war from Germany to France and Russia. Nor did he accept the revisionist interpretation of America's entry into the war. He remained committed to the idea that the key questions leading to America's intervention were neutral rights and national security and not the influence or power of munitions makers or bankers. The controversy over war guilt and America's intervention split the historical community during the 1920s and 1930s, but Shotwell preferred to remain aloof from the debate.[29]

28. J.T.S. to Oron J. Hale, March 26, 1958, Box 232, J.T.S. Papers.
29. It was not until Shotwell became deeply involved in the debates over neutrality legislation in the 1930s that he permitted himself to express his personal feelings on the questions raised by the revisionists. See J.T.S., "History Used as a Guide in the Modern World," *Credit Executive* 30 (March 1936): 71–72.

When he initiated the *Economic and Social History of the World War* Shotwell had announced that the Endowment hoped the study would throw light on the causes of the conflict. As the work progressed, however, he decided that a survey of the causes could not be incorporated because of "the continued political controversy which has arisen in this field." Only by avoiding such political and diplomatic questions could genuine international cooperation be secured. Basically the problem stemmed from two sources. On the one hand, the German and Austrian governments had partially opened their archives on the understanding that the war history would not deal with political controversies arising from the responsibility of the war.[30] The series, therefore, faced the same problem as other "official" or "sanctioned" histories in that it exchanged its freedom to deal with controversial questions for the privilege of seeing classified material. On the other hand, the Endowment itself maintained a strict policy of avoiding all political and partisan matters. As general editor, Shotwell had to cut out all charges and counter-charges between the late belligerents. He was forced to use his red pencil on almost every volume and refused to publish several of them because of their partisan nature.[31]

Not only did Shotwell's policy limit the scope of the history, but it also helped foster general apathy toward the monumental project. The war history, while receiving impressive reviews, never proved a good commercial venture and almost every one of the volumes fell dead upon the market. Part of the problem lay in the Endowment's policy of sending its publications gratuitously to several hundred governmental, educational, and public libraries throughout the world.[32] The Endowment itself was not greatly disturbed over the limited number of sales, for it regarded the history not as a commercial venture, but as an "investment contributed to the cause for which

30. CEIP, *Year Book,* 1924, p. 143; *Year Book,* 1926, pp. 106–7.
31. J.T.S. to Ernest Mahaim, November 3, 1926, Box 53; J.T.S. to W. Alison Phillips, March 20, 1926, Box 46; J.T.S. to Henri Houser, November 1, 1927, Box 68, J.T.S. Papers.
32. Total sales of the War History were $80,000. J.T.S. to George A. Finch, January 12, 1951, Box 230, J.T.S. Papers.

the Endowment was established."[33] Shotwell, however, took great interest in the commercial aspects of the project and was bothered by its failure to attract public interest. Only if his history was widely read could it substantially contribute to the cause of peace. From the very beginning he had justified the study in terms of its possible impact upon public opinion. Yet once publication began the monographs seemed to attract little recognition from anyone but the reviewers.

Eventually Shotwell convinced himself that the poor sales were due to the public's desire to forget about the past war, but the commercial success and popular interest in the "revisionist" books of Harry Elmer Barnes, Charles Beard, C. Hartley Grattan, and Charles Tansill belied his explanation. The lack of public interest stemmed not from any general desire to forget about the war, but from the war history's overall lackluster and avoidance of controversy. Few people could get excited about W. R. Scott and J. Cunnison's *The Industries of the Clyde Valley during the War* or Michel Augé-Laribé and Pierre Pinot's *Agriculture and Food Supply in France during the War.* Although these monographs had some historical value and did provide future scholars with a good deal of important data about World War I, they were not the type of books to attract a wide audience or to get people thinking about the fundamental nature of war.

The work on the war history lasted some eighteen years. In 1937, when Shotwell finally announced its completion, there existed 152 volumes composed of over 300 monographs from 18 different countries. Most of the monographs appeared in the language of the national series. There were volumes in English, Italian, French, German, Norwegian, Swedish, Danish, Czech, and Hungarian. The Russian series, however, was published in English. Only three American studies appeared in the war history: Walter D. Hines' *War History of the American Railroads,* John M. Clark's *The Cost of the War to the American People,* and Leland Mereness' *Introduction to the American Official Sources for the Economic and Social History of the World War.* In addition to the 35 members of the wartime cabinets,

33. Finch, "History of the Carnegie Endowment," 1: 229; George A. Finch to J.T.S., March 24, 1923, Division of Economics and History, Economic and Social History of the War, 1923, #32, CEIP Archives.

dozens of university scholars, many of whom had served in wartime administrations contributed to the series. Although not as successful as he had originally hoped, Shotwell believed that the series was of inestimable value. It had conclusively proven that war and democracy were incompatible in the modern world. The "final lesson" of the war was that no nation could gain security "so long as the technique of war is practiced by great nations."[34]

Shotwell gradually came to the conclusion that if the public would not read the war history, then he would have to publicize its findings himself. Working on the project had made him more conscious than ever of the need to prevent another holocaust and the need for men of knowledge to work out the formulas for the preservation of peace.

Even more important in terms of his future activities, his position as general editor brought him into contact with scores of government officials and influential men in Europe. It gave him access to European statesmen on a basis accorded few American officials. This ability to get to see important European dignitaries and to get them to listen to his ideas proved invaluable to his subsequent antiwar work and helped persuade him that as a private citizen he could make a definite and positive contribution to the building of peace machinery in the post-war world.

34. CEIP, *Year Book,* 1924, pp. 139–40.

7
Amateur Diplomacy

"Most Americans," wrote Shotwell after living in Europe for nearly five years, "are continually asking that the world should 'settle down' so that they may be free from the problems of international politics, but the problem is not like buying a new house or moving in and settling down. It is more like his purchasing a factory which has to work and continue its output."[1] Unlike most Americans of his generation Shotwell did not view peace as the natural and normal state of mankind. Nor did he depreciate the importance of foreign policy or the vital role played by power in protecting a nation's interest. As an historian he was keenly aware of the dominant place that war occupied in human history. He recognized that it was "interwoven in the warp and woof of the fabric of our civilization" and was the instrument "by which liberty has been achieved and democracy established." To rid the world of war would require a fundamental change

1. J.T.S., "Open Conference on Disarmament and Security," August, 1924, Box 1, J.T.S. Papers.

and could not be accomplished "merely by insisting upon idealistic attitudes."[2]

Yet Shotwell never doubted that war could be abolished or that perpetual peace was within reach. Although he rejected such idealistic assumptions as the natural inclination of nations toward peace and the fundamental evil of power politics, he believed that all international disputes were subject to peaceable, just, and satisfactory settlement. He also subscribed to the idea that there existed an essential harmony of interests between nations and that once public opinion was made aware of this truth it would no longer view war as a proper or necessary instrument of national policy.[3]

It was on the question of peace machinery, however, that he found himself most at odds with public sentiment in America. Viewing international relations from his European base rather than from his American home, he came to believe that a strong system of collective security was a prerequisite for world order. Peaceful nations needed assurance that if attacked they would not have to face the aggressor alone. A clearly defined system of collective security would not only bring aid to a victim of aggression, but, more important, would act as a deterrent to those contemplating war in order to achieve their national goals. Only by the creation of such a deterrent could nations disarm without fear.

According to Shotwell the American conception of disarmament and security was much too limited and narrow. The advantageous geographic position of the United States and its historical experience led most American's to conceive of war as merely a temporary interlude in the harmonious relations between nations. They seemed to believe that peace would come as soon as nations eliminated or drastically reduced their guns and warships. Europeans, on the other hand, constantly lived under the threat of war and realized all too clearly that peace rested upon national security rather than upon the arith-

2. J.T.S., "Locarno and After," *Association Men* 51 (February 1926): 269–70.
3. For an analysis of the "idealist" assumptions on war and international relations see Roland N. Stromberg, "The Idea of Collective Security," *Journal of the History of Ideas* 17 (April 1956): 250–63. See also Hans J. Morganthau, "Another 'Great Debate': The National Interest in the United States," *American Political Science Review* 46 (December 1952): 961–62.

metic ratio of armaments. Living in Europe made Shotwell familiar with the Continental conception of security and led him to sympathize with the French position. "The French," he declared, "have long been trying to teach us the simple lesson that there must be security before there can be disarmament, but it is a lesson which we find hard to learn, simply because we have security and do not need to arm, at least by land to maintain it. All that we need to do is to make sure that the Atlantic and Pacific Oceans are not dried up."[4]

Another prerequisite for peace was an adequate substitute for war. Only if nations could settle their disputes without recourse to arms could the revolution in world affairs succeed. Shotwell rejected the conception of a peace based upon the mere maintenance of the status quo. Such a peace, he declared, could not be preserved and would only lead to the "perpetuation of abuses, of injustices established by force of arms in previous wars." Peace would remain precarious as long as nations did not have some means other than armed conflict to settle their differences. The alternative for war, he added, "must leave us an adjustable world and not a static one." This involved "a larger and larger degree of international cooperation and international machinery."[5]

The basic problem, according to Shotwell, centered around the machinery set up at Geneva. Not only was the security system embodied in the League of Nations incomplete, but as long as the United States, Germany, and Russia remained outside the world organization the possibilities of establishing a lasting peace were slim. Throughout the early twenties he pushed the idea of "association with the League," a plan he first suggested at the Paris Peace Conference.[6] Those nations refusing to assume the full responsibilities involved in League membership might become "associates" of the League by participating in recurring conferences on such questions as disarmament, trade, health, and finance. By so doing they would maintain their freedom of action, yet broaden international cooperation and help build a foundation for lasting peace. Given the strong opposition

4. J.T.S., "The Problem of Security," *The Annals of the American Academy of Political and Social Science* 120 (July 1925): 159.
5. J.T.S., "The Challenge to Peace," *Our World* 6 (December 1924): 8.
6. J.T.S., *At Paris*, pp. 110–11, 121–22, 140–42, et passim.

in America to political entanglements, he believed that this plan offered the only practical means for bringing the United States into closer cooperation with Europe and the League of Nations.[7]

Neither the League Secretariat nor the administration of Warren G. Harding showed much official interest in the proposal. The President applauded the idea of nations joining together "to prevent war, preserve peace, and promote civilization," but he would not "sanction" the League Covenant. Responding to the demands of the irreconcilables in his party, he told Congress on April 12, 1921, that "In the existing League of Nations, world-governing with its super powers, this Republic will have no part."[8] Secretary of State Charles Evans Hughes had supported American membership in the League with reservations, but under pressure from the irreconcilables and the President he decided to adopt a policy of nonrecognition toward the world organization. For several months the Harding administration even refused to answer letters from League officials. Gradually, however, this policy was abandoned, and the United States began cooperating with the League on nonpolitical projects. "Unofficial" observers from America attended conferences on numerous humanitarian problems such as opium traffic, public health, and the white slave trade. Although this policy somewhat resembled in practice Shotwell's idea of "association with the League," the American government refused to formalize its position and insisted that the sending of observers implied no official recognition of the League.

Not only Shotwell, but numerous European supporters of the League as well as League officials recognized weaknesses in the Geneva structure and saw the necessity of revising the League Covenant. Germany's failure to make reparations payments, followed by the French invasion of the Ruhr in January, 1923, forced European statesmen to reevaluate the political situation and to take a careful look at the work being done by the Temporary Mixed Commission established by the League to study the problem of disarmament and

7. J.T.S. to David Hunter Miller, July 18, 1922, Box 81, Miller Papers, Library of Congress; *Manchester Guardian,* September 5, 1922, clipping in Box 36, J.T.S. Papers.
8. U. S., Department of State, *Papers Relating to the Foreign Relations of the United States: 1921* (Washington, 1936), 1: xvii–viii.

security. In September, 1923, the Commission completed its work and incorporated its suggestions into a "Draft Treaty of Mutual Assistance."

The proposed treaty declared all aggressive war a crime and stipulated that every signatory state should give military support to any other signatory attacked by an aggressor. War, which the League Covenant sanctioned as a last resort, was no longer permitted for any reason. To implement this broad prohibition, the Draft Treaty vastly increased the authority of the League Council, empowering it to designate the aggressor, to decide on the application of economic sanctions, to determine what military forces each signatory should provide, to organize the transportation of troops, to furnish financial help for the victims, and to appoint a commander-in-chief of the united forces. As a definite step toward disarmament, the treaty provided that no nation could claim the benefit of its provisions until it had undertaken to reduce its armaments in accordance with a plan worked out by the Council. Finally, to meet the French demand for special bilateral treaties of guarantee, the Temporary Mixed Commission agreed that any group of signatories might negotiate special regional agreements among themselves as long as they were open and registered with the League Council.[9]

The Fourth Assembly of the League of Nations considered the proposed treaty at length, accepted it, and sent it on to the various governments for comment. Displeasure, however, expressed itself almost immediately. Many European leaders had serious doubts about turning over such enormous power to the Council. Others pointed out that its very strength would further alienate America from the European security system.[10]

Shotwell, who was then in Europe working on the *Economic and Social History of the World War,* followed the debates closely and decided that the treaty had little chance of success unless certain basic changes were made. He also believed that a clearer statement of

9. Francis P. Walters, *A History of the League of Nations* (London, 1952), 1: 217–28. For text of the Draft Treaty of Mutual Assistance see *International Conciliation* 201 (August 1924): 360–69.
10. Walters, *History of the League,* 1: 225–28; Fleming, *The United States and World Organization,* pp. 193–95.

America's position would be helpful. In order to provide these needed corrections, he returned to the United States in January, 1924 and began organizing a committee to study the joint problem of disarmament and security. He contacted several of his personal friends and many known "internationalists," warning them that unless they could come up with a better formula the entire collective security system might collapse. To Tasker H. Bliss, the American representative on the Supreme War Council during World War I, he stated that while he had no "delusions as to the difficulty of the problem," he could not "satisfy his conscience" without an effort to do his share.[11]

In addition to Bliss, he contacted John Bates Clark, Isaiah Bowman, Joseph Chamberlain, a professor of international law at Columbia, Stephen Duggan, director of the Institute of International Education, General James G. Harbord, former Chief of Staff of the American Army, Frederick Keppel, former Assistant Secretary of War and president of the Carnegie Corporation, David Hunter Miller, a New York lawyer and fellow Inquiry member, and Henry S. Pritchett, president of the Carnegie Foundation. Before the full committee met, Shotwell and David Hunter Miller discussed some of the major problems and decided to draft a treaty of their own. They divided their treaty into two parts: measures applicable to those who were and those who were not members of the League. Aggression was declared a crime, and each signatory power was required to automatically abstain from all economic and commercial intercourse with any declared aggressor. Each nation, however, could decide for itself what military or naval measures, if any, it should take.[12]

The committee as a whole met throughout the spring of 1924 and in June completed its "Draft Treaty of Disarmament and Security."[13] A good deal of Shotwell's original draft found its way into the finished product, as did parts of the Draft Treaty of Mutual Assistance. The

11. J.T.S., "Memorandum on the Draft Treaty of Mutual Assistance and Alternative Plans," April 12, 1924, Box 268, Tasker H. Bliss Papers, Library of Congress; J.T.S. to Tasker H. Bliss, Box 267, Bliss Papers; *New York Times,* June 18, 1924, p. 4.
12. J.T.S. to Tasker H. Bliss, May 26, 1924, Box 267, Bliss Papers.
13. "Draft Treaty of Disarmament and Security," *International Conciliation* 201 (August 1924): 343–51.

American plan, however, differed significantly from the latter in that it not only denounced war as a crime, but provided a clear and precise definition of aggression. Shotwell, as well as most of the other members, recognized that an acceptable definition and a reliable procedure for determining when an act of aggression had occurred were essential for a functional system of collective security. "So long as there was no agreement as to what constituted the crime of aggression," Shotwell pointed out, "there could be no criminal aggressor. So long as defense was indistinguishable from attack by clever camouflage or statesmanship, there could be no distinction legally between the two."[14]

Acting upon Miller's recommendation, the committee agreed to incorporate a juridical determination of aggression and made the crucial test the willingness to go before the World Court.

Article Five of the Draft Treaty declared:

> In the absence of a state of war, measures of force by land, by sea or in the air taken by one State against another and not taken for purposes of defense or for the protection of human life shall be deemed to be acts of aggression.
>
> Any Signatory which claims that another Signatory has violated the terms of this Treaty shall submit its case to the Permanent Court of International Justice.
>
> A Signatory refusing to accept the jurisdiction of the Court in any such case shall be deemed an aggressor within the terms of this Treaty.
>
> Failure to accept the jurisdiction of the Court within four days after submission of a claim or violation of this Treaty shall be deemed a refusal to accept the jurisdiction.[15]

Although the definition made the determination of aggression automatic and overcame the difficult and complex problem of evaluating the merits of each side in a dispute, it failed to confront the basic question of intentions. A nation entirely in the right might believe that

14. J.T.S., "Challenge to Peace," p. 6.
15. Article 5 of "Draft Treaty of Disarmament and Security," *International Conciliation* 201 (August 1924): 344.

unless it attacked first its opponent would attack, or that a situation might develop whereby it would lose its case through default. According to the juridical definition, however, a nation was guilty of committing a crime if it resorted to war no matter what its reasons. The Shotwell-Miller formula simply asked who had resorted to war first, not why he had done so or whether he was justified.

Shotwell recognized that his definition avoided the question of intentions, but defended it on the grounds that the preservation of peace depended upon the willingness of nations to seek means other than war for solving their disputes. "The elimination of force between individuals or sections of the community," he argued, "has been due not so much to the elimination of causes of quarrel as to the bettering of the procedure by which disputes are settled." The Draft Treaty of Disarmament and Security sought to replace historical and traditional methods for redressing international grievances with pacific ones. It made no pretense at redressing the grievances themselves. It assigned "not responsibility for a war but the responsibility of a nation for going to war."[16]

The basic problem with Shotwell's approach was that international relations had little similarity to the relations between individuals within a state. No law existed to govern the relations between states, nor did any supranational authority exist to guarantee the maintenance of justice. Shotwell recognized this, but felt that war was such an overwhelming evil that nations should renounce it first and then later develop machinery for meeting their grievances. Such a step, however, would require nations to cease behaving in their traditional manner, with little compensation in terms of security in return. Few countries were willing to make such a sacrifice during the postwar period, the United States the least of all.

Besides defining and outlawing aggression, the Draft Treaty of Disarmament and Security included provisions for the reduction of armaments, inspection, the making of separate treaties of mutual assistance, and the establishment of a recurring conference to study disarmament proposals. Most important, however, was the provision on sanctions. Everyone on the committee agreed that collective

16. J.T.S., "A Practical Plan for Disarmament," in ibid., pp. 340–41.

security depended upon some form of enforcement, but most felt that Shotwell's original suggestion of automatic economic sanctions was too harsh and would never win acceptance either in America or Europe. After much discussion the committee finally agreed upon the idea of "permissive sanctions," first put forward by David Hunter Miller. The Draft Treaty provided that all commercial, trade, financial, and property interests of a *declared* aggressor would lose, both in the territories of the other signatories and on the high seas, "any privileges, protection, rights or immunities accorded by either international law, national law or treaty." Each signatory, moreover, would have the right to adopt economic and military sanctions against the aggressor at its discretion.[17]

Shotwell quickly saw the advantages of a negative sanction and became one of its staunchest defenders. The most attractive aspect of the idea was that it involved no specific commitment to collective security and therefore had a good chance of gaining support in the United States. In addition to avoiding the question of political entanglements, it provided an effective sanction by removing an aggressor's guarantee of rights and threatening its economy in a vital area. "The effect of this upon business interest," Shotwell predicted, "would be instant. No trader could be sure that his ships would receive entry into the ports of another Signatory or that his investments in their keeping would not be immediately attached. In a world built up on a basis of credit, the result would be for the aggressor unavoidable panic, of greater or less degree." The added threat of further economic or military sanctions, moreover, would serve as a strong deterrent to any nation contemplating war.[18]

The American plan attracted immediate attention both in the United States and Europe. On June 17, 1924, the League Council, meeting in special session, voted to distribute copies of the proposed treaty to all League members and recommended that it be taken up for discussion by the Fifth Assembly scheduled to meet in September. The following day the *New York Times* published the full text of the

17. Article 8 of "Draft Treaty of Disarmament and Security," in ibid., pp. 344–45.
18. J.T.S., "A Practical Plan," pp. 354–55.

treaty and gave it strong editorial support. During the summer the Foreign Policy Association put out a pamphlet explaining its various provisions and organized discussion groups to explore the possibilities of implementation. The Federal Council of Churches also gave it wide distribution, as did the Carnegie Endowment for International Peace.[19]

While Shotwell expected to receive support from the pro-League organizations, he was greatly surprised to receive encouragement from Salmon O. Levinson, the leader of the Outlawry of War movement, and Senator William E. Borah, one of the League's most vocal opponents. Levinson found fault with the proposed treaty because it failed to "outlaw all wars," but he also felt that it was "most encouraging and of very great significance."[20] Borah was even more outspoken in his praise, calling it "the most encouraging event in the movement for peace which has taken place for many a day."[21]

Most likely such devout opponents of collective security as Levinson and Borah saw the Draft Treaty as an alternative to the League of Nations and supported it on that basis. Shotwell and the members of his committee, however, viewed it as strengthening the collective security machinery in Geneva and providing a basis for American cooperation. The important thing was that the document was imprecise enough so that it could win support from both sides. Even Shotwell admitted that the treaty did not depend on League action and could be held intact without reference to the League at all.[22] In other words, Shotwell's committee, in its attempt to bridge the American and European conceptions of security, had inadvertently found a bridge between the diverse factions of the peace movement. It was a bridge, however, built upon a very weak foundation, one that could not stand up against the strains and stresses of public debate.

Despite the frequent statements made by Shotwell and his col-

19. *New York Times,* June 18, 1924, p. 4, June 19, 1924, p. 20; J.T.S., *Autobiography,* pp. 184–85.
20. Salmon O. Levinson to William E. Borah, June 20, 1924, Salmon O. Levinson Papers, University of Chicago.
21. William E. Borah, "Toward the Outlawry of War," *New Republic* 39 (July 9, 1924): 179.
22. J.T.S. to James Brown Scott, July 1, 1924, Division of International Law, 1924, #4377–78, CEIP Archives.

leagues about the unofficial nature of the treaty, many of those who studied its provisions quickly realized that the entire scheme rested upon the support and participation of the American government. The most important question raised, therefore, was whether or not the Coolidge administration would agree to the scheme. Several members of the Temporary Mixed Commission, including Robert Cecil, denounced the entire project, declaring that it could do nothing but hamper European efforts at working out a feasible formula for disarmament.[23] But not all League delegates were ready to condemn the American effort. Several preferred to withhold judgment until some definite statement came from Washington. Some of those who had criticized the Draft Treaty of Mutual Assistance also turned against the American plan. They argued that the treaty would only perpetuate the status quo with all its injustices and all its attending evils. Others questioned whether the test of aggression was really accurate or fair. Could the nations of the world simply disregard the question of intentions and declare a nation an outlaw regardless of its reasons for resorting to force? Was the Court really an adequate substitute for war?[24]

The questions and criticisms leveled at the American plan were profound and hit at the very heart of the Draft Treaty of Disarmament and Security. In an article for the *Nation* Shotwell attempted to clarify the various parts of the treaty and explain the long-range goals of his committee. He agreed that compulsory sanctions might provide more security than his own scheme, but pointed out that if the United States would not accept such a formula it would prove meaningless in a crisis. Permissive sanctions were as far as the United States Senate would go, and if clearly defined these could be quite effective. He asked his readers not to exaggerate the importance of the proposed treaty. It was simply a treaty of disarmament and not a plan for universal compulsory arbitration. "It is an agreement not to commit aggression," he pointed out, "and it includes a readily recognized definition of aggression. It does not insure justice but it denies states

23. Robert Cecil to J.T.S., June 18, 1924, Box 268, Bliss Papers; J.T.S. to Raymond B. Fosdick, July 30, 1924, Box 1, J.T.S. Papers.
24. Frank Simonds to J.T.S., July 13, 1924, Box 267, Bliss Papers.

the right to attempt to secure what they think justice [is] by force of arms, it is only the beginning—if it is that—of a long process, by the substitution of something else for force in international affairs."[25]

The major weakness of both the American Draft Treaty and Shotwell's defense was that he never clearly defined just what that "something else" was which would replace war. The World Court was one possibility, but he denied that his treaty provided for compulsory arbitration. The Permanent Advisory Conference upon Disarmament was only a study group and could provide no real alternative to the use of force. Although he frequently stated that he did not wish to maintain the status quo, he was forced to support the system set up at the Paris Peace Conference until feasible alternatives to war were actually established. He wanted to abolish war immediately, but he gave no indication of how long it would take to work out the alternatives. Until that time came, the logic of his own position forced him to ask those discontented with the system to accept it as the lesser of two evils.

The convening of the Fifth Assembly on September 1, 1924, brought some of the highest ranking statesmen in Europe to Geneva. Ramsay MacDonald of Great Britain and Edouard Herriot of France, both recently elected to head their respective governments, attended the meeting. Fresh from London where they had agreed to the Dawes Plan only two days before, both men were determined to adopt some new plan for disarmament and security. Their decision to attend the Assembly meeting and the prospect of a major revision of the League Covenant brought many other European dignitaries to the Swiss city.[26] Among the hundreds of spectators who came to witness this momentous gathering were Shotwell, David Hunter Miller, and General Tasker H. Bliss. They arrived in Europe in late August and began sounding out various delegates about their attitude toward the American plan. The reaction was mixed. Herriot informed the three amateur diplomats that his government could not support the relatively weak

25. J.T.S., "Working Towards Disarmament," *The Nation* 119 (July 30, 1924): 113.
26. John Spencer Bassett, *The League of Nations: A Chapter in World Politics* (New York, 1928), p. 236; Fleming, *The United States and World Organization*, pp. 196–97.

sanctions provided in their draft treaty. Arthur Henderson of Great Britain and Joseph Paul-Boncour of France were more favorably inclined to the concept of "permissive sanctions," but also opposed the final draft on the grounds that it tended to diminish the importance of the League.[27]

In their opening remarks both MacDonald and Herriot voiced their support for the Shotwell-Miller definition of aggression and urged that it be used as the basis for a new League protocol on disarmament and security. Acting on their recommendation the League's technical committees dissected the American treaty and debated its various provisions. Most attention focused upon the definition of aggression. Several delegates supported the Shotwell-Miller formula over the one presented by the Temporary Mixed Commission, because it not only offered a clear-cut test for aggression, but eliminated the Council as the determining body. Praise for the plan, however, was by no means unanimous. One delegate agreed that the Council should not be given the power to determine an aggressor, but saw no reason to believe that the Court was any more competent. Another pointed out that while the scheme contained an absolute prohibition on aggressive war, it contained no counterpart procedure for settling disputes.[28]

Out of the League debates came the "Protocol for the Pacific Settlement of International Disputes," or the Geneva Protocol as it was popularly called. Although it attempted to define aggression, it omitted the Shotwell-Miller emphasis on the Court. Instead it broadened the concept of arbitration and defined the aggressor as the nation which went to war in violation of its obligations as a signatory of the Covenant or the Protocol. In addition, it clearly outlined rules for determining an aggressor. If a state committed acts of war either without using the arbitral machinery provided for in the Protocol or in defiance of a verdict of the Court or Arbitration Committee, or if it refused to obey an order of the Council to halt its forces, it would

27. J.T.S., *Autobiography,* pp. 187–88; American Research Committee, "Agenda," November 13, 1924, pp. 1–4, Box 267, Bliss Papers (attached to letter from Pauline Sterns to Tasker H. Bliss, November 11, 1924).

28. Bassett, *League of Nations,* pp. 236–38; Clyde Eagleton, "The Attempt to Define Aggression," *International Conciliation* 264 (November 1930): 20–27.

automatically label itself an aggressor. Only an unanimous vote of the Council could keep any one of these actions from constituting aggression.

The League delegates also sought to deter aggression by binding all the signatories to a firm defensive alliance. Upon the call of the Council the signatory states were bound not only to apply sanctions under Article 16 of the Covenant, but also to cooperate "loyally" and effectively "in resistance to any act of aggression." The only qualification to this collective security system was a provision for "graded responsibilities," which declared that each state's contribution was to be made "in the degree which its geographical position and its situation as regards armaments allow." No state, however, could decide not to join in the sanctions.[29]

Shotwell, who had returned to the United States in September, followed the work of the Fifth Assembly in the columns of the *New York Times.* On October 3, he read that the meeting had adjourned after unanimously voting for the Protocol and that the delegates were returning home to discuss ratification with their respective governments. The provisions of the Geneva Protocol disturbed rather than pleased him. He realized that it was an immensely important document, but feared that perhaps the delegates had moved too quickly and too far. He especially regretted their rejection of the idea of permissive sanctions. Not only did American support now look dim, but there was a good chance that several European nations would reject the treaty. As he told Tasker H. Bliss, the picture would have looked much brighter had "the Geneva Assembly been less ambitious."[30]

Although Shotwell expressed much skepticism about the treaty in his private correspondence, he praised it strongly in his public statements. He told a *New York Times* correspondent that it was a new "Magna Charta" of national security and a major step in the direction of outlawing war. Several weeks later he declared that the Protocol

29. Text of "Protocol for the Pacific Settlement of International Disputes" appears in *New York Times,* October 11, 1924, p. 3. See also Eagleton, "Attempt to Define Aggression," pp. 22–24; and Fleming, *United States and World Organization,* pp. 197–201.
30. J.T.S. to Tasker H. Bliss, October 3, 1924, Box 267, Bliss Papers.

was "the most ambitious and most courageous effort ever made by Governments to get rid of war."[31] The other members of the American committee had the same contradictory attitude. As Bliss explained to Hamilton Fish Armstrong, they definitely disliked the Protocol, but feared that any public criticism would influence others and harm the general movement for Covenant revision. In addition, they feared that complete defeat for the Protocol might discourage any future moves towards disarmament.[32]

The fate of the Geneva Protocol was sealed in November when Stanley Baldwin and his Conservative party replaced Ramsay MacDonald's Labour Government. Opposition of Commonwealth members, fear of trouble with the United States if the British government tried to enforce the sanctions called for by the Protocol, a reluctance to underpin the territorial settlement of Eastern Europe, and a deep-seated dislike for compulsory arbitration all led the new Foreign Minister, Austen Chamberlain, to formally reject the treaty in a prepared speech read to the Council on March 12, 1925.[33]

As soon as the Baldwin government came into power Shotwell realized that the Protocol had little chance of success. Believing that the only hope for salvaging the work already done lay in finding a compromise between the American plan and the Protocol, he decided to continue meeting with his Committee on Disarmament and Security. In April, 1925, with the aid of Mendelssohn-Bartholdy, the executive secretary of the German editorial board, he set up a German committee to parallel the work of his own group. He invited several leading citizens to join, including former Chancellor Wilhelm Cuno, the lord mayors of Cologne and Hamburg, Konrad Adenauer and Carl Petersen, Walter Simons of the German Supreme Court, and Professor Theodore Neimeyer, president of the German Society for the Law of Nations. He also established a similar committee in France to aid with the work. These European committees openly debated many of the questions relating to disarmament and security and pro-

31. *New York Times,* October 11, 1924, p. 3, January 11, 1925, sec. 8, p. 9.
32. Tasker H. Bliss to Hamilton Fish Armstrong, November 21, 1924, Box 267, Bliss Papers.
33. Walters, *History of the League,* 1: 283–85; Bassett, *League of Nations,* pp. 244–47.

duced several important technical studies. They both maintained close contacts with the diplomatic authorities in their respective countries and strongly influenced the negotiations which eventually led to the Locarno Agreements of October, 1925.[34]

Shortly after the rejection of the Geneva Protocol and the establishment of the German and French committees, Shotwell decided to discuss his activities with the State Department and Secretary of State Charles Evans Hughes. He had not done this before because he felt that the Draft Treaty of Disarmament and Security should remain "free of all official connections." Although the entire plan depended upon the acceptance of the United States government, he pushed it at Geneva without any support from the Coolidge administration. He was probably wise in staying away from the State Department, for Hughes and his subordinates strongly opposed the work of the amateur diplomats and had no intention of supporting the principles embodied in the Draft Treaty of Disarmament and Security.

When he finally went to see Hughes, the Secretary of State greeted him with a frown and declared that he thought Shotwell had been guilty of violating the Logan Act, which prohibited private citizens from carrying on unauthorized negotiations with foreign governments. Although the government had never enforced the law or prosecuted anyone since its passage in 1799, Shotwell had anticipated the Secretary's accusation and had studied the law before calling at the State Department. Unable to keep from smiling, he replied that the law did not apply to anyone working with the League of Nations, for the United States had not formally recognized its existence as an international agency.[35]

While Hughes might have pursued the matter and challenged Shotwell's interpretation of the law, he decided to let the matter drop rather than open a Pandora's box by trying to press charges. Shot-

34. J.T.S., "Confidential Memorandum on the German Committee for Arbitration and Security," n.d., I.F.2.a, #40412, CEIP Archives; J.T.S., "Memorandum on the Creation of the French Committee on Arbitration and Security," n.d., I.F.2.a, #40416 and #41285A, CEIP Archives; J.T.S., "Reflections on War and Peace," in CEIP, *Perspectives on Peace, 1910–1960* (London, 1960), pp. 22–23.
35. J.T.S., *Autobiography,* p. 195.

well's discussions with French and British diplomats were far from innocent, but the Secretary of State found it much easier to accept his report and hope that he would restrict his activities in the future to the writing of history. Shotwell's venture into amateur diplomacy, however, was much more than just a passing fancy. He never took the Logan Act seriously because he strongly believed that there existed "a sphere of action to be developed by private citizens in the consideration of those principles which underlie sound governmental policy." He believed that as modern governments extended their sphere of action, and as international problems became increasingly complex, technical studies conducted both by governmental and private agencies would become increasingly imperative.[36]

He knew there was some danger in unofficial and unauthorized negotiations, and believed that the scope and activity of private citizens should be "carefully circumscribed so as not to interfere with responsible governmental action." Yet he also believed that such activity would ultimately prove invaluable in solving the complex domestic and international problems of the day. He maintained that if private citizens limited their activities, they would eventually gain the support of their respective governments. While this thesis justified his own actions, Shotwell soon found out that the problem of limitation was not as simple as he originally believed. Many of his subsequent activities on behalf of international peace not only failed to win the support of the American government, but proved extremely embarrassing to the State Department as well.

36. J.T.S., "Confidential Memorandum on the German Committee for Arbitration and Security," September, 1925, I.F.2, #41285A, CEIP Archives.

8
Setting America Straight

In the decade following the First World War, the American peace movement came of age. Horrified by the costs, tired of the effort, disillusioned by the outcome, most Americans retained a faith that the world would return to normalcy and accept alternatives to war. It was a time for peace, and until the depression made the search for jobs seem more important than the avoidance of war, peace groups found strong public support. Not all peace advocates, however, shared James Thomson Shotwell's enthusiasm for the League of Nations or his desire to strengthen the peace machinery at Geneva. In fact, the basic assumptions and peace philosophy of the various opponents of war showed as much diversity as the tactics they employed.[1]

Some of the more conservative opponents of war put little faith in

1. J.T.S. to Hester D. Jenkins, April 25, 1930, Box 232, J.T.S. Papers. See also Robert E. Bowers, "The American Peace Movement, 1933–1941" (Ph.D. dissertation, University of Wisconsin, Madison, 1949), p. 9; Merle Curti, *Peace or War: The American Struggle, 1636–1936* (New York, 1936), p. 277; Robert H. Ferrell, *Peace in their Time: The Origins of the Kellogg-Briand Pact* (New Haven, 1952), pp. 13–30. Charles Chatfield's *For Peace and Justice: Pacifism in America, 1914–1941* (Knoxville, Tenn., 1971) also chronicles the diversity within the ranks of the antiwar movement.

disarmament or collective security. Instead they advocated the substitution of law for war and favored such devices as the codification of international law, treaties of arbitration, and the cultivation of international knowledge and understanding. Others, while sharing some of the assumptions of the conservative antiwar advocates, believed that the cause of peace should be pursued more vigorously. But even this group differed over priorities. Some, like Shotwell, favored collective security and looked to the League as the one hope for civilization; others saw the World Court as the cure-all; and still others opposed both the League and the Court and insisted that the only way to end war was to outlaw it and disarm. A small minority saw the road to peace through isolation and called for the abandonment of trade and the idea of freedom of the seas, while another group maintained that peace required fundamental changes in the political and economic system.[2]

By far the most prominent and wealthy peace organizations were those committed to internationalism of one form or another and to the ideals of Woodrow Wilson. While not all of them promoted American entry into the League of Nations, they shared a common faith in international cooperation and a belief that the techniques of discussion, arbitration, and conciliation would banish war from the world. Among the more effective organizations emphasizing the internationalist approach to peace were the World Peace Foundation, originally established with a one million dollar grant from the Boston publisher Edwin Ginn and the official distributor in the United States of all League of Nations publications; the Foreign Policy Association, founded one month after the 1918 Armistice and dedicated to "spreading knowledge of foreign affairs among the mass of intelligent people throughout the country"; the Woodrow Wilson Foundation, started in 1923 with nearly a million dollars and a desire to promote the ideals of Wilson by aiding scholars interested in international studies; and the Council on Foreign Relations, which published *Foreign Affairs* magazine and sought to interest an elite group of businessmen, educators, and government officials in world affairs.[3]

2. Curti, *Peace or War,* pp. 277–78.
3. Robert A. Divine, *Second Chance: The Triumph of Internationalism in America* (New York, 1967), pp. 18–23; Ferrell, *Peace in their Time,* pp. 23–26.

Even more important and influential in promoting the League and internationalism in America were the League of Nations Non-Partisan Association and the Carnegie Endowment for International Peace. Founded early in 1923, the Non-Partisan Association sought to win popular support for the League of Nations with the ultimate aim of convincing the government to enter the world organization established at Geneva. The organizers and leaders of the Association, John H. Clarke, a former Supreme Court Justice, Hamilton Holt, one of the founders of the League to Enforce Peace, and George W. Wickersham, a lawyer and former Attorney General of the United States, pressed for greater cooperation with League agencies engaged in humanitarian activities, the planning of a disarmament conference, and American entry into the World Court. Among its varied activities, the Association published a bi-weekly *League of Nations Herald,* prepared literature for the public school system, and ran contests and examinations on League information. One month after its founding, it claimed a membership of two thousand, and by 1925 it was annually distributing over a million pieces of literature.[4]

Equally active, but much richer, was the Carnegie Endowment for International Peace. Started in 1910 with a ten million dollar grant from Andrew Carnegie, the Endowment maintained an annual budget of over half a million dollars. It not only subsidized publications like the *Economic and Social History of the World War,* but published a monthly bulletin, *International Conciliation,* which printed texts of important treaties and international acts as well as commentaries upon them, maintained a Paris Center for European Peace, established endowed university chairs in international relations, financed exchange visits of European and American educators and newspapermen, sponsored International Relations Clubs, provided books on international affairs to libraries throughout the United States, financially aided smaller peace organizations, and generally promoted the League of Nations, the World Court, arbitration, freedom of trade, and numerous other peace ideas.[5]

4. Divine, *Second Chance,* pp. 6–18; Selig Adler, *The Isolationist Impulse: Its Twentieth Century Reaction* (New York, 1957), pp. 198–99.
5. Ferrell, *Peace in their Time,* p. 21; Robert H. Ferrell, "The Peace Movement," in Alexander DeConde, ed., *Isolation and Security* (Durham, N.C., 1957), pp. 99–100.

Because of his control of the Carnegie Endowment's purse strings, his broad contacts with American and European political leaders, and his sheer physical vigor, Nicholas Murray Butler, president of both the Endowment and Columbia University, ranked as one of the most important workers in the American peace movement. Although somewhat skeptical about the collective security idea during the World War, Butler became a strong supporter of the League of Nations during the 1920s, and along with James Brown Scott, a prominent lawyer and director of the Endowment's Division of International Law, and Shotwell, who by the mid-1920s had become director of the Endowment's Division of Economics and History, guided the organization from 1925, when he replaced Elihu Root as president, through the Second World War.

Shotwell's relationship with Butler was cordial, but never intimate. As president of Columbia, a post he acquired in 1901 when Shotwell was just a graduate student, Butler assumed an almost condescending attitude toward the faculty which neither Shotwell nor many of the other members appreciated. Shotwell found him too pontifical, too vindictive, and overly opinionated. He particularly resented Butler's lack of interest in the *Economic and Social History of the World War.*[6] Yet Shotwell worked well with his superior and shared many common traits with him. Not only did both men have somewhat the same appearance, but they were equally formal in their personal relations. They were both, moreover, extremely eloquent and could deliver polished speeches without notes, almost spontaneously.[7]

They shared another major characteristic in that they both seemed to venerate the successful and the powerful. They each carefully developed their relationships with important business and political leaders and took great pride and satisfaction in their entree into the world of wealth and power. They differed, however, in that while Butler loved pomp and ceremony, Shotwell preferred a quieter approach. Their relationship with European statesmen reflected this difference. Whenever Butler came to France, the Endowment's Paris office always knew well in advance when he was coming and how he

6. J.T.S., "Reminiscences," (continuing interview, June 8, 1949), 2: 7.
7. Herman, *Eleven Against War,* pp. 26–27; Ferrell, *Peace in their Time,* pp. 22–23.

would arrive. Butler expected not only to have his hotel reservations confirmed and a car waiting, but also to have his arrival formally announced so that a press interview could be held at the station. After a few days in Paris, the Endowment would make an appointment for Butler to go to the Quay d'Orsay to see the Foreign Minister, by whom he was usually received. On the appointed day he would drive over in a limousine, enter through the front door, have his interview, and then leave by limousine. "In effect," noted Malcolm Davis, the Endowment's European representative, "everyone in a position to observe affairs at the Foreign Ministry would know that Dr. Butler, the head of the Endowment, had called on the Foreign Minister and had an interview with him and then had driven away."[8]

With Shotwell, the schedule differed tremendously. More often than not, the Endowment staff in Paris had no idea he was coming and received word only when Shotwell called from the station to announce that he had arrived. Two or three days later, he would disappear from the Endowment office, not telling anyone where he was going. He would walk to the Foreign Ministry and visit with a friend in one of the auxiliary offices or services. Other than the individual acquaintance whom he had gone to see, few people were likely to know that he was in the building. Later it would be discovered that he had gone from his friend's office to that of the Foreign Minister. Upon leaving the building, he would hurridly look for a taxi and drive away. "Sometimes later it would be discovered that he had had a fairly important talk with the Foreign Minister, and that quite possibly something of significance had happened."[9]

Despite the differences in approach, both Shotwell and Butler had important connections and worked vigorously for the cause of peace. They combined their personal contacts with the Endowment's abundant resources to make it the foremost peace organization in the United States.

The Carnegie Endowment, the World Peace Foundation, the League of Nations Non-Partisan Association, and the Woodrow Wil-

8. Davis, "Reminiscences," pp. 114–15.
9. Ibid., pp. 115–16.

son Foundation were joined by two church groups in promoting internationalism. The Church Peace Union, established in 1914 with a two million dollar Carnegie grant, sponsored the World Alliance for International Friendship through the Churches which was very active during the 1920s. In addition, the Federal Council of Churches of Christ established a Commission on International Justice and Goodwill which worked diligently to end war and limit armaments. While all of these groups shared a general commitment to internationalism and world organization, they divided on the importance of disarmament and differed over the emphasis the movement should place on the question of militarism.[10]

Yet the most striking characteristic of these organizations was the homogeneity of their members. Most had old-stock Protestant-American backgrounds and were descendants of English and Scottish settlers. Shotwell may have been one of the few foreigners by birth, but his background and ancestry was not significantly different from the native Americans. Unlike the internationalist movement in Europe which gained strong support within the ranks of labor, in the United States bankers, lawyers, newspapermen, professors, and ministers predominated. There were few salesmen or clerks in these organizations, and almost no workmen. Businessmen tended to be those deeply involved in international trade and world markets. Most internationalists, moreover, lived in the northeast, with only small and scattered groups in university towns and in the more cosmopolitan centers of San Francisco, Chicago, and New Orleans. Perhaps it was the very homogeneity of the internationalists which accounts for their failure to really understand public opinion and to realize that most Americans did not share their views, but were rather simply confused by the complexities of foreign affairs. Although they represented a minority of the American population, these internationalists had access to enormous sums of money and could exert great influence.[11]

10. Ferrell, *Peace in their Time,* p. 26.
11. Divine, *Second Chance,* pp. 22–23; Bowers, "American Peace Movement," pp. 227–28.

Much more numerous and much less rich than the eastern-establishment, internationalist-oriented peace organizations were the peace societies which relied heavily on dues from its members rather than foundation money for their operating funds. These organizations, which seemed more radical in their pursuit of peace than their wealthier counterparts, also supported international cooperation and even certain international agencies. What made them appear more radical was their crusading zeal and the sense of urgency which they put into their efforts. Most of them, moreover, shied away from collective security and placed a strong emphasis on pacifistic solutions such as disarmament, codification of international law, and the outlawry of war.

The National Council for the Prevention of War, headed by Frederick J. Libby, a congregationalist minister who had become a Quaker during the World War, acted as a coordinator for these peace organizations. Next in importance to the National Council was the American Branch of the Women's International League for Peace and Freedom, headed by Jane Addams, the social worker and pacifist, and Emily Balch, who served as president of the branch. Among the other organizations which rejected collective security, leaned towards pacifism, emphasized disarmament, and spoke out forcefully against militarism were the National Committee on the Cause and Cure of War, headed by the well-known feminist Mrs. Carrie Chapman Catt, the Fellowship of Reconciliation, the War Resisters League, the Committee on Militarism in Education, the Parliament of Peace and Universal Brotherhood, the Peace Heroes Memorial Society, and Women's Peace Association.[12]

The peace movement may have grown both in size and activity during the 1920s, but individual organizations could agree on little more than their general goal. Diversity rather than unity characterized the movement. Factionalism became so widespread that many antiwar leaders interpreted their primary aim as finding areas of agreement and bringing peace within the movement. Not until that

12. Curti, *Peace or War,* pp. 272–73; Ferrell, *Peace in their Time,* pp. 26–30; Jean-Baptiste Duroselle, *From Wilson to Roosevelt: Foreign Policy of the United States, 1913–1945* (translated by Nancy Lyman Roelker, Cambridge, Mass., 1963), p. 175.

was achieved could their common goal be reached. There was little chance, however, that those individuals and groups rejecting capitalism could join with the "international liberals," who by and large supported the existing system. Nor was there any real possibility that the pacifists would join with the advocates of collective security. Increasingly, the likliest prospect for a unity program appeared in a coalition of those who supported the World Court and the League of Nations and those favoring the "Outlawry of War."

The phrase "Outlawry of War" was coined by an energetic, civic-minded, Chicago lawyer, Salmon O. Levinson, who came to the idea during the First World War. In December, 1921, while the Washington Naval Disarmament Conference was in session, Levinson published a pamphlet outlining the three main ingredients of his proposal. He called upon the nations of the world to make the institution of war illegal, to codify international law, and to establish an effective world court. He envisioned a court independent of the League of Nations and modeled on the United States Supreme Court, with compulsory jurisdiction over all international disputes.[13]

Although Levinson originally supported the League and the need for sanctions to back up outlawry, he gradually came to the conclusion that sanctions against a state were not practicable. Instead he called for a program of "enforcement" based upon good faith, public opinion, nonrecognition of changes made by the use of force, punishment by each state of its own war fomenters, and the use of whatever means necessary, including force, to put down a "mad-dog state."[14]

The key to Levinson's scheme rested in his view of war as an "institution" for settling disputes. It was in its institutional context that he wished it outlawed. "War," he told one of his supporters, "is an institution in the same sense as the church, the school or the home. It will never cease to be an institution until it becomes illegal, until

13. Salmon O. Levinson, *A Plan to Outlaw War* (Chicago, December 25, 1921), issued by the American Committee for the Outlawry of War. The most complete statement of the outlawry theory appears in Charles Clayton Morrison, *The Outlawry of War: A Constructive Policy for World Peace* (Chicago, 1927). See also John E. Stoner, *S. O. Levinson and the Pact of Paris: A Study in the Techniques of Influence* (Chicago, 1942), pp. 184–211.
14. Stoner, *Levinson,* pp. 208–10.

it is condemned by international law as disreputable and criminal."[15] Because he viewed war as an institution, Levinson refused to make distinctions between "righteous" wars and "unrighteous" wars, or between aggressive wars and defensive wars. He strongly opposed the attempts of Shotwell and his colleagues to find a definition of the term "aggression." According to his plan all institutional wars would become illegal and criminal.

Yet Levinson disclaimed any belief in pacifism and strongly argued that his plan in no way impaired the right of self-defense. In fact, he declared that the right of self-defense was "inherent and ineradicable." It was the "law of God and paramount to all the laws of man."[16] To illustrate his argument, Levinson often cited the case of dueling, which for many years had been the institution for settling grievances between individuals. Once dueling was made illegal, individuals were forced to use the courts for justice. The right of self-defense, however, had never been denied. If war was outlawed, he maintained, a nation would still have the right to defend itself against attack, but this would no longer be war in an institutional sense.[17]

Shotwell and those supporting collective security had a difficult time in comprehending Levinson's scheme and most believed that the Chicago lawyer had gotten himself involved in a semantic bind. They, too, upheld the right of self-defense, but could not understand why he refused to make a distinction between aggressive and defensive wars—a distinction fundamental to their own peace philosophy. They could not understand why he would not admit that a nation defending itself against attack was as much involved in war as two nations resorting to arms of their own free will. Since they conceived of war as a conflict of arms and not as a legal "institution," collective security and the renunciation of aggression became vital components of their peace plans. Economic, political, and military sanctions could not be replaced by public opinion and good faith.

15. Salmon O. Levinson to Mrs. Lewis M. Simes, April 20, 1925, Levinson Papers.
16. Salmon O. Levinson to Charles W. Eliot, January 28, 1925, Levinson Papers.
17. Salmon O. Levinson to Mrs. Lewis M. Simes, April 20, 1925, Salmon O. Levinson to Melle J. Decroix, October 12, 1927, Levinson Papers.

Despite their many differences, the advocates of outlawry and those of collective security began discussing the possibility of a unity program as early as 1923. Levinson and his friends strongly desired to gain support for an outlawry resolution introduced into the Senate by William E. Borah of Idaho and seemed willing to make a deal with the pro-League group. Shotwell, for his part, saw possible advantages in passage of a Presidential proposal, sent to Congress by Warren G. Harding on February 24, calling for adhesion to the Permanent Court of International Justice. Although the Presidential recommendation contained several reservations drawn up by Secretary of State Hughes and designed to reassure the irreconcilables that American participation would involve no legal relations with the League or the assumption of any obligations under the Covenant, Shotwell hoped that joining the Court would eventually lead to greater participation in European affairs. He recognized that support of the President's proposal by Borah and the outlawrists might prove decisive, and he, too, began seriously considering the possibility of mutual cooperation.

Despite some preliminary steps taken toward working out a unity program, antagonism between Levinson and Shotwell continued throughout 1923 and most of 1924. Although Borah and Levinson supported the Draft Treaty of Disarmament and Security, Shotwell used the occasion of its publication to attack the outlawry formula as impracticable and unrealistic.[18] When the League of Nations issued the Geneva Protocol, the outlawrists retaliated. On October 9, Levinson suggested to Borah that he attack the Protocol and the League, for they were issues which offered a "renewed opportunity for slaughtering the Democrats . . . as in 1920." Borah agreed, and looking toward the November election he announced his opposition to any plan based on the false assumption that peace could be implemented by force. Whereas he had hailed Shotwell's Draft Treaty as a major advance toward peace, he condemned the Protocol as one of the "worst things that has been proposed so far."[19]

With the Presidential election decided in favor of Coolidge, and

18. J.T.S., "A Practical Plan for Disarmament," *International Conciliation* 102 (August 1924), pp. 317–19.
19. Quoted in John Chalmers Vinson, *William E. Borah and the Outlawry of War* (Athens, Ga., 1957), pp. 98–99.

with Borah sent back to the Senate for another six years, both Shotwell and Levinson began to reassess their positions. Opposition had gotten neither very much. Borah's resolution made no progress in the Senate and America seemed no closer to supporting the European collective security system than it had in 1920. On November 6, therefore, Shotwell took the initial step in framing a harmony program by asking Levinson to set up a meeting between the two groups. As he later told Borah, the time had come "for those who really want to get rid of war to join their forces in a common attack upon the enemy, rather than spend themselves, as has been too much the case in the past, in mutual criticism."[20] On November 24, Shotwell, Frederick Keppel, president of the Carnegie Corporation, and William B. Hale, a publisher and banker, met with Levinson, Charles Clayton Morrison, editor of the *Christian Century* magazine, and Borah in Washington. Shotwell agreed to support Borah's resolution on the condition that the Senator refrain from criticizing the work done at Geneva and issue a statement recognizing the Geneva Protocol. He admitted that fundamental differences existed between the outlawrist's attitude toward the League and his own. But until the League again became a popular issue, he saw no reason why he could not vigorously support Borah's resolution if the Idaho Senator would encourage Europe "to go on to eliminate war from its own system rather than await any effort at salvation from the United States."[21]

Although Borah remained skeptical about the degree of cooperation possible with the pro-League group, Levinson was enthusiastic. He partially dropped his intense suspicions of Shotwell and wrote to one of his associates that the Columbia professor, "with his intense love of peace, his sincerity, his intellectual attainments and his invaluable experience abroad," had done more than anyone to promote the reconciliation of the diverse peace groups.[22] Yet Levinson did not completely put his trust in the pro-League faction. He fully realized that while Shotwell was "earnest and sincere," he could not "shake

20. J.T.S. to Salmon O. Levinson, November 6, 1924, Box 20, Raymond Robins Papers, State Historical Society of Wisconsin, Madison, Wisconsin; J.T.S. to William E. Borah, November 26, 1924, Levinson Papers.
21. J.T.S. to William E. Borah, November 26, 1924, Levinson Papers.
22. Salmon O. Levinson to Irving Fisher, December 4, 1924, Levinson Papers.

off either the effects of his European associations or experiences or the boundless affection he has for the child of his brain, to wit: the definition of an aggressor." He warned his friend Raymond Robins, an influential Republican and vigorous advocate of Outlawry, that "whatever Shotwell's sincerity we have to be on our guard for the ulterior and final objective of his latest move toward us."[23]

The agreement of November 24 lasted only a short time. Shotwell technically kept his part of the bargain and in several addresses urged the various factions of the peace movement to unite in support of Borah's resolution. He refused, however, to go further than this and made perfectly clear that he still supported the League and the World Court.[24] Borah, for his part, had no intention of either "soft-pedaling" the League nor pushing his outlawry resolution very vigorously. He justified his delay by explaining that Hughes would soon leave office and that it would be best to postpone action until the Secretary's retirement. Levinson's own initial enthusiasm quickly waned. Continuous attacks on the outlawry program by the *New York Times,* which he believed voiced New York pro-League sentiment, led him to question the sincerity of his new partners. He feared, moreover, that his flirtations with Shotwell had alienated Borah, and decided that reconciliation would have to await a more opportune time. His suspicions of Shotwell renewed, he told John Dewey that his colleague was simply the dupe of the pro-Leaguers and was being "unduly used for their undisclosed, sinister purposes."[25]

By February, Levinson had completely reversed himself on working with the pro-League advocates. He was now certain that any program they advocated, no matter how innocent it looked on the surface, was promoted with the ultimate aim of getting the United States into the League by a "trap door." "So subtle, so indirect, so dishonest are the surreptitious League crusades made in this country," he wrote to his European agent, Harrison Brown, that the

23. Salmon O. Levinson to John H. Holmes, December 5, 1925, Salmon O. Levinson to Raymond Robins, December 5, 1924, Levinson Papers.
24. *New York Times,* January 11, 1925, sec. 8, p. 9, January 24, 1925, p. 3.
25. Salmon O. Levinson to Raymond Robins, December 23, 1924, Box 20, Robins Papers; Salmon O. Levinson to John H. Holmes, January 15, 1925, Salmon O. Levinson to John Dewey, January 20, 1925, Levinson Papers.

pro-League advocates could not be trusted in anything they did. The outlawry movement could not afford to work with them, for "if you compromise Outlawry you lose it."[26]

That Levinson was correct in his analysis of Shotwell's motives there can be no doubt. Shotwell made very plain in November that he supported Borah's resolution only as a temporary expedient and that he "looked forward to some differences of opinion" with the outlawrists on the League question "if and when that became a popular issue once more."[27] He and his colleagues, moreover, intended to do all they could to make it a popular issue. Shotwell believed that ultimately the United States would have to join the League, and he openly favored such a move "at the earliest possible moment." Acceptance of the World Court, outlawry, and disarmament were important only because they could serve as stepping-stones to eventual participation in the Geneva experiment.[28]

Despite his strong statements in February, the following month Levinson again reversed himself on reconciliation. He was now certain that the Senate would not block adhesion to the Court protocol and decided that as much as he disliked working with Shotwell it was the only way to save his program. Although Borah refused to compromise on the Court issue, Levinson, together with Charles Clayton Morrison and Raymond Robins, began negotiations with Shotwell in order to work out a new and more clearly defined "harmony program."[29] The compromise, reached after several weeks of hard negotiations, called for the immediate adherence to the World Court Protocol with the Harding-Hughes-Coolidge reservations. It also provided that within two years after adherence, the United States and the other signatories were to endorse the basic principles of outlawry and call an international conference for the purpose of embodying these principles into a general treaty. Specifically, the signatories were to outlaw war "as an institution for the settlement of international

26. Salmon O. Levinson to G. Harrison Brown, February 5 and 28, 1925, Levinson Papers.
27. J.T.S. to William E. Borah, November 26, 1924, Levinson Papers.
28. J.T.S. to Mrs. E. F. Armstrong, December 15, 1924, Box 34, J.T.S. Papers.
29. Salmon O. Levinson to J. Reuben Clark, March 21, 1925, Levinson Papers.

controversies by making it a crime under the law of nations," codify international law, and provide the World Court with affirmative jurisdiction over international controversies between sovereign nations. If these conditions were not met within two years, the United States would have the option of withdrawing from the Court. Its withdrawal would become automatic if the outlawry program had not come into effect within five years.[30]

Although Levinson was enthusiastic about the unity platform, Borah remained skeptical and refused to agree to its provisions. On June 25, Shotwell conferred with the Senator, but Borah would agree to nothing more than establishing a "practical program." He told both Shotwell and Levinson that he could not support the Court as it was then constituted, not even for two years.[31] Since the pro-League party had accepted the compromise mainly because they desired to have Borah on their side in the Court battle, and since Levinson did not wish to take any action which would alienate the Idaho Senator, the "harmony program" at best could serve only as a temporary alliance. Both sides, however, were willing to wait until the convening of Congress in December before taking any definite action one way or the other.

With the platform of unity established, though admittedly precarious, Shotwell turned his attention toward the problems of Southeastern Europe. In the autumn of 1925, with a substantial grant from the Carnegie Endowment, he took an extended trip to the Balkans. His journey had a dual purpose. First, he wanted to arrange for several monographs for his *Economic and Social History of the World War.* Second, and equally important, Nicholas Murray Butler, having just assumed the presidency of the Endowment, wanted him to discuss possible Endowment projects with the various Balkan leaders. During his two month journey, Shotwell, accompanied by his wife, traveled to Rumania, Bulgaria, Yugoslavia, Greece, and Turkey. Treated as a visiting dignitary, he conferred with national leaders, organized editorial boards for his war history, outlined the aims of the Endow-

30. J.T.S. to Tasker H. Bliss, June 29, 1925, Box 269, Bliss Papers; *New York Times,* July 15, 1925, p. 10; Stoner, *Levinson,* pp. 144–45.
31. Borah to Levinson, June 25, 1925, Levinson Papers.

ment, and gave several addresses on the nature of war and peace in the modern age.[32]

Besides arranging several volumes for his war history, Shotwell's major accomplishment was winning over the leaders of the Orthodox Church in Yugoslavia, Rumania, and Bulgaria. In all three countries the church leaders agreed to take up the question of defining aggression in their respective synods and pledged to ask the secular leaders of their countries to perfect the machinery for settling disputes peaceably.[33] W. S. Culbertson, the United States minister in Bucharest, amazed at Shotwell's success in gaining the support of these prelates, reported to Secretary of State Frank B. Kellogg that the Columbia professor had actually enlisted "the active co-operation of the entire Eastern Orthodox Church as well as other organizations and individuals in the cause of international peace."[34]

As soon as he returned to the United States, Shotwell again became embroiled in the debate over the World Court and disarmament. By December, 1925, Coolidge had come out strongly for United States membership in the Court without reference to outlawry. Levinson, fearing that his plan would never gain serious consideration unless made conditional upon America's adherence to the Court protocol, desperately tried to renew interest in the harmony program. On December 3, he called a meeting of several antiwar leaders, including Shotwell, Norman Thomas, Raymond Robins, and Sherwood Eddy, and proposed that a special committee take the outlawry reservation directly to the President for consideration.[35]

Nothing came of his proposal. With Coolidge supporting the Court without outlawry, and with the prospects for a Senate resolution looking bright, Shotwell and his associates saw no reason to promote Levinson's scheme. The Chicago lawyer, of course, became bitter. He

32. Nicholas M. Butler to J.T.S., April 21, 1925, Secretary's Office and Administration, 1925, #1981–1982, CEIP Archives; J.T.S., *A Balkan Mission* (New York, 1949), pp. 1–15; Margaret Shotwell to Helen and Margaret Shotwell, October 15, 1925, Box 251, J.T.S. Papers.
33. J.T.S., "Memorandum on the Journey through the Balkan Countries," January 22, 1926, I.F.2. #40439, CEIP Archives.
34. W. S. Culbertson to Secretary of State Frank B. Kellogg, November 4, 1925, #700.0011/-, State Department Archives, National Archives.
35. Form letter from Sherwood Eddy, December 2, 1925, Levinson Papers.

accused the pro-League party of insincerity and breach of faith.[36] But he could do little to stop the dissolution of the coalition. On December 9, Shotwell wrote to Sherwood Eddy that he could no longer support the June agreement. His explanation revealed the fundamental weakness of the coalition from the start. The Court issue, as well as the harmony plan, were only expedients. He judged all peace moves by their ability to bring the United States into closer cooperation with the League. For Shotwell, adherence to the Court protocol, like Borah's resolution, was only the first step in a long process by which America might "ultimately assume the full measure of responsibility." If he was uncomfortable supporting the Court resolution, he was even more uncomfortable endorsing the harmony program.

The Senate's January, 1926, resolution calling for adherence to the Court protocol with severe reservations, and the subsequent failure of the Court members to agree to the American terms, bothered Shotwell very little.[37] The Court debate had not led to any reconsideration of American policy with reference to the League. Since this was his major concern, he paid little attention to the Court issue after the passage of the Senate resolution. Instead he turned to a new issue, the League's call for a Preparatory Commission on Disarmament. Shotwell had long supported the idea of a recurring conference on disarmament. He believed that it was not only the most promising approach to arms limitation, but also offered the best means for bringing the United States into closer cooperation with the League. By working with League members on the problems of disarmament and security, the United States would of necessity have to take a greater interest in European affairs and in the machinery established at Geneva. Cooperation in recurring conferences would have the effect of creating an "associate" status of League membership—a relationship that Shotwell never tired of promoting.

In September, 1925, when he was in Geneva making preparations for his Balkan journey, the League Assembly began discussing the

36. Salmon O. Levinson to Henry P. Van Dusen, December 7, 1925, Salmon O. Levinson to Florence E. Allen, December 12, 1925, Salmon O. Levinson to Sherwood Eddy, December 11 and 12, 1925, Levinson Papers.
37. For a brief discussion of the Court issue in the United States see Fleming, *United States and World Organization,* pp. 135–59.

possibility of calling a general disarmament conference. Several delegates asked him to draw up a program for such a meeting and he gladly took on the assignment. His memorandum, while not widely distributed, did become the basis for proposals presented by the representatives of Holland, Denmark, and Norway, and strongly influenced the resolution pushed through the Council by Joseph Paul-Boncour of France and Eduard Beneš of Czechoslovakia. It did not deal with the question of disarmament itself, but rather with the creation of a preparatory conference on arms limitation that would precede a more general conference. Instead of jumping into actual proposals for the reduction of armaments, Shotwell suggested that the League undertake "to study the ways and means" by which the problem might be effectively considered at a later date. Few delegates, he reasoned, could oppose merely studying how "so desirable an end may be achieved."[38]

In early December, the League Council decided to establish a Preparatory Commission largely along the lines outlined by Shotwell and invited the United States to participate by sending a delegation to Geneva. Shotwell's belief that there would be less objection to a preliminary conference than to a general conference authorized to make disarmament policy proved correct. On December 17 the State Department made the League's invitation public, and on January 4 President Coolidge sent a special message to Congress asking support for the proposed meeting. He pointed out that participation in the work of the Preparatory Commission involved "no commitment with respect to attendance upon any future conference or conferences on reduction and limitation of armaments." Congress responded with an appropriation of $50,000, and on January 30 Secretary of State Kellogg formally accepted the Council's invitation. Coolidge appointed Hugh Gibson, the American Minister at Berne, and Allen W. Dulles, Chief of the Division of Far Eastern Affairs in the State Department, to head the American delegation.[39]

As soon as the League extended the invitation to the United States,

38. J.T.S. to Nicholas M. Butler, September 15, 1925, and J.T.S., "Preliminary Memorandum on the Organization to Prepare for a Disarmament Conference," September 5, 1925, I.F.2. #41264, CEIP Archives.
39. *International Conciliation* 220 (May 1926): 255–62.

Shotwell reassembled his Committee on Security and Disarmament and began working frantically to prepare studies which might be of some use to the American group. Nicholas Murray Butler offered the services of the Carnegie Endowment to Secretary of State Kellogg and arranged for Shotwell, James Brown Scott, and Tasker Bliss to meet with John Foster Dulles in order to determine how the Endowment might best serve the State Department. Dulles met several times with the Endowment's representatives and agreed that Shotwell should send him the full texts of all the committee's memoranda and reports.[40]

David Hunter Miller, Joseph P. Chamberlain, Tasker Bliss, and several other members of the Shotwell committee drew up technical studies on various aspects of the disarmament question and turned them over to the State Department.[41] Of all the reports turned over to Dulles, however, Shotwell's "An American Policy with Reference to Disarmament" presented the most comprehensive analysis of the problem. Shotwell argued that America's past policy of limited naval reductions contributed little to general disarmament. As an alternative approach, he suggested that the government divide the problem into three separate parts: the "reduction and limitation of armaments properly so called," the "control of supplies from country to country," and "some sort of insurance against industrial and chemical mobilization as an element of warfare." By isolating and finding solutions for each category, the government could deal more effectively with the overall problem.[42]

He further suggested that the United States could make a major contribution to peace and disarmament by "restating the conditions of neutrality." As early as 1924, he had argued that the attempts at collective action in Europe made it imperative for the United States to revise its traditional policy of neutrality. To continue that policy

40. Nicholas M. Butler to Frank B. Kellogg, December 28, 1925, Box 36, J.T.S. Papers; Frank B. Kellogg to Nicholas M. Butler, January 7, 1926, IV, #76493, CEIP Archives; Shotwell to Members of the Committee on Security and Disarmament, February 3, 1926, I.F.2. #41273, CEIP Archives.
41. CEIP Archives, I.F.2. #41270–73.
42. J.T.S., "An American Policy with Reference to Disarmament," n.d., pp. 4–5, I.F.2. #41285, CEIP Archives.

might aid and encourage aggression, or equally deplorable might force League members to turn to military sanctions instead of economic and less dangerous ones:

> A State which knew that it could count upon the helpful neutrality of the United States could afford to take lightly the threats of economic pressure from the League, and the League in turn would then be faced with a situation in which it would either have to give up the task of keeping peace, or pursue it sword in hand. This is the blunt fact which we have to face: that if the United States were to refuse to recognize a decree of outlawry pronounced by the League, economic sanctions would be almost useless, and that if economic sanctions are of no avail, the League will have to make war upon its recalcitrant member.[43]

In the context of disarmament, Shotwell saw traditional neutrality as even more dangerous. World War I demonstrated that neutrality could no longer prevent the spread of war, belying the old justification for such a policy. If belligerents could buy in private trade all the armaments they wanted or needed, the security required for disarmament could not exist. America did not have to take part in arms reduction agreements to be responsible for much of their success or failure. In a collective security situation such as Europe was trying to establish, a neutral nation which continued to ship arms to a declared aggressor might well become the "accomplice" of that aggressor. In order to avoid such an "immoral" situation, Shotwell suggested that the United States alter its policy and publicly announce that it would not aid or support any aggressor state.[44]

What use the State Department made of the numerous studies and proposals turned in by the American Committee is not known. The Preparatory Commission met in May, 1926, but negotiations quickly bogged down and the prospects for actually convening a disarmament conference remained dim.[45] Shotwell's analysis of United States neu-

43. J.T.S., "Plans and Protocols to End War: Historical Outline and Guide," *International Conciliation* 207 (March 1925): 107.
44. J.T.S., "An American Policy with Reference to Disarmament," pp. 7–9.
45. The Preparatory Commission on Disarmament met intermittently from May, 1926 to September, 1930. The actual disarmament conference did not convene until February 2, 1932.

trality policy foreshadowed his later position when the question became a major topic of debate. During the next fifteen years he continued to challenge the idea of American neutrality and attacked it with increasing frequency.

In emphasizing the need for a reappraisal of American foreign policy, Shotwell correctly recognized the increasing interdependence of the world and the need for more international cooperation. His specific policy prescriptions, however, were not above question. Collective security was only one of several possible approaches to international cooperation and was not necessarily the most conducive to world peace. Assuming that the League or the Court could always determine the source of aggression in a conflict—an assumption which many people doubted—it was still not necessarily true that the national interest of each and every country would dictate that it oppose aggression at all times regardless of by whom and against whom it might be committed. The automatic nature of collective security, necessary for its deterrent effect, left no room for decision-making at a national level.

Furthermore, Shotwell tended to conceive of his program in theoretical terms and neglected to think it through. He rarely spoke of military sanctions, but rather held out the hope that effective economic sanctions would make military ones unnecessary. He assumed that if the deterrent effect of collective security failed and a nation resorted to war, economic sanctions alone would suffice to bend the recalcitrant government to its knees. Even when he took the theory to its logical conclusion and admitted that military action might be necessary, he assumed that the united power of the peaceful nations would easily and quickly defeat the aggressor. Despite tradition and historical experience, he tenaciously held to the assumption that the vast majority of nations would behave morally and legalistically. He failed to comprehend, moreover, that a truly effective collective security system might lead to the appalling condition of transforming every particular armed conflict into a general war by obliging all members to participate in the collective action. And lastly, he never really confronted the basic dilemma presented by collective security; namely that no nation could afford to rest its security in an unproven system, yet until the nations of the world did exactly that, collective security could never prove itself. Shotwell simply argued that since war in the modern age was so dangerous to everyone, each nation should take the gamble and strive to make it work. But since the consequences of failure might mean national extinction, his argument was not very convincing.

Shotwell's entire conception of international affairs rested on the assumption that ultimately peace depended upon mutual understanding and trust. Peace machinery and solemn promises not to resort to war were meaningless unless understanding and trust guided national action. It was not surprising, therefore, that he took a strong stand against United States policy on the war debt question. No other issue during the twenties created as much distrust and animosity between America and the nations of Europe. Both the Harding and Coolidge administrations expressed a willingness to scale down the interest rate on the $10.3 billion loaned to the allies, but neither President was willing to cancel any part of the principal. Neither administration, moreover, recognized the connection between Germany's reparation payments or American tariff policy and the ability of the allied governments to make payments to the United States. Unable to collect reparations from Germany and unable to create a favorable balance with America, they were forced to renege on their debt payments. This in turn led to resentment and bitterness on the part of both Americans and Europeans.[46]

In August, 1926, Newton D. Baker issued a carefully reasoned plea for revision of the debt settlement on the grounds that the "capacity to pay formula" had led to a "magnificent disaster."[47] Shotwell, who had come out publicly for revision more than a year earlier,[48] took advantage of Baker's statement to form a committee of Columbia University professors to study the question. On December 20, the committee issued a "Manifesto on War Debts," written largely by Shotwell and signed by forty-two members of the faculty including

46. For a general discussion see H. G. Moulton and Leo Pasvolsky, *War Debts and World Prosperity* (Washington, 1932); Benjamin H. Williams, *Economic Foreign Policy of the United States* (New York, 1929), pp. 217–42; Fleming, *United States and World Organization*, pp. 123–31.
47. *New York Times*, August 30, 1926, p. 1.
48. *Ibid.*, May 15, 1925, sec. I, p. 16.

John Bates Clark, Edwin R. A. Seligman, Rexford G. Tugwell, Raymond Moley, Philip C. Jessup, William R. Shepherd, Carlton J. H. Hayes, Robert L. Schuyler, David S. Muzzey, and Franklin H. Giddings. The statement declared the war debt settlements "unsound in principle" and detrimental to America's true interests. The Columbia professors did not come out for complete cancellation, but urged the convening of an international conference to review the entire problem.[49]

The Columbia Manifesto made front page headlines in newspapers throughout the United States, Europe, and even Asia.[50] The *New York Times* gave it strong editorial support, as did the New York *Evening World,* the Baltimore *Sun,* and the Hartford, Connecticut *Times.* The editors of the *Manchester Guardian* believed that the statement was accurate and fair, but questioned whether the Columbia professors really reflected "the mass mind of America."[51] Several college presidents, including James Rowland Angell of Yale and Frank J. Goodnow of Johns Hopkins, endorsed the Manifesto. Daniel L. March of Boston University felt that the statement should have gone even further and proposed that cancellation be made conditional on European disarmament.

Public reaction, however, was by no means entirely favorable. The *New York Sun* proclaimed that any further scaling down of the debts would eventually lead to cancellation, which in turn would only "shorten the road to the next European war."[52] The *New York Herald Tribune* labeled the entire proposal a "fantastic and impractical demand which only an academic mind out of touch with reality could seriously advocate."[53] Official reaction in Washington was hostile. State Department officials proclaimed that the Manifesto would undermine negotiations then going on with the French government aimed at reaching a new debt agreement. Senators Claude Swanson

49. *Ibid.,* December 20, 1926, pp. 1–2. See original draft of statement in Box 1, J.T.S. Papers. See also J.T.S. to Nicholas M. Butler, November 29, 1926, I.F.2. #40440–40441, CEIP Archives; J.T.S. to Tasker H. Bliss, December 10, 1926, Box 270, Bliss Papers.
50. The Shotwell papers contain an extensive newspaper clipping file on the war debt question and the Columbia Manifesto. See Box 1, J.T.S. Papers.
51. *Manchester Guardian,* December 21, 1926.
52. *New York Sun,* December 20, 1926.
53. *New York Herald Tribune,* December 21, 1926.

of Virginia, Arthur Capper of Kansas, and Reed Smoot of Utah condemned the proposal, calling it an "absurdity" which would have the effect of putting the question of debts into the hands of the debtors and would result ultimately in complete cancellation. President Coolidge at first refused to comment on the document, but on December 22 came out strongly against any further revisions. He pointed out that the Columbia Manifesto would do more harm than good because it might raise European expectations at a time when the administration had no intention of changing its policy.[54]

Despite the initial excitement created by the Columbia Manifesto, public interest in the debt question quickly subsided. Any move for debt revision had to come from the government, and the Coolidge administration made it quite clear that no such action would be forthcoming. But the entire controversy, together with the question of disarmament, had brought Shotwell to the public's attention for the first time. Through the public debates of 1925 and 1926, he gained such widespread recognition that even the readers of the Concord, New Hampshire *Independent* knew of him as an "indefatigable internationalist."[55]

The debates in general, however, yielded little in actual results. The possibility of holding a general disarmament conference seemed at best far off in the future; the Coolidge administration seemed as little disposed to cooperate with the League of Nations as it did to revise the debt settlements; American-European relations had not improved and were, in fact, on the verge of getting worse; and the antiwar groups in America still remained divided and antagonistic toward each other. What was needed was some new and dramatic event, one which could arouse the imagination of the American people, shake the administration out of its lethargy, and create a new atmosphere more receptive to peace proposals and international cooperation. With these thoughts in mind, Shotwell once again sailed for Europe, this time to give a series of lectures as the first Visiting Carnegie Professor of International Relations at the newly founded *Hochschule für Politik* in Berlin.

54. *New York Times,* December 21, 1926, pp. 1–2, 4, December 22, 1926, p. 1, December 23, 1926, p. 4.
55. John Carter, "Short Circuiting the War Debts," *Concord Independent* (New Hampshire), May 21, 1927, in Box 1, J.T.S. Papers.

9
Renouncing War as an Instrument of National Policy

On March 1, 1927, James T. Shotwell presented his inaugural address at the *Hochschule für Politik.* The event received widespread attention throughout Germany. Among the dignitaries who packed the auditorium were Chief Justice Walter Simons, former Foreign Minister and Acting President of the Republic in 1925, Reich Chancellor Wilhelm Marx and several of his cabinet officers, the Prime Minister of Prussia, numerous members of the War Ministry and General Staff, and the leading city officials of Berlin. President Paul von Hindenburg was unable to attend, but sent his apologies with a personal representative.[1]

It was an impressive gathering, and Shotwell took the opportunity to discuss various international problems. Asking "Are we at a turning point in the history of the world?" he emphasized the vast and

1. J.T.S., *Autobiography,* pp. 200–201; J.T.S., *Lesson of the Last War* (New York, 1942), p. 12.

significant changes caused by the industrial and commercial revolutions. The result of all this change and development was that a new world community had emerged—an interdependent community where modern industry and science interlocked common interests. Just as science had changed the world of peace through inventions, it had also changed the nature of war. Science had so increased the destructive potential of armed conflict that it could no longer be considered by "civilized" nations as a proper means for achieving national aims. Neither could it be limited to the original combatants. The growing interdependence of the world meant that neutrals would be drawn into belligerency despite themselves. War spread like a contagion, always extending in scope and intensity. "In short," declared Shotwell, "war has ceased to be calculable, as it was in the era of relatively static phenomena . . . It is no longer a safe instrument for statesmanship under such circumstances; it is too dangerous to employ."[2]

Since war no longer offered a "rational" solution to international grievances, Shotwell suggested that peaceful substitutes be found. The major problem was to guarantee that no nation resorted to war to achieve its goals. To accomplish this, he urged the creation of a deterrent to aggression through an effective collective security system. The League of Nations and the Locarno treaties offered a beginning. What was needed now, however, was a "World Locarno," an agreement that would allow those closest to potential danger to join in its suppression, while committing those further away to nothing more than refusing aid to the aggressors. Such a plan, he hoped, would allow the United States to participate in peace-keeping operations, but not get entangled directly in European affairs.[3]

To advocate the abolition of war before the highest ranking military officials in Germany was an ambitious enterprise, but Shotwell seemed to enjoy the challenge. A persuasive speaker, even in German, he won the respect if not the enthusiastic support of his audience. Newspapers throughout the country covered the event and publicized his views.

2. J.T.S., "Are We at a Turning Point in the History of the World?" CEIP, *Year Book,* 1927, p. 106.
3. Ibid., pp. 108–12.

His Berlin reception went so well, in fact, that the *Hochschule* arranged for him to speak in Frankfurt, Leipzig, and Cologne. In each address his conception of a "World Locarno" became clearer and more definite. He believed the time was ripe for a new international agreement. On March 9, the day following his Cologne address, he went to Geneva to confer with Foreign Minister Gustav Stresemann and Albert Thomas, the Director of the International Labor Office. During the discussion he agreed that the initiative for the scheme should come from France rather than Germany, and accepted an offer from Thomas to arrange an interview with Aristide Briand, the French Foreign Minister. A week later, he arrived at the Carnegie Endowment office in Paris and quietly began making preparations for the meeting.[4]

He particularly wished to see Briand at this time because of the increasing strain in Franco-American relations. The French refusal to participate in the naval disarmament conference called by President Coolidge, combined with the continuing dispute over war debts and America's subsequent refusal to consider French disarmament demands presented to the Preparatory Commission, had heightened hostility and bitterness in both countries. Shotwell was convinced that the time had come for some new and dramatic affirmation of the French interest in peace.[5]

On March 18, he wrote to Arthur Fontaine, a French official and former head of the ILO, that efforts at debt revision could succeed only if favorable political circumstances existed. The disagreement between the two countries over disarmament greatly hurt the French cause in America. Little could be done until France made its position clear and removed the stigma of militarism. Shotwell believed that Briand could recapture American public opinion only "by some signal action of outstanding importance," and suggested that the tenth anniversary of America's entry into World War I might provide the proper occasion for such an action. "Could not France issue a state-

4. J.T.S., "Reflections on Peace and War," p. 26; J.T.S., *Autobiography,* pp. 203–6.

5. *New York Times,* February 15, 1927, sec. I, p. 1, February 16, 1927, pp. 1–2; *New York Herald Tribune,* March 18, 1927; J.T.S. to Nicholas Murray Butler, March 15, 1927, I.F.2. #40449, CEIP Archives.

ment in connection with that event, which would make clear the line of its own contribution to the plans for disarmament, and offer to consider the American proposals in so far as they could be fitted into the general plan?" Such a statement would not only allow Shotwell and his friends to make headway on the debt question, but would improve Franco-American relations generally and might ultimately lead to a solution of the disarmament controversy.[6]

Fontaine delivered the letter to Briand, and four days later Albert Thomas informed Shotwell that the Foreign Minister had agreed to an interview. When he arrived at the Quai d'Orsay, Briand greeted him cordially and ushered him into his office. The two men were remarkably similar in appearance. Both were medium in height, stocky, and had a difficult time controlling their untidy hair which they casually pushed to the side. Mustaches half hid their mouths, although Briand's drooped considerably more than Shotwell's. Similarities, however, ended with physical appearance. Paris gossip had it that Briand was a cynical, fast-living old bachelor, whereas Shotwell, completely devoted to his wife and two daughters, was everlastingly an optimist. Briand never enjoyed a reputation for bookishness, but preferred to develop his ideas in conversation or in extemporaneous speechmaking. His American visitor was an equally fine speaker, but prepared his statements more carefully and tempered them with an academic cautiousness. While Briand was the consummate politician who cared little for intellectuality, Shotwell was the intellectual who aspired to make policy.[7]

After some brief formalities, Briand explained that he had read the letter to Fontaine and wished Shotwell to elaborate on his scheme. Shotwell outlined American attitudes, emphasizing that refusal to participate in the upcoming naval disarmament conference convinced many Americans that France was reactionary and militaristic. Using the debt and disarmament issues as his opening, he then suggested that Briand could alter the situation by proposing not merely arms

6. J.T.S. to Arthur Fontaine, March 18, 1927, I.F.2. #40450, CEIP Archives.
7. Clark M. Eichelberger, "James Thomson Shotwell," *Saturday Review* 48 (August 7, 1965): 16; Ferrell, *Peace in their Time,* pp. 62–63; Austin Chamberlain, *Down the Years* (London, 1935), p. 180.

limitation, but the renunciation of war itself "as an instrument of national policy."[8]

The French Foreign Minister seemed to like the idea but questioned if it could be carried out. He asked his guest to draft a memorandum which might serve as a basis for negotiations. Perhaps remembering Hughes' threat in 1925 when he had become involved in the Geneva Protocol negotiations, and fully realizing that he had already violated the Logan Act by discussing disarmament and debt revision with Briand, Shotwell refused to take the initiative in drawing up such a document. He proposed, instead, that the French Foreign Minister make a statement through the Paris office of the Associated Press on the occasion of the tenth anniversary of America's entry into World War I. If Briand accepted this approach, he would draft an outline of his ideas. Briand agreed, and Shotwell went to work on the statement immediately after leaving the Quai d'Orsay.[9]

Within two days he had completed his "Notes for a Suggested Statement on Franco-American Politics," and presented it to Alexis Léger, Briand's confidant and *chef de cabinet.* The statement, written from a French point of view, began with a defense of the French conception of disarmament. Admitting differences between the French and American position on the question, Shotwell concluded that both countries desired the same ends. In order to overcome some of the misunderstanding, he proposed that the two countries alter the direction of negotiations "so as to deal with the more fundamental question of policies of peace instead of the secondary question of disarmament." In line with this idea, he suggested that France propose a formal engagement between herself and the United States "which, according to the expression widely current in America, would 'outlaw war' between them."[10]

8. Shotwell seems to have been the first to use this phrase, adopting it from one of the sections in Karl Von Clausewitz's book *Von Kriege* entitled "Der Krieg ist ein Instrument der Politik." (Book VIII, chapter vi, sec. B).
9. J.T.S., *Autobiography,* pp. 206–9. The most detailed account of the interview appears in Waldo Chamberlain's "Origin of the Kellogg-Briand Pact," *The Historian* 15 (1952–53): 77–82. Most of Chamberlain's information is based on personal interviews with Shotwell.
10. J.T.S., "Notes for a Suggested Statement on Franco-American Policies," March 24, 1927, pp. 1–4, Box 2, J.T.S. Papers. Waldo Chamberlain has published the text of the memorandum in *The Historian* 15 (1952–53): 83–92.

He made clear that he used the phrase "outlaw war" not as it was understood by Salmon O. Levinson and the "outlawrists," but simply in the sense "that the signatories to such an engagement would renounce, for themselves mutually and reciprocally, the use of war as an instrument of national policy." What he really proposed was a treaty embodying the principles of Locarno without obligating the signatories to take specific action against an aggressor. He declared that since the principle of renunciation was "already familiar to the signatories of the Covenant of the League of Nations and the Pact of Locarno," its acceptance in America would lead to a restatement of international law. He then let slip his real interest in the treaty: "The United States without entering these organizations would nevertheless have to consider whether its present privileges of neutrality were consonant with the new conception of war. Undoubtedly neutrality must be re-defined so that the neutral may not, as at present, thwart even the restrictions of disarmament by insisting upon the right to supply the aggressor by arms and other supplies."[11]

Here was a way to commit the United States to the European collective security system. America would not have to partake in economic or military sanctions, but instead would merely refrain from trading with a declared aggressor. It was a familiar program to those who knew Shotwell well or who had carefully read his articles. It was the same one that he had so frequently enunciated during the debates over disarmament, clothed, however, in much more diplomatic terms. Shotwell fully understood the consequences of his proposal. It stemmed not from some naive and idealistic hope to abolish war by treaty, but rather from a desire to find a workable formula by which the United States could become an "associate" of the League and a supporter of the Locarno treaties.

Briand's message, given to the Associated Press for publication on April 6, closely followed Shotwell's draft. The Prime Minister began with a discussion of disarmament and concluded that while the United States and France approached the problem differently, they had essentially the same goals in mind. He also used the terms "outlawry of war" and "renunciation of war as an instrument of national policy" interchangeably, but clearly indicated that he referred to the

11. J.T.S., "Notes for a Suggested Statement," p. 5.

principle embodied in the Locarno treaties and not to Levinson's comprehensive program of renunciation, codification, and court. Although similar to Shotwell's memorandum, Briand's message avoided the implication that by signing such a treaty the United States would indirectly take the first step in joining the European collective security system. Nor did he explicitly state or imply that such a pact would result in changes in international law or that the United States would have to alter its concept of neutrality. Briand's note was more general and more subtle than Shotwell's, and consequently appeared more idealistic.[12]

One can only guess at Briand's reasons for suggesting a bilateral pact of "perpetual friendship" with the United States. Perhaps he accepted Shotwell's argument that some dramatic act of friendship between the two countries would lead to more fruitful discussions on the debt question. Perhaps he hoped to turn attention away from his rejection of Coolidge's disarmament conference. Most likely, however, he hoped to use the bilateral pact to round out the French security system which had evolved since September, 1920, when France signed a secret military alliance with Belgium. By 1927, in addition to her alliance with Belgium, France had signed a "political agreement" with Poland, an outright treaty of alliance with Czechoslovakia, the Locarno agreements, and treaties of friendship with Siam, Rumania, and Yugoslavia. Getting the United States to sign a treaty to renounce war would create, in effect, a negative alliance for France. America might not come to her aid in case of war, but neither would it side against her. Secretary of State Kellogg, for his part, felt certain that the proposal was designed to involve the United States backhandedly in the sort of political arrangement that the State Department had so carefully avoided in the past.[13]

Although Shotwell repeatedly denied that Briand had any ulterior motive,[14] he himself hoped that such an agreement would indirectly

12. For the text of Briand's note see *New York Times,* April 6, 1927, p. 5.
13. In his study of the Pact of Paris, Robert H. Ferrell convincingly argues that Briand's major aim was to involve the United States in a negative alliance with France. See Ferrell, *Peace in their Time,* pp. 54–65, 73–74, 264–65.
14. J.T.S., *War as an Instrument of National Policy and Its Renunciation in the Pact of Paris* (New York, 1929), pp. 117–18; J.T.S., "The Pact of Paris

extend America's responsibilities and bring the United States into closer cooperation with the League of Nations. That he desired Washington to do more than merely make a formal declaration renouncing war was clearly indicated throughout his memorandum for Briand. As he later wrote, his main purpose in speaking with the Foreign Minister was to get him "to take the definite step to inaugurate an extension of the Locarno Treaty, which had given to Europe its first positive and definite realization of the guarantee of international peace in the post-war world."[15]

On April 15 Shotwell arrived back in New York and to his surprise found that Briand's message had received almost no attention in the United States. Although he had decided not to publicize his part in initiating the offer, he immediately went to John Finley, editor of the *New York Times,* and told him in confidence of his discussion with the French Foreign Minister. He quickly won Finley's support and both agreed that Nicholas Murray Butler should attempt to reopen the issue with a letter to the *Times.* Butler's letter, largely written by Shotwell, referred to the Briand proposal as having every merit of "practicability and practicality." He contended that Briand would never have made the offer had he not received the consent of Premier Raymond Poincaré, and, therefore, Americans should view it in all seriousness. Since it did not ask the United States to join the League, the Court, or the Locarno agreements, he did not see how there could be any objections. He believed, moreover, that it would be a fitting way to celebrate the anniversary of America's entry into the great war.[16]

Butler's letter, combined with the editorial support of the *New York Times,* accomplished its purpose. Suddenly interest in the Briand proposal became widespread. The pro-League faction of the peace movement was not alone in drumming up support for the proposed Franco-American treaty of friendship. Levinson read the text of Briand's message just before boarding a ship for Europe and a spring vacation. Seeing that the French Foreign Minister had used the word

with Historical Commentary," *International Conciliation* 253 (October 1928): 447; J.T.S., *On the Rim of the Abyss* (New York, 1936), pp. 132–34.
15. J.T.S., *Autobiography,* p. 206.
16. *New York Times,* April 25, 1927, p. 22; J.T.S., *Autobiography,* pp. 211–13.

"outlawry," he became enthusiastic and devoted all his time in Europe to promoting the idea.[17]

Shotwell viewed Levinson's activities with alarm. Fearing his scheme might get caught up with the outlawry movement, he warned Earl Babcock in Paris to take all necessary measures "to disassociate the Briand proposal from Levinson."[18] The French Foreign Minister, however, realized that he might get caught between the pro and anti-Leaguers in America and attempted to play one group off against the other. On the one hand, he told Levinson that he found Shotwell and Butler burdensome, and on the other, informed Babcock, who served as the Endowment's intermediary in Paris, that Levinson seemed dangerous and had no real influence with the French Foreign Office. By so doing he was able to get both factions to support the April 6 proposal for different reasons. By appealing to each group separately and making each of the leaders feel that he was "in" while the others were not, Briand was able to unite the American peace movement when all other attempts had failed.[19]

Shotwell spent most of April and May promoting the French offer. On May 2 he spoke at a League of Nations Non-Partisan Association dinner and pushed through a resolution approving the proposed Franco-American treaty. The administration's silence on the entire affair, however, proved extremely distressing. In order to get some response, he asked Henry S. Pritchett of the Carnegie Foundation to solicit a Presidential interview for him. Pritchett wrote to Coolidge that Shotwell had seen Briand prior to the release of the April 6 statement and might have some interesting information. The President responded coolly, stating that any matter relating to the foreign affairs of the United States should be taken up with the Secretary of State. Confidentially he told his secretary that until some direct proposal came from the French government he had no intention of conferring with "volunteers."[20]

Since neither Coolidge nor Kellogg was willing to see him, Shotwell called on Robert E. Olds, the Undersecretary of State and a fellow

17. Stoner, *Levinson,* pp. 216–29; Drew Pearson and Constatine Brown, *The American Diplomatic Game* (Garden City, New York, 1935), pp. 17–18.
18. J.T.S. to Earl Babcock, May 19, 1927, Box 2, J.T.S. Papers.
19. Duroselle, *From Wilson to Roosevelt,* pp. 178–79.
20. Ferrell, *Peace in their Time,* pp. 77–78.

Carnegie Endowment Trustee. Olds told him that while the official policy of the State Department was to remain silent until some communiqué came directly from France, Shotwell might help clear up some of the misconceptions that had developed by drawing up a draft treaty as he had done in 1924. Such a treaty might show what Briand's offer would mean in terms of American obligations.[21]

Shotwell jumped at the suggestion. He contacted Joseph Chamberlain and within a week they had completed a rough draft. Shotwell again went to see Olds. The Undersecretary unofficially approved the draft and assured Shotwell that the government would not react adversely to his initiative or prosecute him under the Logan Act. So confident was Shotwell that the government would not do or say anything to spoil his effort that he informed Alanson B. Houghton, the United States Ambassador to Great Britain, that the Coolidge administration had given him its "blessing" without involving itself directly.[22]

On May 25, after some last minute revisions, Shotwell sent a copy of the completed draft to Olds, declaring that he was prepared to accept full responsibility for its contents and that he hoped its publication would not embarrass the Government. As he had told the Undersecretary previously, the idea was "simply to try to set down in the plainest English the meaning of such an offer as that proposed by M. Briand, and then to throw the matter open for public discussion in order that the Government may feel out the public sentiment in this matter without its being involved."[23]

Receiving no reply from Olds, he assumed that the government had no major objections and proceeded with plans for its release. Five days later, at the Columbia University Memorial Day services, Nicholas Murray Butler made the treaty public. It went much further than Briand's original offer of a simple bilateral agreement between America and France. Although Shotwell and Chamberlain structured it in

21. J.T.S. to Nicholas Murray Butler, May 18, 1927, J.T.S. to Ambassador Alanson Houghton, May 21, 1927, J.T.S. to Earl Babcock, May 21, 1927, Box 2, J.T.S. Papers.
22. J.T.S. to Ambassador Alanson B. Houghton, May 21, 1927, Box 2, J.T.S. Papers.
23. J.T.S. to Robert E. Olds, May 25, 1927, #711.5112 France/7 M568 Roll 2, State Department Archives.

the form of a bilateral treaty, they indicated that the second signatory might be any one of the major powers. They explained that while their original intention had been to state just what the French offer would mean in the light of existing Franco-American treaty obligations, they realized as the work progressed that it "might be framed in terms applicable to any other signatory of Locarno and to other non-American powers as well, including even Japan." "Viewed in this light," they went on, "the draft became not merely an effort to clarify the offer of M. Briand, but to state the possibilities of an American Locarno."[24]

Shotwell, in fact, had opposed a simple bilateral treaty from the first. As he suggested in his inaugural address at the *Hochschule für Politik,* the United States should make agreements with several of the major powers. Even before he began working on the draft treaty, he wrote Thomas Jones of the British Ministry that if the Briand offer came to anything he hoped that America would negotiate "a similar arrangement with Britain and perhaps with Germany and Japan."[25] To Ambassador Houghton he wrote that it was "most important not to have a special treaty with any one Great Power." And when he sent his proposed draft to Earl Babcock in France, he stated that the document had been drafted "so that all the Great Powers might sign."[26]

From the beginning, then, his major interest in the Briand offer was in its possibilities for creating an "American Locarno." He neither favored a simple agreement between the United States and France nor seriously believed that war could be abolished by its mere renunciation. Instead he hoped that the Coolidge administration would sign a series of bilateral agreements with the Locarno nations and Japan so that America could cooperate more closely with the collective security system established at Geneva. The Shotwell-Chamberlain draft treaty sought to make American obligations and responsibilities in such a system more clear and precise. While it did not go as far as the Locarno treaties and avoided all the entanglements of the League Covenant, it attempted to extend over the world the "spirit of

24. *New York Times,* May 31, 1927, p. 18.
25. J.T.S. to Thomas Jones, April 26, 1927, Box 2, J.T.S. Papers.
26. J.T.S. to Ambassador Alanson Houghton, May 21, 1927, J.T.S. to Earl Babcock, May 21, 1927, Box 2, J.T.S. Papers.

Locarno." Shotwell argued that it called for no real departure from settled American policies, but rather demonstrated "that an American Locarno could be made the basis of an adjustment of the United States with all the existing instruments of peace that have gone into operation in recent years."[27]

Basically, the draft treaty consisted of three parts: renunciation of war, arbitration and conciliation, and ratification. Specifically excepted from the renunciation clause was self-defense and the Monroe Doctrine. Article 2 defined "self-defense" as the resistance to a violation of a previous promise not to resort to war, "provided that the attacked party shall at once submit the dispute to peaceful settlement or to comply with an arbitral or judicial decision." In other words, the aggressor was that party which resorted to war in violation of its previous pledge to submit all disputes to peaceful settlement. In terms of American obligations Article 3 was the key clause, for it called upon the signatories to pledge that in the event of a breach of the treaty or any other covenant for the compulsory peaceful settlement of international disputes they would not aid or abet the treaty-breaking power. Moreover, if the treaty was violated by one of the signatories, the other would recover "full liberty of action with reference to it." According to its terms the United States would have to revise its traditional neutrality policy along the lines so frequently advocated by the pro-Leaguers. No longer would it be free to trade with a self-confessed aggressor.[28]

The implications of the Shotwell-Chamberlain draft treaty were so clear that even the French Foreign Office was caught off guard. The *New York Times* reported that Briand was extremely upset and viewed the draft as going far beyond the scope of the compact contemplated by himself. French officials, moreover, made clear that the Foreign Minister envisioned a treaty much more limited than the Shotwell plan and simply desired a Franco-American agreement without the broader implications of an American Locarno.[29]

Press reaction in the United States was mixed. Outright support came from the *New York World*, the *Brooklyn Eagle*, and the Dallas

27. *New York Times*, May 31, 1927, p. 18.
28. Ibid.
29. Ibid., June 2, 1927, p. 10.

News. The editors of the *New York Times* remained cautious in their praise, calling it an "intelligent and high-minded effort to bring a great humane feeling within the realm of practical realization."[30] Washington reacted with restraint, but expressed some irritation. Either Shotwell had misunderstood Olds' silence or the Undersecretary had not carefully read the document. Once released, both the President and the State Department seemed greatly annoyed. The day of its publication Coolidge declared that he was "aware certain individuals, particularly in New York—including Professor Shotwell of Columbia—are preparing proposals for treaties between this government and other countries which are usually referred to as treaties for outlawing war." He refused, however, to discuss them and directed all such individuals to take up the matter with the State Department.[31] The *Brooklyn Eagle* reported that Washington's reception of an "American Locarno" was definitely not encouraging: "That a mere professor in Columbia University, of all places, should have had the temerity to draft a model treaty gives many people in Washington an acute pain."[32]

The publication of the draft treaty, together with the release of two other competing ones—one written by Francis B. Sayre, professor of Law at Harvard, and the other put out by the American Foundation —forced the French Foreign Office to make clear exactly the type of agreement it favored. On June 21 Briand gave the American chargé d'affaires in Paris a draft treaty entitled "Pact of Perpetual Friendship between France and the United States." It was short and simple, consisting of two substantive articles and a third article on ratification. Article 1 provided that "The high contracting powers solemnly declare in the name of the French people and the people of the United States of America that they condemn recourse to war and renounce it, respectively, as an instrument of their national policy towards each other." Article 2 declared that "The settlement or the solution of all disputes or conflicts of whatever nature or of whatever origin they may be which may arise between France and the United States of

30. See extensive clipping file on reaction to draft treaty in Box 8, J.T.S. Papers; *New York Times,* May 31, 1927, p. 20.
31. Pearson and Brown, *American Diplomatic Game,* pp. 21–22.
32. *Brooklyn Eagle,* June 3, 1927, in Box 8, J.T.S. Papers.

America shall never be sought by either side except by pacific means."[33]

Although Briand's proposed pact was much shorter and less complicated than Shotwell's, its structure was basically the same. It also consisted of three essential parts: renunciation of war, arbitration and conciliation, and ratification. The differences between them were of the same nature as those between Shotwell's memorandum of March 24 and Briand's April 6 message. In both cases the French Foreign Minister omitted all explicit references to America's relations with the security system of Europe and avoided all questions of possible obligations ensuing from adherence to his proposed treaty. The two documents reflected the different interests and aims of their respective authors. Shotwell clearly wanted to tie America into the European security system through such devices as a definition of aggression and permissive sanctions. Briand, on the other hand, was not concerned with America's overall relations with Europe, but simply wanted to guarantee his own nation's relations with the United States. He feared, moreover, that the American people would never agree to a negative alliance and therefore couched his proposal in idealistic terms in order to make it look like nothing more than a pact of friendship. His analysis proved correct, for while the Shotwell-Chamberlain draft treaty never gained much popularity in America, the peace movement organized solidly behind the French offer.

Levinson returned to the United States on June 14 and went immediately to see Borah and Kellogg. Despite the skepticism of both men, the "Captain of Outlawry" began an energetic campaign to win support for the proposed treaty. The increased activity and demands of the peace organizations, however, did not alter the administration's policy of complete silence on the subject. Kellogg informed the President that he opposed making any treaty along the lines outlined by either Shotwell or Briand. The Senate, he argued, would never accept either proposal.[34]

33. U. S. Department of State, *Papers Relating to the Foreign Relations of the United States, 1927* (Washington, D.C., 1942), 2: 616. A fairly complete record of the correspondence leading up to the Pact of Paris is also provided in *International Conciliation* 203 (October 1928): 460–531.
34. Frank B. Kellogg to President Calvin Coolidge, June 27, 1927, #711.5112 France/34, State Department Archives.

Although Shotwell and Levinson retained a strong antipathy for each other, they agreed that only Congressional pressure could break the administration's silence. Levinson tried desperately to win over Borah, but the Idaho senator distrusted Briand and had serious doubts about the wisdom of the proposed bilateral treaty. Shotwell proved more successful with Senator Arthur Capper of Kansas and persuaded him to back an antiwar resolution prepared by himself, Butler, and Chamberlain. On November 21, Capper publicly released the joint resolution as his own, and two weeks later, on December 8, introduced it into the Senate. It consisted of three major sections. First it called for the United States to negotiate treaties with "France and other like-minded nations" to renounce war as an instrument of public policy and "to adjust and settle its international disputes by mediation, arbitration, and conciliation. . . ." Second, it proposed that the United States accept the definition of aggression which had appeared in Shotwell's Draft Treaty of Disarmament and Security of 1924 and in the Locarno agreements. Lastly, it called upon the administration to conclude with France and other like-minded nations treaties declaring that nationals of the contracting governments would not, in giving aid and comfort to an aggressor nation, receive the protection of their governments.[35]

By late December Kellogg came to the conclusion that some response to Briand's offer was necessary. Public pressure had increased and many Senators demanded that the administration take some action. To get out of the dilemma in which Briand had placed him, and to avoid a negative alliance with France, the Secretary of State informed Paul Claudel, the French Ambassador to Washington, that the United States would gladly agree to renounce war as an instrument of its national policy, but favored a multilateral treaty including "all the principal Powers of the world."[36]

There followed a series of exchanges in which the French Foreign

35. J.T.S., *War as an Instrument of National Policy,* pp. 94–95; J.T.S. to Charles Gide, November 30, 1927, Box 68, J.T.S. Papers; Arthur Capper to Tasker H. Bliss, December 23, 1927, Box 271, Bliss Papers.
36. U. S. Department of State, *Foreign Relations of the United States, 1927,* 2: 626–27. For a discussion of the origin of the idea of multilateralism see Ferrell, *Peace in their Time,* pp. 138–42.

Office gradually agreed to have others join in a treaty renouncing war as long as the United States and France signed first and as long as only "aggressive" wars were renounced. Kellogg, however, continued to insist upon true multilateralism and complete outlawry without any qualifications. On January 21, Claudel delivered a frigid note stating that although France would reluctantly accept any procedure which might be practicable, she feared that a treaty outlawing all wars would violate her pledge made both in the League Assembly and in the Locarno agreements to resist "aggressive" wars.[37]

This last note seemed to end all hope for agreement. Even Shotwell viewed it as nothing less "than an effort to withdraw from the whole negotiation."[38] On February 5, however, the *New York Times* published an article signed by Senator William E. Borah suggesting to France a way to honor her Continental alliances and adhere at the same time to a multilateral pact renouncing all wars. He maintained that a breach of the pact would automatically release the signatories from their obligations thereunder. By signing such a treaty, in other words, France would only suspend her commitments, which would become active again if any one of the signatories violated the agreement.[39]

The following day the *Times* published a long letter from Shotwell praising the Senator's formula. He went much further than Borah, however, and attempted to prove that no real conflict existed between the European security arrangements and the proposed pact to abolish war. He believed that Kellogg and all those who sided with him reserved the right of self-defense for all nations. Implicitly or explicitly, therefore, some definition of aggression had to be understood and he believed that the juridical definition as worked out in the Geneva Protocol and the Locarno treaties was the best. Since League wars were only acts of collective defense, they too, according to his analysis, were excluded from the proposed outlawry pact.[40]

37. U. S. Department of State, *Foreign Relations of the United States, 1927,* 1: 6–8. See also *International Conciliation* 203 (October 1928): 466–72.
38. J.T.S., *War as an Instrument of National Policy,* p. 133.
39. William E. Borah, "One Great Treaty to Outlaw War," *New York Times,* February 5, 1928, sec. 9, p. 1.
40. Ibid., February 6, 1928, p. 18.

Levinson's blood boiled as he read Shotwell's attempt to twist Borah's meaning and promote his own definition of aggression. The "Captain of Outlawry" was so exasperated that he confessed to Harrison Brown that his patience with Shotwell was at an end:

> He slobbers all over Borah and his proposal and he slobbers right back into his own stuff and expects us to go wrong by patting us on the back. The best thing I can do with Shotwell is to forget him.[41]

Ignoring the wrangling between the two antiwar leaders, Kellogg seized upon the Borah formula and renewed negotiations with France for a multilateral treaty outlawing all wars. Despite their personal antagonism, Levinson and Shotwell, together with Jane Addams, Carrie Chapman Catt, and most other antiwar leaders, united behind the proposed treaty. They addressed college, civic, and professional groups across the country, organized pressure on Senators and Congressmen, held mass meetings, and wrote articles for both newspapers and popular magazines. Working together, they succeeded in building a solid base of support for the proposed renunciation of war treaty.[42]

Even more important in bringing the negotiations to a successful conclusion was Kellogg's conversion to the idea of a multilateral pact. At first he suggested it simply to appease the antiwar agitators in America, but by February, 1928, he had become enthusiastic, viewing it as a great gift to the world.[43] On April 13, he sent the text of a draft treaty to France, Great Britain, Germany, Italy, and Japan. It closely resembled the original French offer except that it took the form of a multilateral treaty instead of a bilateral one. Article I provided that "The High Contracting Parties solemnly declare in the names of their respective peoples that they condemn recourse to war for the solution of international controversies, and renounce it as an instrument of national policy in their relations with one another." The second sub-

41. Salmon O. Levinson to Harrison Brown, February 8, 1928, Levinson Papers.
42. Duroselle, *From Wilson to Roosevelt,* p. 180.
43. Ferrell, *Peace in their Time,* p. 164; Lewis Ethan Ellis, *Frank B. Kellogg and American Foreign Relations, 1925–1929* (New Brunswick, N. J., 1961), pp. 205–9.

stantive article provided that "The High Contracting Parties agree that the settlement or solution of all disputes or conflicts of whatever nature or of whatever origin they may be, which may arise among them, shall never be sought except by pacific means."[44]

One week after Kellogg's treaty went out, Briand responded with a counter-draft which included several reservations including the right of self-defense, French obligations under the League Covenant and its various alliances, and the right of release in case of breach. Kellogg was so intent upon getting his treaty accepted that while he denounced the Briand counter-offer as unacceptable, he indirectly agreed to most of the reservations. Negotiations continued throughout the spring of 1928, and by early summer most of the major nations had responded affirmatively to the Kellogg draft, albeit with reservations of their own. Having received the necessary acceptances, Kellogg and Briand announced that the signing of the antiwar pact would take place in Paris on August 27, 1928.[45]

During July and August a debate developed over the meaning of the various reservations contained in the letters of acceptance. Kellogg maintained that the notes lacked the force of formal reservations and were nothing more than unilateral declarations. Most Americans accepted the Secretary's interpretation and sought the meaning of the new treaty in its two substantive articles. Several international law experts, including Professors Edwin M. Borchard of Yale, Philip Marshall Brown of Princeton, and John Bassett Moore of Columbia, took issue with Kellogg. They maintained that the reservations played a significant part in the treaty's meaning and could not be overlooked.[46]

Shotwell immediately threw himself into the debate and sided with the international lawyers. His reason for taking sides was more than academic. From the outset he had sought to give the Kellogg-Briand negotiations a wider meaning and never gave up hope that somehow the antiwar pact could move the United States closer to the League

44. U. S. Department of State, *Foreign Relations of the United States, 1929,* 1: 23.
45. Ibid., pp. 32–39, 90–95; Ferrell, *Peace in their Time,* pp. 173–76; David Bryan-Jones, *Frank B. Kellogg: A Biography* (New York, 1937), pp. 244–45.
46. Ferrell, *Peace in their Time,* pp. 192–94.

of Nations. He now argued that since the reservations removed "self-defense" and "defensive" wars from the purview of the treaty, some sort of accepted definition of these terms became imperative. To find such a definition he looked to the preamble of the treaty, which declared that any nation violating the pact would lose all benefits incurring from it. Here was his own juridical definition: that nation which violated its previous pledge not to go to war had in effect branded itself an aggressor. Any resistance to such an act was defense. Shotwell also maintained that the preamble might be interpreted so as to lead to a revision of America's neutrality policy. If it inherently provided a definition of aggression, then the United States had a moral duty not to become a silent partner of an aggressor. By using the reservations and the preamble to interpret the antiwar pact, he was able to bend its meaning and bring it fully in line with the draft treaty he had prepared with Joseph Chamberlain.[47]

For many of those in the peace movement the signing of the Pact of Paris on August 27 marked the beginning of a new era. Shotwell, however, noted the event with mixed emotions. Kellogg, impervious to the arguments of the international lawyers, made it perfectly clear that the treaty contained no sanctions and no commitment to go to war. In fact, he declared that the pact itself did not in any way involve the United States in European affairs.[48] Only three days before the signing, Shotwell wrote to Henry Cabot Lodge that although he had proposed the idea to Briand, he could in no way be considered the originator of the plan as it eventually evolved. He had criticized the pact "so long as there seemed to be any chance of modification" and supported it only as a first step in the movement to abolish war.[49]

Although he took an active part in the campaign for ratification, he irritated many peace advocates by constantly emphasizing the limitations of the treaty and urging that further steps be taken to insure against the future outbreak of armed conflict.[50] He was not

47. J.T.S., "How the Anti-War Compact Binds Us," *New York Times,* July 29, 1928, sec. 8, p. 1.
48. *Ibid.,* August 2, 1928, p. 1.
49. Henry Cabot Lodge, "The Meaning of the Kellogg Treaty," *Harper's Monthly Magazine* 158 (December 1928): 32.
50. J.T.S. to Colonel Edward M. House, July 19, 1928, Drawer 17, J.T.S. folder, Edward M. House Papers, Yale University.

alone, however, in recognizing the pact's limitations. Senator W. C. Bruce of Maryland, who favored collective security, predicted that the treaty would be "about as effective to keep down war as a carpet would be to smother an earthquake."[51] Senators Carter Glass of Virginia and James A. Reed of Missouri concurred in Bruce's analysis, the former stating that the treaty wasn't worth a "postage stamp in the direction of accomplishing permanent international peace," and the latter referring to it as an "international kiss."[52] Despite their disparaging remarks, few Senators were willing to flaunt public opinion and vote against the treaty. When Senator Borah called for a vote, on January 15, 1929, 85 Senators gave their advice and consent. Only one—John Blaine of Wisconsin—cast a dissenting voice.[53] Two days later President Coolidge signed the ratifying document and by the summer the other fourteen signatories had ratified. Herbert Hoover, who had taken office in March, announced the antiwar treaty in force as of 1:22 P.M., July 24, 1929.

Shotwell's part in the successful negotiations did not go completely unnoticed. In May he received a gold medal from the National Institute of Social Sciences "for distinguished services rendered in the field of economics and as one having a world-wide reputation for the faithful and effective work in the support of the cause of peace among the nations of the world."[54] It was an honor he well deserved. He had initiated the Briand offer and had been responsible for getting the negotiations off the ground. But in success he had also found failure, for the Kellogg-Briand pact in no way resembled his own proposal for an American Locarno. It was, in fact, little more than an "international kiss"; an effort, as Franklin Delano Roosevelt declared, to make America "feel self-righteous by a general declaration abjuring war" without requiring Americans to make any sacrifices to attain peace.[55]

No one saw the danger in accepting the Pact of Paris as the final

51. *Congressional Record,* 70th Cong., 2nd Sess., vol. 70, part 2, December 15, 1928, pp. 678–81.
52. Ibid., January 5, 1929, p. 1186, January 15, 1929, p. 1728.
53. Ibid., January 15, 1929, p. 1730.
54. *New York Times,* May 1, 1929, p. 11.
55. Franklin Delano Roosevelt, "Our Foreign Policy: A Democratic View," *Foreign Affairs* 6 (July 1928): 582.

realization of world peace more than Shotwell. If Americans sincerely wanted peace they would have to accept the responsibilities thrust upon them by the new world order. Solemn declarations were not enough. They could not assure world peace and yet avoid responsibility should that assurance fail. The ratification of the Kellogg-Briand pact was only the beginning of its history. It presented a program rather than a completed fact. "In the last analysis," he proclaimed, "the establishment of international peace is not a negative but a positive act—not mere renunciation of an outworn technique but the acceptance of peace-time methods in international relations. It will mean more, not less, of these relations in the future."[56]

56. J.T.S., "The Pact of Paris," *The Inquiry* 5 (February 1929): 20.

At the dedication of the James T. Shotwell Library, with Joseph E. Johnson and Grayson Kirk, President of Columbia University, 1954. Courtesy the Carnegie Endowment for International Peace

At Andrew Carnegie Birthday Celebration with Thomas J. Watson of IBM and Mrs. Walter Elliot, 1954. Courtesy the Carnegie Endowment for International Peace

10
An International Mind

Shortly after the signing of the Kellogg-Briand Pact, Harcourt, Brace and Company published *War as an Instrument of National Policy and its Renunciation in the Pact of Paris,* Shotwell's first major work on international relations. The book traced the complicated negotiations leading to the signing of the antiwar treaty and analyzed the various reservations contained in the notes of acceptance. The conclusion was clear. The treaty did not guarantee peace; it provided only the necessary first step. A stable peace depended not upon pious declarations, but upon the development of alternatives for war, greater international cooperation, and an effective collective security system which included all the great nations of the world.

Neither the thesis nor the conclusions of Shotwell's study were particularly new or original. Woodrow Wilson and the international liberals had said much the same thing throughout World War I. The fascinating aspect of the book was its tone and approach. It articulated a world view which had become quite respectable among a small group of prominent intellectuals and political commentators. It was a view which played down domestic concerns and placed international relations above all other issues. Solutions to domestic economic and social problems could not precede solutions to international problems. If the threat of war continued or if armed conflict actually broke out, domestic questions would count for little. It was a view, in other words, which interpreted "national interest" as an anachronistic concept. Only if each nation interpreted its national interest in terms of the national interests of all other nations could perpetual peace and the good society be realized.

If *War as an Instrument of National Policy* did nothing else, it revealed that Shotwell had developed what Nicholas Murray Butler often called the "international mind."[1] Shotwell, in fact, went much further than most of his contemporaries in externalizing American interests. His lectures, articles, books, and even personal correspondence during the 1920s reveal an almost complete disregard for domestic matters. He gave little thought to the decline of reform in America; he never seriously discussed the growing materialism of American life or the increasing political and economic centralization of the Harding-Coolidge era; he rarely mentioned prohibition, censorship, or Ku-Kluxism; he took no interest in domestic politics other than in its direct relation to world affairs; and he left no record of any interest in the Sacco-Vanzetti trial. He seemed neither disillusioned nor optimistic about the state of American society in the 1920s; he simply wasn't concerned with the problems which bothered other American intellectuals at the time.

Shotwell was by no means insensitive to social and economic inequities. Nor was he opposed to social reform. He fully understood, moreover, that "social justice" would have to come at a national level before it could be realized on an international level. Yet he remained primarily concerned with world politics. Whereas he carefully defined the problems facing the community of nations and worked diligently to make his policy statements as clear as possible, he never bothered to define precisely what he meant by social progress. He seemed content to make generalizations about the need for social and eco-

1. For Butler's definition of the term see Nicholas Murray Butler, *The International Mind: An Argument for the Judicial Settlement of International Disputes* (New York, 1912), p. 102.

nomic changes, but rarely brought to these problems the "scientific" attitude or the enthusiasm he reserved for international questions. As Benjamin Stolberg noted, Shotwell, and many other internationalists like him, seemed satisfied to "put forth social smoke screens for social solutions."[2] His argument at the Paris Peace Conference that an international child labor law and the creation of the ILO would relieve the discontent among the masses and check world-wide revolutions, revealed his inability to confront social problems directly and his misunderstanding of the nature of postwar revolutionary ferment.

Like most Wilsonian internationalists, Shotwell strongly believed in the necessity of economic expansion. He not only viewed the Open Door policy as the best means for solving problems at home and taking advantage of economic opportunities abroad, but also as a valuable means of promoting world peace and international prosperity. Although he admitted that national economic expansion was "the imperialism of the modern world," he still maintained that the process would ultimately enrich all concerned by creating interlocking international interests. He preferred to overlook the fact that economic imperialism often caused conflict, encouraged exploitation, and even led to war. Instead he saw the "world of credit" as leading to "a world of peace."[3]

The stock market crash of 1929 and the world-wide depression which followed merely convinced him of the truth of his arguments. He viewed the depression as due not to the over-expansion of major industries, the weak banking structure, the maldistribution of income, or the poor corporate structure, but to the First World War. The economic decline, he proclaimed, was "the last battle of the World War itself."[4] Like Cordell Hull, then a Senator from Tennessee, he believed that the best means of achieving prosperity was to open the markets of the world to free trade. He went further than Hull, how-

2. Benjamin Stolberg, Review of *The Origins of the International Labor Organization* by James T. Shotwell, ed., *Saturday Review of Literature* 11 (February 9, 1935): 478.
3. J.T.S., "Does Business Mean Peace?" *Outlook and Independent* 151 (March 31, 1929): 407, 436.
4. J.T.S., "The Last Battle of the World War: An Address," May 31, 1932, pp. 3–4, IV, #62333, CEIP Archives.

ever, and argued that lasting prosperity depended upon the elevation of the masses in all countries. "It is a short-sighted view," he argued, "which would keep the backward nations in a condition of economic dependence upon any one nation or group of nations. The ultimate aim should be to strengthen the whole economic fabric, for only by such a process can we avert that saturation which inevitably produces industrial depression throughout the world. . . . There is only one way by which prosperity can continue to meet the increasing demands of increasing organized industry, and that is by a parallel increase of the buying power of the common man the world over."[5]

Just how the buying power of the common man could be raised he never made clear. He also assumed, as did Hull, that free trade itself would create international good will and promote peace. Businessmen recognizing the interdependence of the economic system would take a strong stand against war and serve as a positive force for peace. Both men preferred to ignore the fact that increased international economic activity might create as much friction and conflict as it did international cooperation. Neither one, moreover, seemed to clearly understand that peace was as much a condition for international trade as freedom of trade was a necessary condition for peace.[6]

Shotwell's interest in international economic policy and world politics was not confined to Europe and the Western Hemisphere. Recognizing the importance of the Far East, he became deeply involved in the work of the Institute of Pacific Relations, an organization created in 1925 to "study the conditions of the Pacific peoples with a view to the improvement of their mutual relations."[7] Although he missed the Institute's first biennial conference, he attended the second one in

5. J.T.S., "The Conditions of Enduring Prosperity," *International Conciliation* 267 (February 1931): 60–63.

6. For an analysis of Hull's economic theories see William R. Allen, "Cordell Hull and the Defense of the Trade Agreements Program, 1934–1940," in Alexander De Conde, ed., *Isolation and Security* (Durham, N.C., 1957), pp. 107–32.

7. "Handbook of the Institute of Pacific Relations," in Bruno Lasker, ed., *Problems of the Pacific, 1931: Proceedings of the Fourth Conference of the Institute of Pacific Relations, Hangchow and Shanghai, China, October 21 to November 2* (Chicago, 1932), pp. 521–27; Chester H. Rowell, "The Kyoto Conference of the Institute of Pacific Relations," *International Conciliation* 260 (May 1930): 235–36.

1927 as chairman of the Research Committee of the American branch of the organization. Two years later, he received a substantial grant from the Carnegie Endowment and sailed for Japan two months before the scheduled convening of the third biennial conference in order to study firsthand the political and economic situation in Asia. His travels took him not only to numerous Japanese cities, but to China, Korea, and Manchuria as well. He held interviews with various academic, business, and political leaders, including Kijuro Shidehara and C. T. Wang, the Japanese and Chinese Foreign Ministers.[8]

The Kyoto Conference, which met from October 28 to November 9, 1929, was the largest held by the Institute. For the first time delegates from the entire Pacific world attended, including representatives from Australia, Great Britain, Canada, China, France, Japan, Korea, Mexico, the Netherlands, New Zealand, the Philippines, Soviet Russia, and the United States. Both the League of Nations and the International Labor Organization sent observers. More than 190 delegates attended the conference meetings and the round-table discussions.[9]

Of the many issues taken up, the two most important and controversial were extraterritoriality in China and control of Manchuria. In the discussions on both subjects Shotwell played a key role. The question of extraterritoriality had become quite serious in 1929 when China announced its decision to terminate all existing extraterritorial rights by January 1, 1930. Chinese leaders maintained that these priviliges violated her sovereign rights and retarded her progress toward self-government. By November, 1928, China had negotiated treaties with Italy and Belgium abolishing their extraterritorial privileges, and by February, 1929, Luxemburg, Spain, Denmark, and Portugal had also agreed to end their special legal status in China. Although most nations had either lost their privileged position in China, or had voluntary given it up, the United States, Great Britain, and France continued to share the benefits of extraterritoriality and made

8. J.T.S., *Autobiography,* pp. 236–53; J.T.S. to Nicholas Murray Butler, September 20, 1929, I.F.2. #40523, CEIP Archives; J.T.S., "Diary," 1–2, I.F.2. #41287, CEIP Archives.
9. Rowell, "Kyoto Conference," pp. 239–40.

clear that they had no intention of accepting unilateral termination. The three western powers maintained that under the existing judicial system their citizens could not be guaranteed justice in Chinese courts. Basing their position on a report of an international Commission on Extraterritoriality which met in 1926 to study Chinese law and judicial procedure, they refused to agree to any new treaty arrangements until China had reformed her judicial system so as to avoid interference by executive and military authorities and had adopted modern codes of civil and commercial banking law, patent law, criminal law, and land-expropriation law.[10]

In the debates at Kyoto, the Chinese delegates argued that in the past many countries, including Japan, Turkey, and Siam, had ended extraterritorial privileges without agreeing to preconditions. They pointed out, moreover, that progress already had been made in administrative and judicial reforms and that codes of law had been drawn up as suggested by the international commission. Several western delegates replied that they had seen no proof of change in the administration of justice and that the government of China had made no attempt to guarantee the independence of the judiciary. Hoping to bring the two sides closer together, Shotwell presented a compromise plan.

The plan grew out of his discussions with several government officials, including Dr. C. T. Wang, the Chinese Foreign Minister. He suggested that the question of extraterritoriality could be viewed in two ways. The Chinese viewed it as a matter of politics, symbolizing western exploitation and imperialism, while the western powers saw it as a juristic matter concerning the administration of justice and the protection of their citizens. The solution lay in finding some way by which the juristic claims of the western powers could be established within the framework of the Chinese political system. He strongly believed, therefore, that it was in China's best interest to carry out the

10. *New York Times,* October 20, 1928, p. 1, December 1, 1928, p. 6, February 10, 1929, p. 5, May 4, 1929, p. 7, May 6, 1929, p. 7, September 17, 1929, p. 4; Wesley R. Fishel, *The End of Extraterritoriality in China* (Berkeley, 1952), pp. 90–126; Robert H. Ferrell, *Frank B. Kellogg–Henry L. Stimson,* vol. 11 of *The American Secretaries of State and Their Diplomacy,* ed. Robert H. Ferrell, 16 vols. (New York, 1963), pp. 74–80.

legal reforms suggested by the international commission of 1926. Such an action, he argued, would not only help internally, but could serve as the basis for international negotiations.[11]

Until the new law matured, he proposed that China adopt a temporary expedient and set up several special courts to deal with property rights and problems of foreign business interests. Such an action might convince the western powers of the government's sincerity and lead them to give up extraterritoriality without fearing unjust treatment for their citizens. In line with this proposal, he advocated the establishment of special courts in areas of foreign concentration such as Shanghai, Tientsin, Mukden, and Canton. These courts would have the authority to apply new Chinese law and would be given some enforcement power. Recognizing possible objections to purely Chinese courts, he proposed that initially the government appoint justices from international panels submitted either by the World Court or the Court of Arbitration. Gradually they would be replaced by Chinese justices until China had full control over the new courts.[12]

Reaction in China to Shotwell's compromise was immediate and mixed. Both Walter A. Adams, the American Consul in Nanking, and Edwin S. Cunningham, the American Consul-General in Shanghai, reported that the idea of an interim measure before the complete abolition of extraterritorial rights had won the support of many prominent Chinese citizens.[13] The Consul-General in Canton, Douglas Jenkins, substantiated his colleagues' evaluations. He reported that while some of the more radical groups rejected any form of extraterritoriality, "many well-informed and responsible Chinese" seemed favorable to a "plan along the lines advocated by Professor Shotwell, who after all has merely become the spokesman for many people who

11. J.T.S., *Extraterritoriality in China* (Concord, N. H., 1929), pp. 16–18.
12. Ibid., pp. 19–20; J.T.S., "Note on Memorandum 'Extraterritoriality in China,'" Box 116, Papers of the American Institute of Pacific Relations, Columbia University (hereafter cited AIPR); J. B. Condliff, ed., *Problems of the Pacific, 1929* (Chicago, 1929), pp. 345–55.
13. Walter A. Adams to J. V. A. MacMurray, November 11, 1929, p. 13, #893.00 P. R. Nanking/19, State Department Archives; Edwin S. Cunningham to J. V. A. MacMurray, November 26, 1929, #793.003/219, State Department Archives.

have considered such an evolution of our extraterritorial relations with China for years."[14]

Comments in Chinese newspapers followed the lines suggested by Jenkins. Conservative journals such as *The North-China Daily News* gave the Shotwell plan strong editorial support, while *The China Truth,* a radical paper edited by several foreign-educated Chinese, strongly condemned it. The editors of *The China Truth* identified Shotwell as a leading member of that "group of pacifists who are always busy in devising all sorts of methods for better relationship among nations." They maintained that if China had to appoint justices from a panel of experts nominated by the World Court, the new courts would forever remain outside Chinese control. Although they did not question Shotwell's sincerity, they believed that he had given so much priority to European questions that he lacked sufficient insight into Oriental problems.[15]

Such a conclusion was not entirely fair. Shotwell had devoted a good deal of time to studying the question of extraterritoriality and had carefully surveyed the alternatives. If his plan did not satisfy the strong nationalist desires of many Chinese, it was due to his realization that the western powers would never agree to complete and immediate abolition of their rights in China. His major aim was to find some temporary measure which would legally end extraterritoriality and gradually lead to full Chinese sovereignty. Like so many of his European schemes, his proposal at Kyoto was an attempt to bridge two contrary and conflicting points of view. That he partially succeeded was revealed in statements released by both the Chinese and American governments. In its note of December 28, 1929, announcing the termination of extraterritoriality, the Chinese government implied that it would be willing to experiment with a plan along the lines suggested at the Kyoto Conference. The American State Department, for its part, suggested that it too would be willing to consider a plan for the gradual relinquishment of extraterritorial rights "either as to

14. Douglas Jenkins to J. V. A. MacMurray, November 14, 1929, #793.-003/204, State Department Archives.
15. *The North-China Daily News,* November 9, 1929, clipping in State Department Archives, #793.003/219; *The China Truth* (Canton), November 9, 1929, clipping in State Department Archives, #793.003/204.

designated territorial areas or as to particular kinds of jurisdiction. . . ."[16] Despite these conciliatory expressions, the western powers ignored the Chinese proclamation and maintained the legal status quo for some thirteen years, when under the pressures of another world war the United States and Great Britain acceded to Chinese wishes.[17]

The Kyoto Conference spent its last days discussing the Manchurian question, which by late 1929 had also become quite serious. Following the Institute's general policy, the delegates avoided the most controversial political issues and concentrated instead on the economic and social aspects of the problem. Although Shotwell recognized the limitations of an unofficial meeting such as the Kyoto Conference, he deluded himself at times as to both its importance and possibilities. He often spoke as if the agreements reached during the discussions pointed to practical solutions which the various national leaders might adopt. If only the ruling circles in the Far East, or for that matter in Europe, would follow the example set by the delegates at Kyoto and substitute "rational" discussion for "emotional" response, no problem would prove too difficult to solve peacefully.[18]

At times Shotwell seemed to forget that the Kyoto Conference succeeded precisely because the delegates did not have to settle any issues or reach any definite conclusions. The conference proved only that Chinese and Japanese citizens, for the most part intellectuals and businessmen, could discuss problems affecting their respective countries without coming to blows; it by no means pointed to actual solutions nor did it demonstrate that these problems could be solved peacefully to the mutual benefit of both parties.

With the Kyoto Conference over, Shotwell once again turned his

16. Stanley K. Hornbeck to J.T.S., November 15, 1930, Box 116, AIPR Papers; State Department press release, November 13, 1930, Box 116, AIPR Papers; J.T.S., "Speech delivered before the Federal Council of Churches of Christ in America at Madison Square Hotel," January 9, 1930, III, #55218, CEIP Archives.
17. The United States and Great Britain signed separate treaties with China abolishing extraterritorial rights on January 11, 1943. See Fishel, *End of Extraterritoriality,* pp. 1–2, 170–217.
18. J.T.S. to Nicholas Murray Butler, December 6, 1929, I.F.2. #40529, CEIP Archives; J.T.S., "Speech delivered before the Columbia University Faculty Club," January 8, 1930, III, #55217, CEIP Archives.

attention to the question of disarmament and to the London Naval Conference which convened on January 21, 1930. Although he put little faith in the mathematical approach to disarmament, he became distressed as news from Great Britain made it clear that Secretary of State Henry L. Stimson and the American delegation were sticking to the old Hughes' formula of maintaining parity with Great Britain and fixing maximum limits upon certain types of vessels instead of working for significant armament reductions. Increasingly it became clear that the delegates were avoiding the essential elements of the disarmament question and had become embroiled in controversies over the appropriate ratios of armaments and the size of guns for different classifications of ships.[19]

In protest against the direction of negotiations, Shotwell, Raymond B. Fosdick, former Under-Secretary General of the League of Nations and an official in the League of Nations Association, James G. McDonald, chairman of the Board of the Foreign Policy Association, and Mrs. Carrie Chapman Catt drew up a petition calling upon the United States to work for actual reduction and not the mere limitation of armaments. Eventually some 1,200 prominent American business, academic, and political leaders signed the document.[20] On March 4, the four antiwar leaders sent another appeal to the American delegation warning them that the American people would not accept mere parity. Instead they demanded substantial reductions in naval vessels, including the abolition of all battleships, cutbacks in other types of ships, and acceptance of the conference method to relieve tensions during crisis situations.[21] In addition to these petitions, Shotwell wrote numerous articles for the *New York Times* in which he seriously questioned the mathematical approach to disarmament and convincingly argued that as long as political conditions remained the

19. Robert H. Ferrell, *American Diplomacy in the Great Depression: Hoover-Stimson Foreign Policy, 1929–1933* (New Haven, 1957), pp. 87–100; Elting E. Morison, *Turmoil and Tradition: A Study of the Life and Times of Henry L. Stimson* (Boston, 1960), pp. 325–30. For Shotwell's views on disarmament see "Disarmament Alone No Guarantee of World Peace," *Current History Magazine* 30 (September 1929): 1024–25.
20. *New York Times,* March 3, 1930, p. 1.
21. Ibid., March 5, 1930, p. 3.

same, disarmament talks could have but little success in promoting peace.[22]

Neither Hoover nor the American delegation in London paid much attention to the appeals of the antiwar leaders. In April, Stimson agreed to a treaty along the lines established by Hughes in the Five-Power Treaty of 1922. The new agreement provided Japan with a slightly better ratio in total capital-ship tonnage, extended limitations in tonnage to smaller naval craft, continued the postponement on replacement of capital ships for another five years, and permitted each power to exceed the established tonnage levels if in its opinion new construction by other powers affected the requirements of national security.[23]

While the delegations at the London Naval Conference argued over the technical aspects of parity, Shotwell returned to full-time teaching at Columbia University. Throughout his eleven years of antiwar work he had often thought about returning to an academic career and during the late 1920s had even offered an occasional course at Columbia on such topics as "The Economic and Social History of the World War" and "The Contemporary World Community and International Problems."[24] Now, as the spring semester approached, he decided to devote an increasing amount of time to his old profession. Although he received encouragement from Nicholas Murray Butler and other members of the Columbia faculty, several antiwar leaders tried to dissuade him from taking the step. Raymond Fosdick of the League of Nations Association strongly urged his friend to reconsider:

> Anybody can teach history in this generation. Whether it is well taught or badly taught is, relatively speaking, unimportant. The only question that really ought to concern us is whether we are going to have a world in which history or anything else can be

22. J.T.S., "The London Conference," *New York Times,* March 12, 1930, p. 28; J.T.S., "Navies and Policy," Ibid., March 14, 1930, p. 20.
23. The complete text of the treaty appears in U. S. State Department, *London Naval Conference,* State Department Publications Series 6 (Washington, 1931), pp. 203–320.
24. *Columbia University Bulletin of Information: History, Economics and Public Law,* 1925–26, 1929–30; J.T.S. to Newton D. Baker, December 17, 1929, Box 208, Newton D. Baker Papers, Library of Congress.

taught. Your work lies in connection with this infinitely bigger question. Why in God's name do you give your time to the secondary question? There are thousands of historians in the United States but there is only one Shotwell.[25]

Despite the pronounced anti-intellectualism of his colleagues in the peace movement, Shotwell had long believed that it was possible, if not essential, to bridge the gap between scholarly work and activism. His return to Columbia in no way reflected a desire to turn his back on the peace movement. In fact, he no longer offered courses on Medieval History, but concentrated instead on international relations and problems dealing directly with the question of war and peace. He lectured and conducted seminars on such topics as "The League of Nations," "The Development of the International Community," "The Contemporary World Community and International Problems," and the "World War and the Paris Peace Conference." In addition to these courses, he continued to offer his courses on historiography and historical criticism. Shotwell found academic life extremely satisfying, and although fifty-six years old when he resumed teaching, he remained an active member of the Columbia University faculty for the next twelve years. In 1937, he became Bryce Professor of the History of International Relations and finally retired in 1943 as Bryce Professor Emeritus.[26]

Shotwell's academic interest in international relations did not restrict itself to college teaching. He also became very active in the Social Science Research Council. In 1927, in connection with his work for the Institute of Pacific Relations, he agreed to serve as the first chairman of the Council's Advisory Committee on International Relations. Three years later, he became Director of Planning and Research in International Relations and established the basic guidelines for the Council's work in this field.[27] His academic concerns, however, did not reduce his desire to be effective in political affairs. Not only did he keep his position with the Carnegie Endowment for Interna-

25. Raymond B. Fosdick to J.T.S., April 10, 1929, Box 33, J.T.S. Papers.
26. *Columbia University Bulletin of Information,* 1931–42.
27. Social Science Research Council (hereafter cited SSRC), *Decennial Report, 1923--1933* (New York, 1934) 11; SSRC, *Annual Report,* 1930–1931, pp. 31–32.

tional Peace, but he also refused to give up his job as "adviser" to the *New York Times* on League of Nations matters, a position he had taken in the mid-1920s. In explaining his decision to continue his connection with the *Times*, despite pressure from the Social Science Research Council to give it up, Shotwell stated that it "was worth much more to me with statesmen and men of affairs than any academic position which I have ever held."[28] He desired to retain the position, in other words, not so much because he hoped to enlighten the American people through its columns, but because of the status it gave him.

Shotwell remained director of the Council's international relations program until 1933. Using his influence on the Council and on the Carnegie Endowment, he initiated, and eventually edited, a multivolume study of *The Relations of the United States and Canada*. In conjunction with this project he also convinced the Endowment to sponsor and finance several biennial conferences dealing with the political, economic, and social problems facing the North American neighbors. Eventually over forty volumes were published by outstanding scholars in both countries. Professor Chester Martin of the University of Toronto directed the Canadian studies, while Professor Allan Nevins of Columbia University directed the American work.[29]

It was also in his capacity as Director of the Council's international relations division that Shotwell first suggested the establishment of an Institute of European Affairs. Influenced by Briand's proposal for a Federation of Europe, Shotwell hoped that a European organization similar in structure and purpose to the Institute of Pacific Relations would not only promote the "scientific" study of problems common to European nations, but would also create a climate more conducive to an intergrated political and economic community. Like Briand's proposal, very little came of the idea.[30] It did give him and Margaret,

28. J.T.S. to Robert S. Lynd, December 11, 1930, Box 241, J.T.S. Papers.
29. J.T.S., "Confidential Outline of Plan: Survey of the Economic, Social, and Political Relations of Canada and the United States," 1934, Box 293, J.T.S. Papers; J.T.S., *Autobiography*, pp. 292–95; *New York Herald Tribune*, May 6, 1934.
30. J.T.S., *Autobiography*, pp. 256–78; J.T.S., "The Institute of Europe," 1930, Box 116, AIPR Papers; J.T.S., "An Institute of European Affairs," Summer, 1930, III #55855, CEIP Archives. For a discussion of Briand's proposal see Walters, *History of the League of Nations*, 1: 430–34.

however, a chance to return to Europe for a few months. In the early summer of 1931, with a substantial grant from the Carnegie Endowment, he crossed the Atlantic once again. He and Margaret spent the month of July in London, Paris, and Geneva, dining with various dignitaries and attending various meetings and conferences. Late in the month, they were joined by several academic colleagues, including Columbia professors Joseph Chamberlain and Lindsay Rogers, who were to assist Shotwell in establishing European research committees as a first step in creating an Institute of European Affairs. Although Shotwell tried to make clear what he planned, various rumors began to circulate about the true intention of his mission. One such rumor surfaced just prior to their scheduled arrival in Hungary. The Vienna correspondent of the *New York Times* called asking Shotwell to verify a statement out of New York that he and his party had been "authorized to take financial control of Hungary with wide powers." The idea amused and delighted Shotwell, but he assured the correspondent of his nonpolitical intentions and went on to visit Hungary, Czechoslovakia, Poland, and Germany. He organized research committees in all of these countries and made plans for a general conference of central European scholars. The scheme, however, never got beyond these initial stages.[31]

That same summer Shotwell became involved in yet another aspect of international relations when he agreed to represent the United States at the annual conference of the League of Nations' International Committee on Intellectual Cooperation. He took the place of Robert A. Millikan, the Nobel Prize physicist and head of the American branch of the organization. The League had originally established the Committee on Intellectual Cooperation in 1922 in order to promote international understanding and develop contacts between teachers, artists, scientists, and members of other intellectual professions. Although its success was not spectacular, it managed to assist intellectuals in war-torn countries and attracted such reknown figures as Albert Einstein, Madame Curie, Henri Bergson, and Gilbert Murray. Since it was an unofficial body, representing individuals rather

31. J.T.S., "Diary of a Research Expedition to Europe, July–September, 1931," pp. 35–117, Box 262, J.T.S. Papers.

than governments, citizens from all nations, whether or not they belonged to the League, could participate in its work. The unique nature of the organization permitted several prominent Americans including Millikan, Elihu Root, Raymond Fosdick, and Virginia Gildersleeve of Columbia, to organize the American branch in 1926.[32]

Although a strong supporter of peace through international understanding, Shotwell had remained extremely critical of the Committee on Intellectual Cooperation and had refused to take part in its activities. His major complaint was that the organization catered to literary and scientific celebrities, and included very few social or political scientists. He seriously questioned if such an organization could accomplish anything positive for the cause of peace. A program and membership oriented toward the arts and sciences, he argued, could be of no real value to the League, under whose auspices the committee was established. If, on the other hand, the committee would devote more of its time to questions dealing with the political, economic, and social relations between nations, its worth would increase immeasurably. When approached in 1931 about replacing Millikan as America's representative on the central committee, as well as taking over the chairmanship of the American branch, Shotwell replied that unless the organization altered its program he would have to refuse. He agreed to substitute for Millikan at the Geneva meeting of 1931, but made clear that he would use the opportunity to present his views to the leadership of the organization.[33]

Gilbert Murray, the chairman of the League organization, rejected Shotwell's suggestions. He argued that the League had not created the Committee on Intellectual Cooperation to study political questions, but rather "to promote cooperation between men of science and scien-

32. Denys P. Myers, *Handbook of the League of Nations: A Comprehensive Account of its Structure, Operation and Activities* (Boston, 1935), pp. 183–84; Malcolm W. Davis, "The League of Minds," in Harriet E. Davis, ed., *Pioneers in World Order: An American Appriasal of the League of Nations* (New York, 1944), pp. 240–49; League of Nations, Intellectual Cooperation Organization, *National Committees on Intellectual Cooperation* (Geneva, 1937), pp. 6–15.

33. J.T.S. to Eric Drummond, September 13, 1931, Box 205, J.T.S. Papers; J.T.S. to J. David Thompson, October 20, 1931, Box 139, J.T.S. Papers; J.T.S. to Nicholas Murray Butler, October 27, 1931, I.A.2.b., Report #66, CEIP Archives.

tific associations in the different countries."[34] Upon receiving the chairman's reply, Shotwell threatened to sever all ties with the organization. Only the active intervention of Millikan and J. David Thompson, the executive secretary of the American branch, persuaded him to postpone taking action. The chairman of the American branch immediately wired Murray that he fully backed Shotwell's position and strongly urged the League to appoint members more oriented toward the political and social sciences. He not only urged the central committee to reevaluate its position, but warned against underestimating the importance of getting Shotwell to join in the work. The California physicist believed that Shotwell was "far and away the most active, most objective, most constructive and best informed man in America on international affairs approached from the scientific rather than from the political point of view." He predicted that if Shotwell broke with the organization, American participation would decline sharply and the American National Committee might even disintegrate. On the other hand, he was confident that with Shotwell's aid the Committee on Intellectual Cooperation had a chance of transforming "from the most ineffective to the most important and significant portion of the League."[35]

Millikan's letter accomplished its purpose. Despite Murray's skepticism about altering the organization's program, he fully recognized the importance of American participation. He asked the League Council to appoint Shotwell to the central committee with the understanding that his proposals would be given serious consideration and that other social and political scientists would also receive invitations.[36] Having won the organization to his point of view, Shotwell accepted the League's appointment as the new United States representative. Millikan then announced his own retirement as chairman of the American National Committee and appointed Shotwell his successor. In his acceptance speech, the new chairman made it very clear that the committee would concern itself less with the arts and pure sciences and more with the political aspects of international

34. Gilbert Murray to J.T.S., December 16, 1931, Box 134, J.T.S. Papers.
35. Robert A. Millikan to Gilbert Murray, January 7, 1932, Box 134, J.T.S. Papers.
36. Eric Drummond to J.T.S., September 28, 1932, Box 205, J.T.S. Papers.

relations. "With the United States out of the League," he declared, "intellectual cooperation is an open door to the kind of helpful cooperation with the League itself which is free of political entanglements."[37]

As chairman he brought in numerous political and social scientists and established close ties with the Social Science Research Council, the American Council of Learned Societies, the American Council of Education, and the American Coordinating Committee of the Conferences of the Institutes for the Scientific Study of International Relations. His reforms were both thorough and complete. They not only influenced the work of the American group, but also profoundly affected the program and direction of the entire League Committee on Intellectual Cooperation.[38]

While Shotwell worked to reform one of the least effective League committees, events in the Far East threatened to undermine the entire Geneva experiment. Japan's invasion of Manchuria in September, 1931 placed the pro-League advocates in the United States in a very difficult position. Many of them, including Shotwell, admitted the legitimacy of some of the Japanese claims, yet they thoroughly abhorred the method chosen by the Tokyo government to correct the situation. The armed attack not only violated the League Covenant, but also the Nine-Power Treaty and the Kellogg-Briand Peace Pact. They were forced to recognize, moreover, the basic weaknesses in the League's collective security system, for not even France proved willing to apply sanctions against the aggressor.

At first Shotwell supported the Hoover-Stimson position of watchful-waiting in the hope that the more liberal forces in Tokyo would regain control of the government. By December, however, he realized that such a policy had little chance of success and suggested that the United States strongly assert the validity of the Kellogg Pact and the Nine-Power Treaty. He believed, in addition, that President Hoover should cooperate to the utmost with the League of Nations. Applaud-

37. American National Committee on Intellectual Cooperation, "Minutes of Meeting, October 27, 1932," Box 141, J.T.S. Papers.
38. See "Provisional Memorandum of the American National Committee on Intellectual Cooperation," April 5, 1933, attached to Minutes, April 29, 1933, Box 141, J.T.S. Papers.

ing the President's decision to send an American representative to participate in League discussions dealing with the Kellogg Pact, he argued that even more direct cooperation was necessary. The United States, he believed, should embargo arms, supplies of war, and money to any violator of the Pact against whom the League had placed sanctions. Such a policy would not only help to solve the Manchurian situation by giving the League the added prestige of American support, but would also serve as an opening for future cooperation, especially in crisis situations.[39] The administration's failure to act, coupled with Japan's obvious intent to drive out the last vestige of Chinese authority from Manchuria, proved extremely distressing. "What a parody of peace to undermine the authority of the League of Nations in this way," he declared. "American public opinion is confused and uncertain owing to lack of leadership. Never has our country been more in need of courageous and farsighted statesmanship, but it has been denied both in this crisis."[40]

Shotwell fully approved of Stimson's announcement that the United States would not "recognize any situation, treaty, or agreement which may be brought about by means contrary to the covenants and obligations of the Pact of Paris." It was a step in the right direction, but he had few illusions about the nonrecognition doctrine. It could in no way stop Japanese aggression or alter her foreign policy. The only hope for an acceptable conclusion to the conflict, according to Shotwell, lay in League action, and he searched desperately for some formula which would both preserve the integrity of the League as a positive force for peace and yet avoid dramatizing its true weakness by calling for the application of sanctions. In the end, all he could propose was that the League attempt to settle the outstanding economic issues involved in the Manchurian conflict. Solutions to these questions, he hoped, would reduce the importance of the more explosive political questions and thereby pave the way for a general resolu-

39. J.T.S. to Clark M. Eichelberger, December 4, 1931, Box 33, J.T.S. Papers; J.T.S., "America's Responsibility in the Oriental Crisis," *Bulletin of the University of Georgia: Proceedings of the Institute of Public Affairs, May 2–11, 1932* (September 1932), pp. 189–90.

40. J.T.S. to Harold Westergaard, December 23, 1931, Box 95, J.T.S. Papers.

tion of the crisis.[41] It was a nice thought, but given the determination of the Japanese to take all of Manchuria and the widespread support the government received at home, it had as little chance of ending the conflict as Stimson's policy of nonrecognition.

The Manchurian affair and the failure of the League to respond positively confused and frustrated supporters of the world organization. The crisis forced even the most optimistic internationalists to realize that the collective security machinery would not work as originally established and that a major revision of the system was needed. The key to the League's collective security mechanism was Article 16 of the Covenant. Article 16 required all members to isolate "aggressive" nations by means of a complete economic and financial boycott. Further it obligated the League members to assist one another in the execution of the collective action and called upon the Council to recommend what military action should be taken. The events in the Far East revealed several weaknesses in the system. Japan never declared war on China and consequently a dispute arose as to whether Article 16 had actually been violated. Much more important, however, was the fact that none of the European powers proved willing to apply a full and complete economic boycott against Japan and certainly had no intention of allowing the Council to recommend military force to pressure Japan into withdrawing. Many statesmen realized that economic sanctions alone could not force Japan to retreat and that nothing short of war itself could get her out of Manchuria. With Hitler gaining power in Germany and sounding increasingly hostile, neither Great Britain, France, nor Italy were willing to commit their forces to an Asian war.

Not only the Asian conflict, but the new obligations undertaken by the signatories of the Kellogg Pact convinced many of those interested in collective security that the time had come to revise Article 16. While the Covenant permitted war as a last resort—that is after the pacific methods had been tried and failed—the Kellogg Pact prohibited all wars except those of defense. Several nations, especially the

41. J.T.S., "A League Problem," *New York Times*, December 20, 1931, sec. 3, pp. 1–2; J.T.S., "The League at a Mile Post: Its Future Course at Stake," *New York Times*, February 5, 1933, sec. 20, pp. 3, 8.

Scandinavian states and members of the British Commonwealth, believed that the extension of the prohibition of war under the Pact of Paris made the sanctions incorporated in Article 16 all the more difficult to implement because of the wider field for their application. Even before Japan moved against Manchuria, they demanded that the Council take action to harmonize the League Covenant with the Pact of Paris.[42]

During the winter and spring of 1932, Shotwell, at the request of several League delegates, undertook to redraft Article 16. He hoped not only to harmonize the Covenant with the Kellogg Pact, but also to harmonize the American and European points of view on the question of sanctions. His redraft, completed in May, incorporated the idea of graded responsibilities and substantially weakened the provision for economic sanctions. Instead of an automatic, compulsory, and complete economic and financial boycott against the violator of the Covenant, Shotwell's revision called for a number of successive steps, limiting the automatic sanctions to the shipment of arms and supplies of war and the granting of money loans. Decisions concerning all other economic and military measures were left for a conference of governments "especially affected" by the crisis. He believed that by so restricting the compulsory and automatic sanctions League members would prove more willing to go along with them. In addition, he hoped that through the conference method the United States might be brought into closer cooperation with the League, especially in its attempts to halt aggression in areas considered important to America's national interest.[43]

On May 14, 1932, Shotwell sailed for Geneva to study the progress of the General Disarmament Conference which had finally convened in February after nearly seven years of preparation. At Geneva he showed his redraft of Article 16 to Norman Davis, a Carnegie Endowment Trustee and American representative to the Disarmament Conference, and to Eric Drummond, the Secretary-General of the League of Nations. Both men agreed that in theory the revision embodied the

42. Walters, *History of the League of Nations,* 1: 462–63; J.T.S. to Nicholas Murray Butler, June 9, 1932, I.F.2. #40608, CEIP Archives.
43. A copy of Shotwell's redraft of Article 16 is attached to his letter to Butler of June 9, 1932, I.F.2. #40609, CEIP Archives.

lessons of the Japanese crisis and that it might win support in the United States and Great Britain. They feared, however, that the practical problem of securing its adoption might prove insuperable. Shotwell also spoke with several French leaders, including Premier Edouard Herriot. They, too, were skeptical and argued that even if the redraft won acceptance by the League, enormous difficulties and delays would remain in getting it ratified. After several days of searching for a more effective approach, Shotwell decided to drop the attempt to revise the Covenant and incorporated the principles of his redraft into several protocols for direct consideration by the disarmament conference. He hoped that by attaching the provisions to the disarmament treaty the difficult problem of amending the League Covenant could be avoided.

Tactfully he sent his draft protocols to Secretary of State Stimson. He also sent a long explanatory letter declaring that he in no way interfered with the disarmament negotiations and that his discussions with European leaders were restricted to general principles concerning the harmonization of the Kellogg Pact and the League Covenant.[44] Although he did not specifically mention the Logan Act, he clearly wished to deny any possible violations of it. He must have smiled as he carefully prepared his case for the Secretary of State, for he had violated both the spirit and letter of the law more than any other American citizen since its enactment in 1799. Stimson, like Hughes and Kellogg before him, fully recognized Shotwell's guilt, but preferred to ignore it rather than take a chance of arousing public sentiment. If the Secretary of State never bothered to bring up the subject of Shotwell's illegal activities, neither did he show any interest in the proposed redraft of Article 16. Since he refused to pursue the subject, nothing came of Shotwell's effort.

Along with his draft protocols on sanctions, Shotwell sent the Secretary of State a protocol on "moral disarmament." Here he had more success. Because the suggestion that he consider the subject came from Mary E. Woolley, president of Mount Holyoke College and one of the American representatives to the World Disarmament Conference, he did not fear dealing directly with the American delega-

44. J.T.S. to Henry L. Stimson, June 7, 1932 and June 10, 1932, Box 39, J.T.S. Papers.

tion on this issue.[45] The Polish representatives first introduced the idea when they suggested that the conference adopt an international agreement for the suppression of war fomenters. According to the terms of their proposal, each nation would undertake to prohibit the use of the press, radio, cinema, and other channels of public communication to any individual or group which sought to heighten the spirit of discord or instigated acts of hostility.[46]

At first Shotwell refused to consider the suggestion, for he believed that any form of censorship or suppression of ideas was both dangerous and destructive. Such governmental activities, he argued, even when used for good purposes eventually fell into the hands of reactionaries. There could be no sure way to distinguish "between the fomenting of war and the legitimate warning against real dangers."[47] At the request of Mary Woolley, however, he agreed to study the plan and after a good deal of thought came to the conclusion that despite its negative and dangerous features, it contained the seeds of an important idea. Consequently, he drew up a protocol on moral disarmament in which he excluded all aspects of censorship and concentrated upon its possible positive contributions to peace.

Basically his protocol called upon the governments of the world to recommend "to their competent educational authorities the study of the principles and application of pacific settlement of international disputes and of the renunciation of war as an instrument of national policy," and to prescribe a "knowledge of these subjects in all examinations for public office." It also called upon the International Committee on Intellectual Cooperation to further the ideal of pacific settlement and to make annual reports on the steps taken within each nation to promote international understanding and moral disarmament. These reports were to be published by the League of Nations so as to get the full force of public opinion behind the movement and to expose any nation which refused or delayed in taking positive steps to implement the protocol.[48]

45. J.T.S. to Mary Woolley, June 9, 1932, Box 203, J.T.S. Papers.
46. J.T.S., "Memorandum on Moral Disarmament and International Civics," Box 126, J.T.S. Papers.
47. Ibid., 2–3.
48. J.T.S., "Draft Protocol on Moral Disarmament," attached to letter to Henry L. Stimson, June 10, 1932, Box 39, J.T.S. Papers.

When Mary Woolley received Shotwell's draft protocol she passed it on to her colleagues in both the British and American delegations. Preferring his plan to the Polish proposal, they redrafted it into the form of a "Declaration" and presented it to the Committee on Moral Disarmament for consideration.[49] Although pleased that the declaration followed his own protocol, Shotwell strongly objected to the omission of two important clauses. The document neither called for the inclusion of "international civics" on civil service examinations nor did it require that the Secretary-General of the League publish the various reports on the progress of moral disarmament within each nation. Without these two provisions he did not see how moral disarmament could make a serious dent in national attitudes.[50] In order to promote the principle in general, and his own version in particular, Shotwell began contacting national leaders in both the United States and Europe. He addressed numerous civic and peace organizations in America and even obtained an interview with Stimson to present his ideas. Although the Secretary of State at first was not enthusiastic about the idea, Shotwell succeeded in persuading him of the possibilities of his proposals. Shortly after the interview, Stimson wrote to Secretary of War Patrick J. Hurley, and to Secretary of the Navy Charles F. Adams, that if the disarmament conference adopted a protocol on moral disarmament, the United States would accept it.[51]

In June, 1933, after several months recess, the Committee on Moral Disarmament reconvened at Geneva and again took up its work. Shotwell's one-man campaign paid off, for the committee agreed to use his revised memorandum and protocol as the basis for their discussion. After nearly five months more of debate it finally adopted a protocol including his suggestion that civil service examinations contain a section on international civics, but omitting his idea of having the League reports published. The official draft also included a portion of the original Polish suggestion, recommending that the signatories

49. "Declaration on Moral Disarmament," attached to letter from Mary Woolley to J.T.S., July 21, 1932, Box 203, J.T.S. Papers.
50. J.T.S. to Mary Woolley, August 8, 1932, Box 203, J.T.S. Papers.
51. Cablegram from Stimson, December 9, 1932, #500–A 15 A4 Political/22, State Department Archives.

use their influence "to avoid the showing of films, the broadcasting of programs and the organization of performances obviously calculated to wound the legitimate sentiments of other nations."[52]

By the time the Committee on Moral Disarmament adopted its text, most of the supporters of the idea, including Shotwell, had lost interest. Danger signs were everywhere. Japan had completed its conquest of Manchuria and had walked out of the League. Germany was quick to follow and, in October, announced its withdrawal not only from the League but from the World Disarmament Conference as well. It did not take long for the grand meeting to adjourn in complete failure. With events taking such a dramatic turn for the worse, Shotwell could not help but question the practicability of his numerous projects and schemes. Of what use were conferences and open discussions if the nations of the world remained so intent upon reaching their goals that war remained an acceptable instrument of national policy? Of what value were plans for getting the United States into the League through the "back door" if its original members were not willing to apply sanctions or take risks in the name of collective security? What meaning had moral disarmament if the great powers were intent upon building up their armies and navies?

It was a time for reevaluation and, perhaps, a little pessimism. But after much thought and examination, Shotwell remained convinced that a rational and intelligent approach to world problems still held the key to peace. Only international cooperation could prevent the world from once again falling over the rim of the abyss. He admitted that some of his previous suggestions no longer were applicable to the world situation, but he could not give up the idea that his method and approach were still viable. "Instead of talking of moral disarmament," he told the Director of the International Institute of Intellectual Co-operation, "we must analyze the political elements of international relations as they actually reveal themselves today and build the conception of a world community not on the basis of wishful thinking, but facing grim realities and dealing with them in definite terms."[53]

52. See Box 2, J.T.S. Papers for Draft Protocol on Moral Disarmament, November 20, 1933.
53. J.T.S. to H. Bonnet, October 30, 1933, Box 181, J.T.S. Papers.

The time for realism and intelligence in foreign affairs had arrived. Either rational thought and progress would prevail or else the world would return to the barbarity of emotionalism, war, and bloodshed. The next few years would be crucial.

11
Advocate of the Open Door and Covenant Revision

Friends of the League of Nations viewed the election of Franklin Delano Roosevelt with mixed emotions. Although he had made over eight hundred speeches in support of international organization during his campaign for the Vice-Presidency in 1920, over the years he had become increasingly vague about his position on foreign policy and the possibilities of American cooperation in the Geneva experiment. In 1928, he had come out against joining the League, but had also favored extending to the organization "a far larger share of sympathetic approval and definite official help."[1] The depression and the failure of the League to take effective action against Japan only intensified public opposition to entangling alliances and further weakened support for collective security. Under the circumstances Roosevelt found it politically expedient to avoid foreign policy issues during

1. Franklin Delano Roosevelt, "Our Foreign Policy: A Democratic View," *Foreign Affairs* 6 (July 1928): 581.

his campaign. Intent upon achieving New Deal goals of relief, recovery, and reform he made peace with the majority of "isolationists" in his own party and carefully avoided alienating important Republican senators like William E. Borah, Gerald P. Nye, and Burton K. Wheeler, who were all staunch opponents of collective security.

The Democratic Platform for 1932 called for the settlement of international disputes by arbitration, adherence to the World Court, the reduction of armaments, and the bolstering of the Kellogg Pact through consultation and conference in case of violations. It made no mention of the League of Nations.[2] To the chagrin of many Wilsonian Democrats, Roosevelt refused to support even these moderate foreign policy planks. When he rose to give his inaugural address on March 4, 1933, the nation suffered from a country-wide banking crisis, millions of unemployed vainly sought work from coast to coast, and the national economy seemed paralyzed. Deeply concerned with the domestic fate of the United States, the new president omitted any reference to foreign policy other than a brief statement that he would dedicate his administration to "the policy of the good neighbor." His address clearly reflected the New Deal order of priorities, and throughout his first term in office he concentrated on vital domestic issues, leaving most foreign policy problems to his Secretary of State, Cordell Hull of Tennessee.[3] When he did take an interest in specific policy questions, however, he often acted alone, without consulting his State Department advisers and often undermining their efforts.[4]

As America turned inward in an effort to revive its economy, the peace structure established in 1919 began to crumble. The rise of aggressive nationalism in both Europe and Asia shattered the dream of a true international community based upon economic and social justice. As soon as the trains were running on time, Mussolini began to talk of a new Roman Empire. Hitler's rise in Germany and his appointment as Chancellor in January, 1933 quickly brought an end to the internationalist policies of Gustav Stresemann. Japan defied the

2. *Platform of the Two Great Political Parties, 1932 and 1936* (compiled by Leroy D. Brandon, Washington, 1936), p. 338.
3. Cordell Hull, *The Memoirs of Cordell Hull,* 2 vols. (New York, 1948), 1: 194.
4. Robert A. Divine, *The Illusion of Neutrality* (Chicago, 1962), p. 55.

Lytton Commission and the League by recognizing Manchukuo, her puppet government in the conquered territory of China, and shortly after Roosevelt's inauguration gave the required two-year notice of withdrawal from the international organization. The world-wide depression forced even Great Britain, the pioneer in free trade, to follow the other major powers in raising tariff walls. In addition, the British not only decided to suspend the gold standard, but joined other European nations in defaulting on their debt payments to the United States.

These developments convinced most Americans of the wisdom of their rejection of the League of Nations. Ignoring the fact that one of the major reasons for the failure of the Versailles settlement was America's refusal to assume its responsibilities in the postwar world, they accepted that very failure as further proof that the United States should avoid European problems. Pro-League supporters could not help but recognize the futility of their long campaign to educate their fellow Americans on the importance of international cooperation and collective security. Those who did not give up and turn to the challenge of domestic reform and recovery, were forced to reevaluate their position and begin the search for new directions.

Few internationalists better understood the importance of the problem than James Thomson Shotwell. Civilization had reached a crossroad. "The issue before us," he declared, "is whether we shall have to turn back the march of progress and accept once more the anarchy of the old state system, with all its risks and dangers, its accentuation of conflict, and its acceptance of war as the instrument of policy. It is a contest of the future with the past; a future of anxious hope and of reason struggling to reassert itself in human affairs, a past weighted with achievements as well as with tragedy and vital still with the memory of great deeds."[5] Although admitting the need for new policies to meet the changing world situation, he remained convinced that the internationalist outlook held the only hope of creating a just and durable peace. Somehow the people of the United States, or at least their elected officials, had to be convinced of this truth.

Despite his strong backing of Norman H. Davis, a Carnegie En-

5. J.T.S., *On the Rim,* p. 34.

dowment Trustee and important State Department official, for the position of Secretary of State, Shotwell approved of Roosevelt's choice of Cordell Hull. He had met the Tennessee senator for the first time at the Democratic Convention in Chicago the previous July and found him extremely "sound" on questions of international economics. Both men agreed on the need for lowering the barriers set up by the Smoot-Hawley Tariff of 1930 and both saw real danger in the rise of economic nationalism. Shotwell's relationship with Hull never became intimate, but it remained cordial, and he could always count on a fair hearing for his schemes.[6]

With Hull in charge of American foreign affairs, Shotwell hoped that the United States would reverse its economic policy and become the new champion of international free trade. The Secretary's presence at the World Economic Conference at London, which met in the summer of 1933, raised his hopes still higher. He failed to realize, as did Hull himself, that any demand for lower tariffs would conflict with the New Deal emphasis on recovery, which required higher tariffs to combat higher costs at home.[7] Both men were extremely disappointed, therefore, when, on July 3, Roosevelt torpedoed the conference by sending a sharp message criticizing its work and monetary proposals. The President's rebuff fell upon the meeting "like a bombshell" and only Hull's clever maneuvering allowed it to continue for a few more weeks. It finally broke up in failure and a general feeling of hopelessness.[8]

In Europe on one of his perennial good-will trips for the Carnegie Endowment, Shotwell sympathized with Hull's difficult position and spent a good deal of time with him during the last dying days of the conference. On July 27, they sailed together from London on the small

6. J.T.S., *Autobiography*, pp. 303–4; J.T.S. to Colonel Edward M. House, July 2, 1932, Drawer 17, House Papers; Cordell Hull to J.T.S., October 25, 1935, Box 231, J.T.S. Papers; J.T.S., "Diary," entry of June 23, 1942, p. 5, Box 259, J.T.S. Papers.
7. Julius W. Pratt, *Cordell Hull, 1933–1944*, vol. 12 of *The American Secretaries of State and Their Diplomacy*, ed. Robert H. Ferrell, 16 vols. (New York, 1964), 1: 35–36.
8. Ibid., 1: 59–70; James MacGregor Burns, *Roosevelt, The Lion and the Fox* (New York, 1956), pp. 177–78; Arthur Schlesinger, Jr., *The Coming of the New Deal*, vol. 2: *The Age of Roosevelt* (New York, 1959), pp. 221–32.

slow liner, *President Harding,* and on the leisurely journey home spent several hours discussing various domestic and international problems. Ever the opportunist, Shotwell tried to interest the Secretary in a tariff scheme he had developed for presentation to the upcoming biennial conference of the Institute of Pacific Relations. He suggested that "labor conditions should be made one of the basic factors in tariff bargaining; that products made under specified labor conditions—internationally agreed upon—should be given preferential treatment, while articles made under oppressive or exploitative conditions should be subjected to higher duties and impositions." Such a tariff program, he argued, would tend to eliminate labor as an element of international competition and would further the idea behind the International Labor Organization.[9]

Hull found the idea ingenious, but questioned its practicability. He agreed to consider it and urged Shotwell to formally submit it to the State Department. The Office of the Economic Adviser studied it briefly, but rejected it on the grounds that the possibilities for its implementation were remote. In fact, economists both in and out of the government found the scheme extremely unrealistic, and Shotwell quickly abandoned it for Hull's reciprocal trade agreements as the best means for lowering tariff barriers.[10]

The changing conditions in Europe led Shotwell to reduce his activities in purely academic organizations and turn his attention to direct-action groups. He continued to teach at Columbia, serve as president of the American Committee on Intellectual Cooperation, and direct the Carnegie Endowment's Division of Economics and History, but he gradually withdrew from active participation in the Institute of Pacific Relations and the Social Science Research Council. He now devoted an increasing amount of time to seeking solutions to

9. J.T.S., *Autobiography,* pp. 307–8; J.T.S., "Memorandum for Tariff Discussion at the Institute of Pacific Relations," August, 1933, pp. 1–2, Box 142, AIPR Papers. This scheme was later published as "NRA and the Tariff," *New York Herald Tribune,* September 17, 1933.

10. "Memorandum by 'h.f.' " (n.d.), #611.003/2916, State Department Archives. See also Bruno Lasker and W. L. Holland, eds., *Problems of the Pacific, 1933: Economic Conflict and Control. Proceedings of the Fifth Conference of the Institute of Pacific Relations, Banff, Canada* (Chicago, 1934), pp. 117–18.

specific foreign policy problems and less to the academic study of international relations.

Getting the United States into the International Labor Organization became one of his pet projects. Although Secretary of Labor Francis Perkins gave Shotwell no credit for the successful campaign to push the membership resolution through Congress and developed the myth that she "did it alone," it is doubtful that she could have succeeded without his help.[11] Early in 1934, at the request of Senator Key Pittman of Nevada, the chairman of the Senate Foreign Relations Committee, Shotwell drafted a resolution for American participation in the ILO which eventually became the basis for the joint resolution brought before Congress in June. As a lobbyist few surpassed him in energy or persistence. He virtually lived in Washington during the hearings and floor debate on the resolution, cornering House and Senate members at every available opportunity and urging them to support the pending legislation.[12] In a syndicated column in the New York *American*, George Rothwell Brown, an anti-League political journalist, gave Shotwell credit "for having put America into a side-door of the League of Nations. . . ." Shotwell's spirit, reported Brown, "hovered over the proceedings of the House Foreign Affairs Committee, while his corporeal self paced the corridor outside the committee room, as the set-up was being cunningly arranged inside."[13] Whatever the value of the International Labor Organization, Shotwell played a significant, if not a major, part in making the United States a member.[14]

He was much less successful in trying to tie the United States to the League of Nations. Believing that peace and stability depended upon a major reorganization of the League, Shotwell continued to search for a formula which would transform that body into a universal organization with American support. His original idea of "associa-

11. Frances Perkins, *The Roosevelt I Knew* (New York, 1946), pp. 337–46.
12. Interview with Mrs. Isador Lubin, December 26, 1966. Mrs. Lubin was Shotwell's secretary and research assistant during the early 1930s.
13. New York *American*, June 22, 1934, clipping in Box 256, J.T.S. Papers.
14. J.T.S., *Autobiography*, p. 308; J.T.S. to Nicholas Murray Butler, June 29, 1934, Box 117, J.T.S. Papers; Wallace McClure to J.T.S., June 21, 1934, Box 117, J.T.S. Papers.

tion" with the League still seemed like the best approach not only for promoting American cooperation, but also for readjusting the League and making it stronger. His plan, first presented to Colonel House in 1919 and then made public in 1920, called for the creation of recurring conferences which would periodically bring all the major powers together to discuss problems concerning their mutual relations. Only those nations which had particular interests in a certain region would join together to guarantee its peace and security. Guarantees for European security would be made by European powers, while similar guarantees for the Far East and the Caribbean would be made only by those countries most directly involved. Such a plan, according to Shotwell, was far more realistic than asking each nation to provide security for the entire world.[15]

In May, 1934, he elaborated upon his idea of graded responsibilities by incorporating a proposal first made by Joseph Paul-Boncour, at various times Foreign Minister and Premier of France. Boncour suggested the reorganization of the Geneva collective security system around a structure resembling Dante's Inferno. The model he constructed consisted of three concentric circles. Those nations on the outer rim, such as the United States, would be bound only by the Kellogg-Briand Pact. Their sole obligation would be to refuse aid to those nations resorting to war in violation of their pledge to submit all disputes for pacific settlement. The circle inside the outer rim consisted of members of the League of Nations held together by the terms of the Covenant. The innermost circle consisted of those member nations closest to the danger. This last group would add to the Covenant pacts of mutual assistance. Since Shotwell assumed that the greatest threat to peace centered in Europe, he envisioned the nations of this region as providing most of the police measures. In addition to this security system, Shotwell urged the establishment of a "League of Conferences" to deal with "normal" problems of international affairs. He believed that when put together the entire structure would provide adequate security, help solve vital international issues, and,

15. J.T.S., "First Pages from the History of the League of Nations," in *The League of Nations Starts: An Outline by its Organizers* (London, 1920), pp. 57–58.

most important, allow the United States to participate without forcing it to become the policeman for Europe.[16]

Two years later, with the European situation fast deteriorating, Shotwell reiterated his reorganization scheme based on regionalism and graded responsibilities in a book entitled *On the Rim of the Abyss.* Italy's conquest of Ethiopia and Hitler's remilitarization of the Rhineland made it clear that the future of world peace depended "upon the growth of that sense of unity in diversity which places the responsibility for action upon those members who are most directly concerned, but binds all nations together by a common renunciation of war as the instrument of their policy." In such a system the United States would "have the negative duty of not impeding the pacific processes of the world community, but could not be looked to for those positive measures which even the European states are unwilling to take unless they coincide with national self-interest."[17]

Shotwell's analysis and policy proposals were both moderate and logical. His suggested changes in the League structure won support from many internationalists and students of international affairs. Denna F. Fleming of Vanderbilt University felt that Shotwell's book came "to grips with the future of the League and the future of world peace as no volume written in recent years has." Grayson Kirk, then teaching at the University of Wisconsin, felt that if the people of the United States turned a deaf ear on Shotwell's suggestions, they probably were not worthy of escaping "the aftermath of disaster which another world conflagration would bring to belligerent and neutral alike."[18]

Not all scholars agreed with Fleming and Kirk. Several seriously questioned Shotwell's approach. Merle Curti, an astute observer of the peace movement then teaching at Smith College, pointed out that structural changes in the League along the lines of associated membership and regional security left many problems unsolved. Despite the persuasiveness of Shotwell's arguments, the question remained

16. *New York Times,* May 6, 1934, sec. 8, pp. 3, 11.
17. J.T.S., *On the Rim,* pp. 177–79, 319–20.
18. Denna Fleming's review appeared in *The International Outlook,* October 16, 1936, p. 256; Grayson Kirk's review appeared in the *Capital Times* (Madison, Wis.), August 16, 1936, both clippings in Box 255, J.T.S. Papers.

whether these changes would in themselves, even with the benevolent cooperation of the United States, prove adequate. Curti had his doubts, although he admitted that eventually they might prove inevitable and desirable.[19] Frederick Schuman, professor of Political Science at Williams College, went further and argued that regardless of what structural changes were made the League would eventually fail. The problem of peace, he pointed out, was not, and never had been a "problem of procedures, machinery, pacts and covenants." It was rather "a problem of attitudes and values, of the persistence of ancient prejudice and stupidity, and of the timidity of peace-seekers, of the provincialism and short-sightedness of irresponsible blunderers, of the utter bankruptcy of democratic diplomacy." Schuman concluded that "Professor Shotwell's valiant effort to put Humpty-Dumpty together again in a new form is—alas!—wholly irrelevant." His proposal would "not become the charter of a new League, but the epitaph of one which has died. He has mistaken sunset for dawn."[20]

Although most reviewers of *On the Rim of the Abyss* were more sympathetic than Schuman, Shotwell's program attracted little public support and even less official approval.[21] Perhaps Shotwell's major error was that whenever he presented his plan he spoke of its international implications and never of its precise significance for American foreign policy. For had he examined exactly what his plan meant in terms of America's national interest—had he shown how a regional system of collective security could have furthered America's dominance in the Caribbean and reinforced the Open Door policy by justifying actions designed to preserve the territorial integrity of areas within her economic empire—he might have received more support and a more cordial hearing from administration officials. He made clear, it is true, that his plan of graded responsibilities and associated membership removed the most objectionable aspects of Articles 10 and 16 of the League Covenant, but he failed to go beyond idealistic

19. Merle Curti, "Dr. Shotwell's Plan for the Strategy of Peace," *New York Times Book Review,* June 21, 1936, p. 4.
20. Frederick Schuman, Review of Shotwell's *On the Rim of the Abyss,* in the *Annals of the American Academy of Political and Social Sciences* 189 (January 1937): 242–43.
21. For other reviews of *On the Rim of the Abyss,* see clipping file in Box 255, J.T.S. Papers.

and internationalist rhetoric to explain why now, after the League had demonstrated its inherent weaknesses, the United States should reverse its policy and take an active part in the Geneva experiment.

Although Shotwell did not discuss the implications of his scheme in terms of the Open Door policy, he was by no means blind to the importance of economic expansion in American history. In a memorandum for the American delegation to the Conference on World Economy, written in November, 1935, less than a month after Italy invaded Ethiopia, he forcefully supported the Open Door approach. Like most Wilsonian liberals, he assumed that economic expansion would bring domestic prosperity and peace. Not only the United States, but all industrialized nations, including Germany, Italy, and Japan, would benefit in the long run. A "guaranteed open door," he argued, would serve as a "means of relieving economic pressure and removing the excuse for conquest." He hoped that eventually "a real open door regime might be established in all dependent colonial areas." This meant the end to all discriminatory duties in dependent colonies and complete equality of trade in these areas. Going far beyond John Hay's original proposal of 1899, Shotwell suggested that the major industrial powers not only have equal access to the vast markets of independent underdeveloped countries like China, but also compete openly in areas previously controlled and exploited by individual colonial governments.[22]

Although he supported economic expansion and free access to the resources and markets of underdeveloped nations, Shotwell did not approve of exploitation. Like many other advocates of the Open Door policy, he sincerely believed that economic expansion would benefit both the underdeveloped areas as well as the industrialized nations. Together with free trade, economic expansion would give the industrialized countries access to needed resources and markets, but at the same time it would hasten the development of backward nations and promote their economic growth. He was convinced that in a world where science and technology had made the possibilities for progress unlimited, no one had to suffer and all could prosper together.[23]

22. J.T.S., "Memorandum for the American Delegation to the Conference on World Economy," November 2, 1935, I.F.2. #41239, CEIP Archives.
23. J.T.S., "Does Business Mean Peace?" pp. 405–7, 436–37.

Opponents of the League of Nations and of the Open Door policy did not share Shotwell's optimism. In fact, they saw dangerous implications in his approach. Oswald Garrison Villard, the retired pacifist editor of *The Nation,* argued that despite his concern with the international community and the peoples of underdeveloped areas, Shotwell had not freed himself from the old "shibboleths of imperialism."[24] Even more hostile than the former editor of *The Nation* was C. Hartley Grattan, one of the leading "revisionist" historians and a severe critic of capitalism. In his book *Preface to Chaos,* published in 1936, Grattan attacked both the "isolationist" and "internationalist" sides of the American foreign policy debate. Neither group, he maintained, really understood the political or economic realities of the postwar world. He specifically pointed to Shotwell as an illustration of the internationalists' failure to comprehend the dynamic character of the twentieth century. To those who had read some of Shotwell's writings the charge must have seemed strange, for throughout the 1920s and early 1930s he had constantly emphasized the vast changes brought about by scientific and technological innovations. Yet Grattan built a strong case, one similar in many ways to that presented by Merle Curti in his review of *On the Rim of the Abyss.* Although their *Weltanschauung* differed, Curti and Grattan agreed that Shotwell had mistakenly subordinated the internal problems of nations to their external relationships. But whereas Curti argued that Shotwell's suggestions should be "seriously considered" and might in the end "prove inevitable and desirable," Grattan dismissed them as superficial:

> On reading an impassioned advocate of the League like Professor James T. Shotwell one gets the definite impression that he firmly believes that present-day economic relations have been characteristic since the world began and will remain to the end of time. . . . This is not to say that Dr. Shotwell does not recognize change, but rather he is able to see only technological change without conceiving that change of this character may dictate fundamental redefinitions of the relations of the classes within

24. Oswald Garrison Villard, "The League and the Future," *Saturday Review of Literature* 14 (June 13, 1936): 7.

> the several nations. On the other hand, he thinks technological changes are important in dictating cooperation among the nations, especially changes in the technology of communication. In short, he takes up the traditional position that the system of control must remain constant within the nations, but that a new system may be added in international relations. This highly unhistoric view is held, it should be emphasized, by a Professor of History at Columbia University, so it is probably impertinent to expect the lesser fry to do any better.[25]

Grattan also criticized Shotwell for failing to recognize that national capitalism had a logic of its own—one which traditionally led to the creation of international situations charred with the dynamic of war. The League of Nations, according to Grattan, was not "a poor struggling eleemosynary institution dispensing 'justice' in a recalcitrant world," but rather the bulwark of capitalism in Europe—a "league of conflicting capitalist states."

Grattan's intellectual rejection of capitalism strongly colored his view of the League of Nations and its supporters. Yet his analysis of Shotwell's position accurately revealed the latter's underlying assumptions and total commitment to the existing economic order. Shotwell did not reject socialism outright, but he strongly hoped that the establishment of an international organization would prevent violent or sudden threats to the status quo. His support of the International Labor Organization, according to his own testimony, was based upon a desire to stem the rising tide of revolution.[26] Regardless of the possibility of an organization like the ILO actually preventing social upheaval through international agreements on universal labor conditions, it was significant that he conceived of the agency in those terms.

There is no reason to doubt Shotwell's genuine desire for increased social justice and economic equality, for he often made clear his intellectual commitment to these goals. Yet the logic of his own assumptions forced him to support the status quo even when in his own terms that status quo was unfair and needed revision. His hope

25. C. Hartley Grattan, *Preface to Chaos: War in the Making* (New York, 1936), pp. 171–72.
26. J.T.S., "International Labor Organization as an Alternative to Violent Revolution," pp. 18–25.

rested, in part, upon the belief that through economic expansion prosperity would come and with it a general elevation of the masses. The trouble with this position, as Grattan pointed out, was that in the past economic competition had led to conflict, war, and exploitation, and there were no signs during the 1930s that this process would significantly change.

His hope also rested upon the belief that through cooperation the United States and the other major powers could develop viable machinery for the peaceful settlement of disputes. Unfortunately, that machinery still needed much work, and Shotwell could only suggest that dissatisfied powers use diplomacy to alter the world situation. To discourage the use of armed force in the interim, he called for a coalition of nonrevisionist nations to prevent violent changes in the Versailles settlement.[27] In other words, the status quo would have to remain until the necessary machinery was developed. Until then, the dissatisfied states would have to live with their grievances and work to ameliorate their condition through diplomacy without recourse to the traditional threat of force to back it up. Such a program could satisfy few critics of the Versailles settlement. It helps explain why intellectuals like Villard and Grattan viewed Shotwell's arguments as mere "liberal" rhetoric, if not outright hypocrisy.

Shotwell's efforts to revise the League Covenant and foster greater cooperation with Europe soon brought him to the presidency of the League of Nations Association. The primary aim of the Association, organized in 1922 as the League of Nations Non-Partisan Association, was to furnish other groups, institutions, and interested people in the United States information on the activities of the League and the Permanent Court of International Justice. The ultimate purpose of this educational campaign was to secure American membership in these two organizations upon such terms as the then existing administration should deem proper.[28]

Shotwell took an active interest in the Association from the start and served concurrently on both its Executive Committee and Board

27. J.T.S., "The League's Work for Peace," *Current History* 43 (November 1935): 119–24.
28. "The League of Nations Association," July, 1929, pp. 1–2, IV, #61523, CEIP Archives.

of Directors. He found himself, however, in a minority position because of his open advocacy of Covenant revision. The leaders of the Association reluctantly agreed to support United States membership with reservations, but until the mid-1930s firmly rejected major changes in the Covenant. By December, 1932, Shotwell had become so disgusted with their dogmatic stand that he informed the vice-president of his decision to resign unless the Association reversed its policy and began working for fundamental changes in the structure of the League. It was the same tactic he had successfully employed when seeking revisions in the structure of the League's Committee on Intellectual Cooperation.[29]

The failure of the League to act in the Manchurian crisis and the increasing threats posed by Mussolini and Hitler seriously weakened the League of Nations Association. A sharp decrease in membership forced the organization to face the fact that most Americans had no interest whatever in joining an unaltered League. Agitation for Covenant revision in Europe also strengthened Shotwell's hand. In June, 1935, when Raymond Fosdick resigned as president, the Executive Committee and the Board of Directors turned to the Columbia professor for direction and on October 1 announced his appointment.[30]

Already recognized as the leading exponent of collective security in the country, Shotwell's new position added to his influence in the American peace movement. The appointment also brought him into close association with Clark Eichelberger, who had become the executive director in 1933. Eichelberger, a University of Chicago graduate and former social worker, began working for the Association in 1927 as director of the Chicago office. He did an outstanding job in the hostile Middle West and was soon recognized as a persuasive spokesman for the internationalist cause. He and Shotwell formed an effective partnership, with Eichelberger running the daily affairs of the Association and Shotwell concentrating on securing financial support and developing new policies for the Association to pursue.[31]

As one of his first actions as president, Shotwell with the help of

29. J.T.S. to Charles H. Strong, December 14, 1932, Box 35, J.T.S. Papers.
30. *New York Times,* October 2, 1935, p. 20.
31. Divine, *Second Chance,* p. 26.

Eichelberger, drew up a four-point program to strengthen the League and promote American interest in it. The program called for a universal League committed to the Kellogg Pact renouncing war as an instrument of national policy, special arrangements for peaceful modification of the status quo, graded obligations among states for the maintenance of collective security, and finally, the separation of the Covenant of the League from the Treaty of Versailles.[32]

Despite the energy and persistence of the new president and director, the League of Nations Association did little to increase support for collective security. The desire to avoid European political entanglements had become stronger during the 1930s than in the preceding decade. The advent of the great depression, the breakdown of world trade, and the intense concern with domestic recovery turned the eyes of the American people inward. The increasing tensions in Asia and Europe convinced many Americans that nothing could be done to save these areas from again plunging into the abyss, and they saw no reason why the United States should tie itself politically or militarily to a region destined to become embroiled in another holocaust.

Americans wished to avoid war and the surest path seemed to lie in complete avoidance of European disputes. A poll conducted by the *New York Herald Tribune's* "Institute of Public Opinion" shortly after Italy's invasion of Ethiopia revealed that only 10% of those questioned favored armed collective action to stop aggression. To the question of joining other countries to enforce peace only 29% gave their support, while 71% answered in the negative. A combination of disillusionment with the Versailles settlement, anger over European default on war debts, the Nye Senate Committee investigation which found munition manufacturers as the essential cause for America's involvement in the First World War, and a strong dose of "revisionist" history which all but cleared Germany of war guilt led 75% of those questioned to favor a popular referendum as a direct check on the war-making powers of Congress and 47% to support a complete embargo against all belligerents.[33]

32. *New York Times,* May 11, 1936, p. 3; J.T.S., "Plan for Reorganization of the League of Nations," May 11, 1936, Box 145, LNA folder, Newton D. Baker Papers, Library of Congress.
33. Curti, *Peace or War,* p. 300.

With public opinion so strongly opposed to involvement in another European war, and with the majority in Congress of a similar mind, Shotwell's arguments won few converts. He soon realized that his primary responsibilities lay in combating the growing "isolationist" sentiment in America and preventing the passage of legislation designed to check America's freedom of action in times of crisis. It was useless to draw up plans for Covenant revision or schemes for United States involvement in the League of Nations at a time when Americans and their representatives in Congress sought to insulate themselves still further from European political disputes. Educating the people on the implications of an interdependent world and the importance of collective security as a deterrent to aggression would have to await the more important work of stemming the "isolationist" tide.

As the European situation grew more chaotic and dangerous Shotwell turned to the task at hand. Fulfillment of his dream of a new international community built upon social justice and enduring peace seemed further away than ever. His fifteen-year campaign to educate America on the responsibilities of its new world position had come to naught. Instead of facing the realities of power most Americans seemed to prefer to close their eyes to world events, hoping against hope that the consequences of those events would not threaten their own destiny. Although many of his specific policy suggestions were more unrealistic and impracticable than he believed, Shotwell clearly understood that America had become deeply involved in the fate of the rest of the world. If there was one central theme in all his speeches, articles, and books, it was the interdependence of the modern world. The more industrialized a nation became, the less chance it had to insulate itself against the vicissitudes of the world situation. European problems necessarily became America's problems. Interdependence was the price of progress.

Despite the tragic events in Europe and America's refusal to adopt a constructive policy, Shotwell somehow retained his optimism and progressive view of history. "To get rid of war as the instrument of policy," he declared as the world once again leaned over the rim of the abyss, "is the hardest and greatest task that the civilized world has ever set itself. It cannot be achieved overnight. Generations or even centuries will pass before the new era of 'a warless world'—a phrase so glibly used, so little weighted—will be firmly established. Someday the ideal will be reached in an ultimate triumph of human decency, when the pacific substitutes for force and violence will have more of history behind them and nations will be more confident of their effectiveness. It will come even if world wars should occur again, like the waves returning on a shore from which the tide is slowly but surely receding."[34]

Only his strong belief in the unlimited possibilities of the future and the ultimate justification of his work allowed him to face the days ahead with continued dedication, dogged persistence, and seemingly unbounded energy.

34. J.T.S., *On the Rim,* pp. 324–25.

12
Opponent of Neutrality Legislation

The rise of fascism in Germany and the increasing danger of war in Europe focused attention on the disorder within the American peace movement. New schemes had fathered new organizations; and each new organization viewed those already in existence with antagonism and scorn. Each group boldly proclaimed that it alone held the panacea for the age-old problem of international conflict, but few took the time to examine the possible consequences of the plans they proposed. Pacifists and advocates of collective security not only opposed the programs of one another, but worked at cross purposes with those in their own camp.

Yet the events in Europe and the Far East, together with Roosevelt's increased rearmament program and his failure to clearly define his foreign policy position, led many antiwar leaders to search for a common program. The idea of a coalition of American peace forces was not original in the 1930s. The National Council for the Prevention of War, established in 1921 by Frederick J. Libby, had sought to coordinate the activities of several organizations interested in the Washington Disarmament Conference and remained active throughout the postwar period. In 1925, Mrs. Carrie Chapman Catt brought together nine women's organizations in the National Committee on the Cause and Cure of War. During the next ten years her group grew steadily and by means of an elaborate system of local committees reached a vast number of Americans. In 1931, seven leading peace groups organized a short-lived Emergency Peace Committee. Two years later, a Commission on the Coordination of the Efforts of Peace, including such well-known figures as John Dewey, Newton D. Baker, William Allen White, and Quincy Wright, surveyed the existing state of antiwar sentiment and concluded that coordination had to precede success.

Shortly after President Roosevelt took office, twenty-eight national organizations interested in "international justice and peace" formed the National Peace Conference. That same year liberals, radicals, and communists joined in an attempt to create a "united front" through the American League Against War and Fascism. Its platform, calling for demonstrations against the manufacture and transportation of munitions, support for Soviet peace policies, denunciations of imperialism, condemnation of war preparations, and opposition to fascism "in every form" attracted not only labor groups, but also such pacifist organizations as the Fellowship of Reconciliation, the War Resisters League, World Peaceways, and the Women's International League for Peace and Freedom. By 1935, the American League claimed a membership of more than two million. The Emergency Peace Campaign, conceived and organized by Ray Newton of the American Friends Service Committee, proved even more successful in winning the support of antiwar groups. Dominated by, although not restricted to, pacifists, the Emergency Peace Campaign strongly influenced the direction of the peace movement during 1936 and 1937.[1]

As one of the earliest supporters of unity within the peace movement, Shotwell worked diligently for a united front in behalf of international cooperation and the pacific settlement of disputes. "The peace forces," he complained, "war among themselves with an ardor

1. Bowers, "The American Peace Movement," pp. 176–97, 272–87; Curti, *Peace or War,* pp. 272–77; Lawrence Wittner, *Rebels Against War: The American Peace Movement 1941–1960* (New York, 1969), pp. 1–33; Chatfield, *For Peace and Justice,* pp. 256–86.

hardly to be distinguished from that of their attack upon militarism." Wars would continue until there existed "a more generous temper, a less doctrinaire attitude upon the part of both leaders and followers, and a plan of action sufficiently broad to be capable of application by all those varied elements within a nation which make its public opinion operative, as well as by nations that differ from one another in their traditions, laws, and institutions."[2]

Yet Shotwell, like other antiwar leaders, proved willing to compromise only on his own terms. He condemned the pacifists for refusing to "accept as allies those, more moderately inclined, who admit the legitimacy of national defense," and he had little patience for those in the peace movement who rejected "the institutions which have enshrined the hopes of whole nations." What he wanted was a program based upon the principles of collective security and international free trade. He made this perfectly clear in April, 1935, when he suggested to his good friend Newton D. Baker that a scheme based upon "Wilson's program and view of International Relations" might prove just the thing to solidify antiwar sentiment in the United States.[3]

His proposal might never have gone beyond an expression of personal preference had not Nicholas Murray Butler, in his capacity as President of the Carnegie Endowment for International Peace, asked Senator James Pope and Newton D. Baker to draft a platform of unification which would appeal to a wide spectrum of the peace movement. Since both men had previously looked to Shotwell for advice on matters of peace strategy, they agreed to enlist his aid once again. They also consulted Clark Eichelberger, the Director of the League of Nations Association, who had previously agreed to draft a new "Statement of Principles" for the National Peace Conference. These four worked closely together for several weeks and finally came up with a program incorporating both Shotwell's political guidelines and a set of "Recommendations" originally framed at an unofficial international conference held at Chatham House in London the previous March. Besides supporting lower tariffs and free trade unions, the recommendations called for a stronger League, the furthering of inter-

2. J.T.S., *On the Rim,* pp. 36–37.
3. J.T.S. to Newton D. Baker, April 25, 1935, Box 208, Baker Papers.

national cooperation, the promotion of judicial settlements of disputes, arms limitations, social justice for all, and machinery for continuous consultation by the major powers. Having completed the draft proposal, Baker submitted it to the Carnegie Endowment and Eichelberger submitted it to the National Peace Conference.[4]

On June 3, 1935, in a move designed to attract the Carnegie Endowment and to make itself the center of the unification movement, the National Peace Conference formally adopted Eichelberger's proposed "Statement of Principles."[5] Nicholas Murray Butler took the next step by calling a conference for the purpose "of discussing and adopting a united program of action on the part of organizations devoted to promoting international peace and understanding."[6] The meeting, held at Columbia University on October 3, attracted not only antiwar leaders, but also businessmen, academicians, and government officials. They included besides Butler, Shotwell, Eichelberger, Baker, and Senator Pope, Evans Clark of the 20th Century Fund, Frederick J. Libby of the National Council for the Prevention of War, Henry L. Stimson, Norman Thomas, Quincy Wright of Chicago University, Manley Hudson of Harvard, Walter Van Kirk of the Federal Council of Churches of Christ in America, and Thomas J. Watson, President of IBM and head of the American branch of the International Chamber of Commerce. After a long day of debate and consultation this diverse group unanimously agreed that the time had come to make a more determined effort to coordinate the activities of American peace societies. The conference accepted the Chatham House recommendations and the National Peace Conference's "Statement of Principles" as the basis for a new unified program and instructed Butler

4. Clark M. Eichelberger to Nicholas Murray Butler, May 12, 1935, IV, #62568, CEIP Archives; Newton D. Baker to Thomas P. Lamont, June 13, 1935, III, #58384, CEIP Archives. For the Chatham House "Recommendations," see Nicholas Murray Butler, *Across the Busy Years: Recollections and Reflections* (New York, 1935), 2: 224–27.

5. National Peace Conference, "Statement of Principles," June 3, 1935, III, #58412, CEIP Archives; National Peace Conference, *The National Peace Conference—What it is: What it proposes to do* (New York, n.d.), pp. 6–8, in CEIP Archives, III, #70049.

6. F. B. Sayre to Senator James Pope, August 27, 1935, III, #58425, CEIP Archives.

to appoint a committee to arrange a definite program of action based upon these documents.[7]

As instructed, Butler appointed Newton D. Baker to head the special committee, which also included Shotwell, Eichelberger, Pope, Stimson, Van Kirk, Watson, and John Nevin Sayre. The committee, in turn, designated the National Peace Conference as the appropriate body for carrying out the work outlined at the Columbia Conference and after prolonged negotiations convinced the Carnegie Endowment and the Carnegie Corporation to appropriate $7,500 each to help reorganize the NPC. Central headquarters were established in New York City and Walter Van Kirk became the new director. In December, at a meeting in Rye, New York, the Carnegie Endowment accepted membership in the NPC, thereby completing the process of reorganization. Butler became an Honorary President and Shotwell took a position on the powerful Steering Committee.[8]

Unfortunately, neither the financial resources nor the prestige of the NPC, could unite the peace movement behind a program tied, even indirectly, to the League of Nations. Several months before reorganization took place, the issue of neutrality legislation deeply split the antiwar forces and demonstrated the extent of anti-League sentiment in the country. Collective security depended upon the willingness of nations to join together in opposing acts of aggression either through economic or military means. But in August, 1935, Congress passed a joint resolution announcing that the United States had no intention of becoming involved in any foreign conflicts no matter who started them or for what reasons.

Support for neutrality legislation came from many sources. "Revisionist" historians had turned the attention of the nation toward the sinister causes of World War I and convinced many people that the United States could have kept out of the conflict had it remained truly

7. Nicholas Murray Butler, "Memorandum on Columbia Conference," n.d., IV, #70090, CEIP Archives; Walter W. Van Kirk, "The National Peace Conference—Report to the Carnegie Endowment for International Peace," April 1, 1936, pp. 1–3, IV, #70165, CEIP Archives.
8. Ibid.; Walter Van Kirk to Nicholas Murray Butler, December 21, 1935, IV, #70077, CEIP Archives; Nicholas Murray Butler to Newton D Baker, December 17, 1935, IV, #70088, CEIP Archives; Henry Haskell, "Memorandum for President Butler," January 2, 1936, IV, #70103, CEIP Archives.

neutral. The revelations of the Senate munitions investigation further convinced the American people that the blunders of the First World War could have been avoided by restricting the activities of certain business interests. By the summer of 1935 Mussolini's designs on Ethiopia had become clear and war seemed imminent. If the United States was to benefit from the lessons of history, action had to be taken at once.[9]

President Roosevelt and his Secretary of State did not oppose neutrality legislation. In fact, they hoped that such legislation would enable them to control the future course of American foreign policy free from the emotional demands of national honor and the pressure of economic interests.[10] They favored an act giving the Executive discretionary power—power to place an arms embargo on one or all belligerents as the President saw fit. Congress, however, preferred mandatory legislation, and, in August, passed a joint resolution prohibiting the export of "arms, ammunition and implements of war" to *all* belligerent countries. The resolution, which Roosevelt reluctantly signed on August 31, also forbade American ships from carrying such goods to or from a belligerent nation, provided for the creation of a National Munitions Control board with the Secretary of State as chairman, and empowered the President, at his discretion, to warn American citizens against traveling on belligerent ships.[11]

Throughout the debate in Congress Shotwell had urged the passage of a discretionary law. He hoped that neutrality legislation would bring the United States closer to the League. What he wanted was a law flexible enough to allow the President to forbid the exportation of arms and munitions to aggressor governments, while permitting their sale to the victim of aggression. He also wanted legislation that would permit the President to distinguish between acts of belligerency and actions taken on behalf of the League of Nations to stop aggression.[12] On several occasions he went to Washington to lobby for such a discriminatory bill, but met with vigorous opposition on Capitol

9. Divine, *Illusion,* pp. 57–58; Cohen, *American Revisionists,* pp. 144–60.
10. Divine, *Illusion,* pp. 121–22.
11. U.S. *Statutes,* 49, pp. 1081–85.
12. J.T.S., "The Issue in the Crisis," *Survey Graphic* 24 (November 1935): 523, 558.

Hill. Finding the Neutrality Act of 1935 totally unacceptable, he agreed to become chairman of a committee set up by the National Peace Conference in September to study the new law and make proposals for its amendment.

Since the First Neutrality Act was only a temporary measure designed to expire on February 29, 1936, Shotwell hoped to use the committee to promote a more flexible policy. Secretary of State Hull fully shared his point of view and instructed the State Department to provide him with any documents pertinent to the committee's work. In addition, Hull met with the committee several times to discuss possible lines of revision.[13] President Roosevelt's decision to implement the Neutrality Act after Mussolini sent his armies into Ethiopia offered the committee a test case upon which to base its report. The President's inability to prohibit the export of oil and other commodities essential to Italy's war effort but not considered "arms, ammunition, and implements of war" revealed one major weakness in the legislation. The danger, moreover, that League members, following the Council's recommendation to apply economic sanctions against Italy, might become involved in the conflict thereby forcing Roosevelt to extend the embargo to them, provided the committee with another strong argument for revision.

With the help of such prominent international lawyers as Philip Jessup of Columbia University, Quincy Wright of the University of Chicago, and Clyde Eagleton of New York University, Shotwell worked throughout the autumn of 1935 on the neutrality question. Since the National Peace Conference included organizations which both supported and opposed collective security, the committee's major difficulty was in finding a formula that might reconcile these divergent points of view. Most of the work centered around Point 5 of the National Peace Conference's "Statement of Principles." It declared that "The Neutrality policy of the United States should be revised in order that the risk of entanglement in foreign wars may be reduced and in order that the United States may not obstruct the world community in its efforts to maintain peace." The committee

13. J.T.S. to Nicholas Murray Butler, September 25, 1935, Butler Papers, Columbia University.

believed that a practical program worked out along these lines would win the support of all factions in the peace movement.[14]

On December 12, Shotwell submitted "A Suggested Redraft of the Neutrality Act of August 31, 1935" to the National Peace Conference for consideration. The report proposed several lines of policy. It urged Congress to renew the mandatory arms embargo in case of war and to supplement it by giving the President discretionary power to prohibit the export of other essential supplies and credits. Like the embargo on arms, the restriction on these "other articles or commodities essential to the continuing conduct of war" would apply impartially to all belligerents on either side of the dispute. The draft proposal also called upon the President to negotiate a treaty "supplementary to the Pact of Paris" to clarify the rights and duties of neutrals.[15]

The most controversial aspect of the draft was Article 7. It provided the President with an "escape clause" from an overly rigid system of impartial embargoes by empowering him to distinguish between an aggressor and its victim. It stated that if the President determined that one or more of the belligerents were attacked in violation of the Kellogg Pact, and if a majority of the other nonbelligerent parties to the treaty concurred in his finding, then he might, with the consent of Congress, revoke the embargo against the victim or victims of aggression. Such an action, Shotwell hoped, would not only give the President more flexibility, but would also facilitate closer cooperation between the United States and the League of Nations.[16]

The National Peace Conference referred the draft to its constituent organizations for study and discussion. These groups agreed that Congress should extend the neutrality legislation for a definite period of time and that it should authorize the President, at his discretion, to embargo loans and essential war materials to warring parties. They could not agree, however, on whether the United States should apply these prohibitions impartially to all belligerents or whether under certain circumstances it should lift them from nations attacked in

14. "Report of the National Peace Conference by its Committee for the Study of Neutrality Legislation," December 12, 1935, *International Conciliation* 316 (January 1936): 18–19.
15. Ibid., pp. 22–23.
16. Ibid., pp. 25, 43.

violation of the Pact of Paris. Since the Conference could not reconcile the division of opinion between those supporting mandatory legislation and those supporting a more permissive and flexible policy, it decided to take no stand whatever on this particular question.[17]

The failure to gain support for a more flexible policy annoyed Shotwell so much that he seriously considered severing his ties with the Conference in order to organize "the support of those who do not allow their ethical emotions to blur their sense of reality."[18] He took no action, however, for he became convinced that no matter what he and his associates did Congress would pass a more rigid law and tie the United States "against the interests of . . . world peace."[19] The passage of the Second Neutrality Act, signed by Roosevelt on February 29, proved him correct. It not only extended the mandatory embargo, but also precluded the possibility of any Presidential discretion concerning new belligerents entering an existing war.[20] This meant, of course, that any League member becoming involved in the hostilities because of its obligations under the Covenant could not look to the United States for material aid or support. For Shotwell, the Second Neutrality Act was nothing less than a giant step backwards. Following its enactment, he gave up looking for ways to moderate or revise the work of Congress and increasingly attacked the neutrality legislation as a tragic mistake. He argued that the acts of August, 1935 and February, 1936 were both based on historical fallacies perpetuated by "Congressional committees and those who write pamphlets in the name of history." He could not accept the contention that either arms trade or private loans forced America to enter World War I. Such an interpretation led to an oversimplification of history and disregarded political reality. Any generalizations which attributed great events to single causes were bound to be "superficial and misleading."[21]

Far more discerning than most antiwar leaders, he recognized that the greatest fallacy of the neutrality laws lay in the supposition that

17. Ibid., p. 21.
18. J.T.S. to Newton D. Baker, January 13, 1936, Box 208, Baker Papers.
19. J.T.S. to Leo Rowe, January 2, 1936, Box 231, J.T.S. Papers.
20. U.S. *Statutes,* 49, pp. 1152–53; Divine, *Illusion,* pp. 160–61.
21. *New York Times,* February 21, 1936, p. 7; J.T.S., *On the Rim,* pp. 47–49.

there existed no connection between the security of the United States and the configuration of power in Europe. "Far from being a policy of pure negation," he declared, "our safety in the time of foreign war calls for measures of precaution better thought out than those of the cyclone cellar. The need is for a citadel of defense planned with an architecture more complicated than has been dreamed by those who think that all that is needed is for everyone to retire under cover."[22] Yet he could not bring himself to support a foreign policy which ultimately might lead to unilateral action in defense of the world balance of power. Despite his understanding of the importance of power in international affairs, he opposed Roosevelt's rearmament program and urged the President to harmonize his defense policies with the Kellogg Pact.[23]

Having lost hope in modifying American neutrality policy, Shotwell not only attacked it as politically harmful, but now saw it as economically disastrous as well. He pointed out that effective neutrality would require the extension of embargoes to various materials such as oil, cotton, and other products essential for carrying on war. Whereas he supported these prohibitions during the National Peace Conference debates, he now saw great danger in them. Assuming, as did many Americans, that domestic prosperity depended upon overseas economic activities, he worried about the consequences of a really viable neutrality policy. If neutrality legislation could keep the United States out of war, he agreed that it might be worth the sacrifice. But he seriously questioned if this was a realistic possibility. The great danger of such legislation was that it blinded Americans to the fundamental fact that modern war was as "contagious as the plague," and that war industries were as interdependent as peace industries. In the final analysis neutrality had a dual weakness. It could not keep the United States out of future wars and it would greatly disrupt America's foreign trade.[24]

22. J.T.S., "Isolation and Nationalism," *Bulletin of the University of Georgia: Proceedings of the Institute of Public Affairs* 36 (July 1936): 29.
23. National Peace Conference, "An Appeal to the President and Congress of the United States," March 5, 1936, IV, #70145, CEIP Archives.
24. J.T.S., "Isolation and Nationalism Inherent Among Americans," *Columbia Alumni News* 27 (February 21, 1936): 3, 20; J.T.S., *On The Rim,* pp. 56–64, 88–96.

Shotwell's concern about the ultimate effects of neutrality upon American trade revealed, once again, his deep commitment to the established system and his strong belief in the necessity of economic expansion. He viewed with alarm the strong and increasing attacks upon American business which followed the depression of 1929 and the Senate munitions investigation. He attacked outright the "revisionist" interpretation that business and financial interests had forced the United States to intervene in World War I. Business interests in America, he believed, favored peace rather than war. In fact, they needed peace in order to prosper.[25]

His strong defense of American business stemmed not only from his abstract commitment to the capitalistic system, but also from his work with the International Chamber of Commerce and from his close friendship with Thomas J. Watson, President of IBM, head of the American branch of the International Chamber of Commerce, and a Carnegie Endowment trustee. In 1936, both men served on a joint committee on international economic problems set up by the ICC and the Carnegie Endowment, and in the late 1930s they helped organize several other cooperative programs between the two organizations.[26] In addition, they worked on several independent projects together and even drafted an outline plan for a new world organization which they submitted to President Roosevelt in November, 1936.[27] No doubt this close association with American business led Shotwell to reject the "Merchant of Death" thesis.

Shotwell's interests during this period did not restrict themselves solely to political and economic internationalism. Having assumed the chairmanship of the American National Committee on International Intellectual Cooperation largely on his own terms, he turned it into one of the most active and productive branches of the entire organiza-

25. J.T.S., "Neutrality," *Bulletin of the University of Georgia: Proceedings of the Institute of Public Affairs* 36 (July 1936): 3.
26. "Memorandum on the Cooperation of the Carnegie Endowment and the International Chamber of Commerce," n.d., Secretary's Office and Administration, 1936, pp. 163–64, CEIP Archives; J.T.S. to Nicholas Murray Butler, November 25, 1936, I.B.3. #24528–29, CEIP Archives; CEIP, *Minutes*, 28: 33–34, 44–45, and 29: 50–51, 58–59.
27. Thomas Watson to Franklin Delano Roosevelt, November 13, 1936, Roosevelt Personal File #2487, Franklin D. Roosevelt Papers, Franklin D. Roosevelt Library, Hyde Park, New York.

tion. Besides serving as a center of information for inquiries dealing with international problems in the social sciences, arts and letters, and pure sciences, the American Committee worked on numerous projects concerning copyright laws, the use of radio and motion pictures as educational devices, inter-American cultural relations, and textbook revision.[28]

In all of the committee's varied activities its chairman played a major role. One of the first scholars to recognize the possibilities of motion pictures as a "scientific aid to learning" and as a molder of public opinion, he proved extremely successful in using the new medium to promote internationalism. In 1937, he set up a very successful motion picture exhibit at the Paris World Fair depicting various aspects of "American life and achievement."[29] Two years later, he served as the historical consultant for the motion picture "Land of Liberty," an epic of American history produced by Cecil B. DeMille and shown at both the New York and San Francisco World Fairs. He also wrote the commentary for "Made in the USA," a short documentary depicting the dependence of America on other parts of the world for the raw materials required in manufacturing various essential products.[30]

Even more significant than his success with motion pictures was his effort to persuade the Roosevelt administration to give official recognition to cultural problems. In July, 1938, largely due to the pressure exerted by Shotwell and his committee, as well as other groups interested in international cooperation, the President established a Division of Cultural Relations with the avowed purpose of encouraging and strengthening "cultural relations and intellectual cooperation between the United States and other nations."[31] Shotwell also actively

28. "Report of the American National Committee on Intellectual Cooperation for 1938," Box 122, J.T.S. Papers.
29. J.T.S., "Memorandum on the Use of Moving Pictures for Educational Purposes and for International Exchange," Box 122, J.T.S. Papers; J.T.S., *Autobiography,* pp. 288–89.
30. *New York Times,* April 9, 1939, sec. 10, p. 5; J.T.S. to Nicholas Murray Butler, January 23, 1940 & March 15, 1940, Butler Papers; CEIP Archives, VII, #99969–100016. For reviews of "Land of Liberty" and Shotwell's correspondence concerning the picture see Box 260, J.T.S. Papers.
31. J.T.S. to Cordell Hull, February 1, 1935, #800.403/2, State Department Archives; Cordell Hull to J.T.S., October 21, 1938, Box 192, J.T.S. Papers; Ben M. Cherrington, "The Division of Cultural Relations, State Depart-

participated in his committee's efforts to bring American copyright law more in line with international agreements. Although he persuaded Elbert D. Thomas of Utah to introduce the "Shotwell Bill" into the Senate, several interest groups opposed sections of the proposed law and Congress never acted upon it.[32]

While Shotwell devoted a good deal of time to the promotion of intellectual cooperation, his position as president of the League of Nations Association and as one of the leading spokesmen for the Carnegie Endowment kept him in the forefront of the public debate over America's foreign policy. In fact, on the recommendation of Ambassador William E. Dodd, President Roosevelt seriously considered him for the Berlin post as Dodd's successor. Nothing came of this, however, and Shotwell continued to promote collective security as a publicist and lobbyist.[33]

A trip to Europe during the summer of 1936, sponsored as usual by the Endowment, proved extremely depressing and fully awakened him to the dangerous situation developing on the Continent.[34] In March, having withdrawn from the League of Nations and having resumed compulsory military service, Germany repudiated both the Treaty of Versailles and the Locarno Pacts by remilitarizing the Rhineland. Two months later, Mussolini decreed the annexation of all Ethiopia and followed Japan and Germany out of the League. In July, General Francisco Franco launched an insurrection against the republican government of Spain, precipitating a major civil war in which liberals and communists aligned themselves against the fascists.

Because the Second Neutrality Act made no provisions for embargoes in cases of civil war (forcing Congress to pass a special joint resolution), and because it was scheduled to expire on May 1, 1937,

---

ment," *News Bulletin: Institute of International Education* 14 (May 1939): 5–6.

32. *Congressional Record,* 76th Cong., 3rd session, vol. 86, part 1, January 8, 1940, pp. 63–78. See also Edwin P. Kilroe (ed.), "The Shotwell Copyright Bill, March 11, 1938–February 14, 1940" (unpublished manuscript, 4 vols., Columbia University Law Library, New York City).

33. Franklin D. Roosevelt to Cordell Hull, June 17, 1937, #523, Roosevelt Papers; William E. Dodd to J.T.S., November 28, 1937, Box 230, J.T.S. Papers. See also Robert Dallek, *Democrat and Diplomat: The Life of William E. Dodd* (New York, 1968), pp. 295–96, 313.

34. J.T.S. to Steward F. Bryant, July 27, 1936, Box 33, J.T.S. Papers.

the entire question of neutrality once again opened for discussion. As before, Shotwell became a leading figure in the public debate. In February, Senator Elbert Thomas, after conferring with him and other leaders of the Carnegie Endowment and the National Peace Conference, came out for neutrality revision along the lines proposed by the NPC's Committee on Neutrality. He also read into the *Congressional Record* a statement prepared by Shotwell and Quincy Wright calling for discriminatory legislation which would allow the President to embargo shipments of arms, ammunition, and materials not classified as implements of war to "aggressors" only.[35]

Neither Congress nor the majority of American people, however, accepted the arguments for discriminatory legislation. With the European situation deteriorating, most Americans believed that any attempt to take sides between belligerents could only bring the United States into war. The result was the Third Neutrality Act, signed by Roosevelt on May 1. It extended the main provisions of the previous acts indefinitely, prohibited the export of arms and ammunition to the parties in foreign civil wars, and forbade American citizens to travel on belligerent ships instead of merely warning them against such travel. In addition, it included a cash-and-carry provision for a limited two-year trial period.[36] The resumption of the Sino-Japanese War in 1937 and the beginning of Hitler's *Drang nach Osten* in March, 1938, convinced most Americans that Congress had acted correctly. The failure of the League, Great Britain, and France to oppose effectively the moves of Germany and Italy only reaffirmed their belief that America should in no way become involved in conflicts over the European balance of power.

The events of 1936, 1937, and 1938 presented serious theoretical problems for the advocates of collective security. The Italian-Ethiopian War shook their belief that economic sanctions alone could stop aggression. They rationalized that sanctions had failed because the United States and the League refused to include such materials as oil and cotton on the embargoed lists, but they could not have completely

35. *Congressional Record* (Appendix), 75th Cong., 1st session, vol. 81, part 9, February 15, 1937, pp. 216–17.
36. U.S. *Statutes,* 50, pp. 121–28.

ignored the fact that only armed intervention could have stopped Mussolini. Sanctions only alienated Italy from the western powers and in the end benefitted Germany. By applying sanctions, the League had broken its united front against Hitler and gave him the opportunity to remilitarize the Rhineland. The Chancellor's action further revealed the difficulties involved in applying the theory of collective security to practical situations. Armed resistance by Great Britain and France might have forced Germany to retreat, but there existed the problem of harmonizing such an action with the principles underlying the very basis of the League of Nations. The remilitarization of the Rhineland was not, in reality, an act of aggression. Hitler simply marched into his own territory. On the other hand, Hitler might have complained legitimately that any military action taken to stop him was itself aggression and a violation of the Kellogg Pact.[37]

As Europe leaned over the rim of the abyss, Shotwell intensified his efforts to awaken his fellow countrymen to the crisis at hand. Long before most Americans, he clearly saw the threat posed by Germany, Italy, and Japan to Western Europe and the United States. Neither neutrality legislation nor isolationist rhetoric blinded him to the deep stake the United States had in other parts of the world. No matter how peaceful America's intent, it could not keep out of a war which endangered the very survival of Great Britain and France. He presented his case on June 15, 1938, in an unsigned editorial in the *New York Times:*

> It is important that the statesmen of aggressor countries should realize that today, no less than 1917, there are specific and vital American interests in all parts of the world which would almost certainly be affected by war on a large scale. It is important that they should realize the real depth of American loyalty to the whole set of principles and methods and traditions which goes by the name of democracy.
>
> No remoteness from the scene of potential European conflict can isolate the United States from the consequences of a major war. No Neutrality Act can prevent the American people from favor-

37. Roland N. Stromberg, *Collective Security and American Foreign Policy: From the League of Nations to NATO* (New York, 1963), pp. 91–103.

ing their natural allies. In any ultimate test of strength between democracy and dictatorship, the good-will and the moral support —and in the long run more likely than not the physical power of the United States—will be found on the side of those nations defending a way of life which Americans believe to be worth living.[38]

While he clearly perceived America's vital interest in the European balance of power, Shotwell never declared himself in favor of a clear-cut alliance with Great Britain or France. His reluctance stemmed from both the realization that neither the American people nor Congress would accept such a proposal as well as his own personal refusal to abandon the theory of collective security. Despite his awareness of the importance of the European configuration of power to American security, he rejected the concept of the balance of power as a nineteenth-century idea unsuited for the modern world. Condemning the appeasement policy of Great Britain and France, he continued to view the Geneva experiment as the only hope for peace. "We must re-think our way through not in despondency but with faith in mankind and justice," he declared several days after Neville Chamberlain and Edouard Daladier capitulated to Hitler at Munich. "The League of Nations stands for that and it will come through or universal anarchy and the blotting out of our civilization is the alternative."[39]

Shotwell fully supported Roosevelt's annual message to Congress on January 4, 1939, in which the President called for a revision of the Neutrality Act so that the United States might aid the opponents of aggression through methods short of war. In the spring and summer he joined in the national campaign for repeal of the arms embargo and strongly supported the activities of the American Union for Concerted Peace Efforts, a group committed to "an active foreign policy for the United States to oppose aggression, to promote economic justice between nations and to develop adequate peace machinery."[40]

Despite the efforts of Roosevelt and his supporters, Congress refused to revise the Neutrality Act. The President had little choice

38. J.T.S., "A Way of Life," *New York Times,* June 15, 1938, p. 22.
39. *New York Times,* October 14, 1938, p. 17.
40. Ibid., March 16, 1939, p. 11; J.T.S. to William Hinckley, December 7, 1938, Box 225, J.T.S. Papers.

but to proclaim American neutrality shortly after Hitler precipitated a general war in Europe by attacking Poland. On September 21, Roosevelt called Congress into special session and once again urged repeal of the arms embargo. He also requested the extension of the cash-and-carry formula so that it covered all goods, including arms and implements of war. Such a policy, he believed, would permit the United States to aid England and France without becoming directly involved in the war. Once again the advocates of collective security organized. Shotwell, Eichelberger, and several other members of the American Union for Concerted Peace Efforts established the Non-Partisan Committee for Peace through the Revision of the Neutrality Act and persuaded William Allen White, the well-known editor of the *Emporia Gazette,* to become its chairman. With its central office at 8 West 40th Street in New York City, the same address as the League of Nations Association and the American Union, the Non-Partisan Committee led a vigorous campaign to pressure Congress into quick action. Within six weeks it had achieved success. On November 4, 1939, President Roosevelt signed the Fourth Neutrality Act, giving him virtually all that he had asked.[41]

Internationalists applauded the new law as a major step in the right direction. They soon realized, as did most other Americans, that it was but the first step in a long series which ultimately would carry the United States from a position of neutrality to one of nonbelligerency and finally to one of active intervention.

41. The most complete account of the Non-Partisan Committee appears in Walter Johnson's "William A. White Defends America" (Ph.D. dissertation, University of Chicago, August, 1941), pp. 47–70. This was later published in popular form without footnotes as *The Battle Against Isolation* (Chicago, 1940).

13
The Search for Lasting Peace

"The fundamental lesson of this tremendous crisis," Shotwell told a CBS radio audience on the evening of August 28, 1939, "is that there is no hope for lasting peace in the world unless civilization can put something in the place of war. This, even more than the tragic drama of youth being mobilized for slaughter, and homes prepared for destruction, is the outstanding fact that has become clear to all thinking people in these anxious days. So long as war is the ultimate tribunal to which nations take their conflicting claims, no amount of moral denunciation will rid the world of it. Outlawry of war without provision for justice is a futile thing."[1]

Three days later Hitler sent his troops crashing into Poland. The Second World War had begun.

In the United States public opinion quickly divided between those who favored strict neutrality and avoidance of any actions which

1. J.T.S., *The Fundamentals Behind the Conflict: An Address by James T. Shotwell Delivered over Columbia Broadcasting System, August 28, 1939* (New York, 1939), p. 2.

might ultimately lead to American intervention (a program spearheaded by the America First Committee) and those who favored revision of neutrality along the lines advocated by President Roosevelt and the Non-Partisan Committee for Peace Through Revision of the Neutrality Laws. Although Shotwell did not endorse direct military involvement, he supported any and all efforts to aid the Allies by measures short of war. He worked closely with the Committee to Defend America by Aiding the Allies, an organization established in May, 1940 by Clark Eichelberger and William Allen White. The White Committee, as it was popularly known, supported the destroyer-base deal and campaigned vigorously for lend-lease and the complete repeal of the neutrality laws. During the winter of 1940–41, Shotwell continued to side with the White faction of the Committee which opposed direct American intervention. By the spring, however, he realized that the twin objectives of Allied victory and American peace were irreconcilable and decided to follow Eichelberger and the other more militant members of the organization down the interventionist road.[2]

Although Shotwell participated in the debate over America's wartime policy, he focused most of his attention on the nature of the peace which had to follow. As early as the summer of 1939, he and Eichelberger made plans to organize a Commission of Enquiry to study "the bases of a lasting peace and the organization of international society."[3] Lack of funds prevented the organization from becoming functional, but in November several groups including the League of Nations Association, the American Union for Concerted Peace Efforts, and the Church Peace Union helped organize the Commission to Study the Organization of Peace with Shotwell as chairman, Eichelberger as director, and William Allan Neilson, president emeritus of Smith College, as head of the executive committee. Shotwell and Neilson

2. J.T.S. to J. W. Defoe, March 29, 1940, Box 230, J.T.S. Papers; J.T.S. to William A. White, July 30, 1940, Box 317, William A. White Papers, Library of Congress; Interview with Clark Eichelberger, December 22, 1966, New York City. For an account of the interventionists see Mark Lincoln Chadwick, *The Hawks of World War II* (Chapel Hill, N. C., 1968).

3. Clark Eichelberger to Nicholas Murray Butler, August 31, 1939, IV, #62984–62985, CEIP Archives.

announced the formation of the new organization in early January and listed among the Commission members, Quincy Wright, William Allen White, John Foster Dulles, Dean Virginia Gildersleeve of Barnard College, Evans Clark, executive director of the 20th Century Fund, Frank G. Boudreau, executive director of the Milbank Memorial Fund, Thomas W. Lamont, chairman of the board of J. P. Morgan and Company, and Harry D. Gideonse, president of Brooklyn College. The new organization hoped to "clarify and enlighten public opinion, to explain the world in which we were living and to propose the way for building the structure of peace."[4]

From the outset the Commission to Study the Organization of Peace attracted widespread interest. Between January and May of 1940 it conducted a series of radio programs over the Columbia Broadcasting System designed to clarify the war issues, promote the Allied cause, and discuss some of the major problems connected with postwar planning.[5] Although the Commission limited its membership to "persons qualified for expert study," by 1943 it boasted of more than 120 participants including government officials, international lawyers, political scientists, educators, businessmen, editors, and leaders of farm, labor, church, and women's groups.

Monthly discussion meetings were held in New York City and regional commissions, with their own officers and staffs, were organized in fifteen other major cities across the country. Through its national and regional groups, the Commission sponsored public meetings and persuaded the various communciation media to carry its educational program throughout the nation. Newspapers from Birmingham, Alabama to Oklahoma City, from the Bronx, New York to Helena, Montana, and from Winnipeg, Canada to London printed Commission news releases and commented upon Commission activities. Shotwell estimated that its material reached over 9,000 rural weeklies and about 1,000 dailies. A Speaker's Bureau supplied met-

4. Clark Eichelberger to Henry S. Haskell, November 30, 1939, IV, #62996, CEIP Archives; *New York Herald Tribune,* January 3, February 14, 1940; "Minutes of the Commission to Study the Organization of Peace," November 5, 1939, Box 195, J.T.S. Papers. Box 241 of the Shotwell Papers contains an extensive clipping file on the Commission to Study the Organization of Peace (hereafter cited CSOP).
5. The series of fifteen broadcasts under the general title of "Which Way to Lasting Peace?" can be found in Box 195, J.T.S. Papers.

ropolitan areas and over 600 local communities. Special training courses provided speakers, discussion leaders, and program chairmen with extensive material on subjects dealing with the war and the making of peace. In addition, the Commission drew up and distributed a wide variety of studies on such problems as international health, human rights, trust territories, disarmament, security, and economic readjustment.[6]

Shotwell became so preoccupied with the Commission's work that he decided to free himself from some of his other obligations. On January 1, 1940, he resigned as president of the League of Nations Association. Even with this cutback, he could not keep up with the demands of teaching, lecturing, and planning for the postwar period. In May, overwork and anxiety over the progress of the war led to a complete physical collapse.[7] His breakdown was remarkably similar to the one he suffered in the summer of 1917 when he had exhausted himself as chairman of the National Board for Historical Service. He recovered rapidly, but decided to take his doctor's advice and disengage himself further from the numerous committees and commitments which had become part of his daily routine.

The process of slowing down did not come easily, for at sixty-five Shotwell had more energy than most men half his age. His work had become essential to his existence, and the rapid pace of public controversy a way of life. Less than two weeks after his collapse, he informed his secretary that doing nothing drove him "crazy" and that although unable to work for more than an hour at a time, he felt compelled to resume some of his activities.[8] Early in 1941 he suffered a mild relapse and agreed to go to Mexico. The stated purpose of the trip was to study possible fields of work for the Carnegie Endowment for International Peace, but the main reason was to get away from New York and Washington and the problems of war.[9] While in Mexico, Shotwell arranged for the Endowment to sponsor numerous economic and

6. CSOP, "Memorandum on Plans for the Commission," January, 1941, VII, AA, #123370A, CEIP Archives; "Work of the Commission to Study the Organization of Peace," December 6, 1941, VII, AA, #123379, CEIP Archives.
7. J.T.S. to Waldo G. Leland, May 20, 1940, Box 129, J.T.S. Papers.
8. Edith Ware to Waldo G. Leland, May 20, 1940, Box 129, J.T.S. Papers.
9. Interview with Helen Harvey Shotwell and Mrs. Margaret Summers, July 26, 1971, Poughkeepsie, New York.

cultural studies as a means of bettering relations between the United States and its southern neighbor. The State Department became interested in several boundary questions raised by these Endowment studies and eventually negotiated a new treaty arrangement with Mexico.[10]

The two months in Mexico seemed to do Shotwell good and he quickly regained his old spirit and energy. As a matter of caution, however, he further reduced some of his activities. His duties as director of the Division of Economics and History of the Carnegie Endowment were not very demanding and provided a steady, if not extremely large, income, and he, therefore, decided to retain this position.[11] He did, however, reduce his teaching obligations and in June, 1942, retired from the Columbia University faculty as Bryce Professor Emeritus of International Relations. The *New York Herald Tribune* commented upon the event and declared that it was "as hard to visualize Professor James T. Shotwell in retirement as it is to think of Niagara no longer flowing."[12] The war itself limited the activities of the American National Committee on Intellectual Cooperation, but after his collapse he turned most of his remaining duties over to Waldo Leland, who replaced him as chairman in June, 1943.

His illness had almost no affect on his participation in postwar planning activities. Freed of his other obligations, he devoted his time to the Commission to Study the Organization of Peace and to drawing up a blueprint for a "practicable" peace settlement. By far the most important task undertaken by the Commission was the publication of its general reports. A committee composed of Shotwell, Eichelberger, Quincy Wright, Clyde Eagleton, Harry D. Gideonse, Malcolm Davis, and Carter Goodrich, professor of economics at Columbia University, prepared these statements of policy which were then debated by the Commission as a whole and released to the public. In November, 1940, the Commission published its first or "Preliminary Report." It

10. J.T.S. to Nicholas Murray Butler, "Mexican Studies," March 17–April, 14, 1941, Box 245, J.T.S. Papers; J.T.S. to Nicholas Murray Butler, May 14, 1941, Box 245, J.T.S. Papers.
11. Until 1946 J.T.S. received an annual salary from the Endowment of $7,000, but he also received an extremely liberal expense account. In March of that year the Executive Committee boosted his salary to $12,000.
12. *New York Herald Tribune,* June 9, 1942.

announced that the Commission planned to exert what influence it could "to ensure that the United States, whether or not forced to enter the present struggle, shall not again fail to play its part in any opportunity which may offer to organize a durable peace." To that end the Commission intended "to do its utmost to lead the American people to see more clearly than they did twenty years ago that, for selfish and unselfish reasons alike, all their efforts must have as their ultimate goal the creation of a better world in which to live—a world in which international cooperation will be able to use human intelligence and natural resources for the economic security and free development of all men."[13]

Shotwell's approach, ideas, and even phraseology permeated the entire report. It rejected the idea of world government as politically impracticable, but emphasized the necessity of limiting national sovereignty. Future peace would depend upon the willingness of nations to accept the jurisdiction of international tribunals and renounce the use of force in all cases except self-defense. Besides outlining various limitations upon sovereignty, the report called for the creation of several institutions to maintain peace and security. These included an international court "with jurisdiction adequate to deal with all international disputes on the basis of law," an international legislature "to remedy abuses in existing law and to make new law whenever technical progress requires the adjustment of international practice," an adequate police force and economic sanctions "to prevent aggression and to support international covenants," and appropriate authorities "to administer backward areas ceded to the world federation." In addition, it called for the creation of a number of welfare agencies to deal with such problems as transportation, health, labor, commerce, and finance.[14]

Throughout 1941 the Commission studied the various technical and political problems involved in establishing a world organization along the lines projected in its "Preliminary Report." In June, Shotwell released a seven-point program drawn up by himself and several

13. CSOP, "Preliminary Report," *International Conciliation* 369 (April 1941): 195.
14. Ibid., pp. 195–202.

of his associates. It paralleled Wilson's Fourteen Points of nearly a quarter of a century before and anticipated the Roosevelt-Churchill Atlantic Charter by two months. Like the Atlantic Charter, it called for the abandonment of force in international affairs, the development of substitutes for war, free commercial relations between nations, self-determination, and the defeat of the "forces of lawlessness." In addition, it advocated an International Bill of Rights, guarantees for racial, religious, and political minorities, intellectual cooperation between nations, and American assistance for postwar reconstruction.[15]

The similarity of the Commission's seven-point program and the August pronouncement of the Anglo-American leaders was deceptive. Roosevelt and Churchill had not come to any decision about a postwar settlement other than to agree that after the war the United States and Great Britain should cooperate "in policing the world until the establishment of a better order."[16] Their major purpose, as had been Wilson's when he issued his Fourteen Points, was to set up idealistic objectives which would appeal to liberals everywhere. The practical effect of the Atlantic Charter was to commit the United States more fully to the side of the Allies and bring it one step closer to war. Only one month after its release, Roosevelt instructed the American navy to "shoot on sight" at any German or Italian vessels entering American waters.

The Japanese surprise attack on Pearl Harbor and America's subsequent entry into the war gave added importance to the work of the Commission to Study the Organization of Peace. Two months after Congress declared war on Japan, the Commission released its second report on the "Transitional Period." It dealt with the important period between the end of the war and the establishment of the new world order outlined in the Preliminary Report. During this period rebuilding would take place and the foundations laid for a permanent international organization. The Commission believed that to avoid disaster the Allies would have to make preparations for reconstruction and rehabilitation before the war ended. Almost prophetically it

15. *New York Times,* June 7, 1941, p. 6.
16. Winston Churchill, *The Grand Alliance,* vol. 3: *The Second World War* (Boston, 1950), p. 444.

suggested that Allied dissension might prove the most serious threat to a successful and progressive postwar settlement. The victors might fail to unite in the necessary work; they might quarrel among themselves; or even more likely, they might refuse to surrender their power to a permanent international organization.[17]

In February of the following year, the Commission issued its third report on "The United Nations and the Organization of Peace." Relying heavily on the principles contained in the Atlantic Charter, the Commission called upon the Allies to meet "as soon as possible" in order to begin making preparations for the peace settlement.[18] America had not as yet committed itself to a postwar substitute for the League of Nations, but on November 1, 1943, the Roosevelt administration joined the governments of Great Britain, Russia, and China in releasing the "Declaration of Four Nations on General Security." The document pledged the Allies to continue their united action "for the organization and maintenance of peace and security." In addition, it clearly recognized the "necessity of establishing at the earliest practicable date a general international organization" for that purpose.

The members of the Commission to Study the Organization of Peace applauded the statement. Equally encouraging were the resolutions presented in Congress by Senator Tom Connally and Representative J. William Fulbright calling for American participation in whatever international agencies might be set up during or after the war for the future preservation of peace and prevention of aggression. With a good deal of enthusiasm, therefore, Shotwell and Eichelberger released, on November 20, the Commission's fourth report entitled "Fundamentals of the International Organization." In addition to elaborating upon the Commission's seven-point program for a future peace settlement, it provided a precise blueprint for a new world organization. Their plan proposed an assembly open to all nations, an executive council composed of a limited number of nations including "those nations that bear the heaviest share of responsibility for the

17. CSOP, "Second Report: The Transitional Period," *International Conciliation* 379 (April 1942): 149–67.
18. CSOP, "Third Report: The United Nations and the Organization of Peace," *International Conciliation* 389 (April 1943): 203–35.

restoration and maintenance of peace," and a secretariat to study international problems and provide information and secretarial services. All regional organizations were to conform to the same fundamental purposes as the general organization and cooperate with it in their fulfillment.[19]

The State Department carefully studied the Commission's reports and made use of them in their own peace-planning work. On November 3, 1944, less than a month after the release of the Dumbarton Oaks proposals, Under Secretary of State Edward R. Stettinius, Jr. praised the Commission for its "objective and scientific approach to the problems of an international organization."[20] In addition to receiving copies of all the Commission's studies and reports, the State Department heard directly of the Commission's work from Shotwell, who in June, 1942 had been asked by Secretary of State Hull to serve on the Department's Advisory Committee on Post-War Foreign Policy.

The State Department had begun to consider the problems of postwar foreign policy long before the United States entered the war. In December, 1939, stimulated by private groups interested in postwar problems such as the Federal Council of Churches of Christ in America and the Council on Foreign Relations, Hull had created within the Department a "Committee on Problems of Peace and Reconstruction." The Secretary charged this high-level committee with surveying "the basic principles which should underlie a desirable world order to be evolved after the termination of present hostilities" and with examining "proposals and suggestions made from various sources—both official and unofficial—as regards problems of peace and reconstruction."[21] In January, Hull publicly announced the creation of an "Advisory Committee on Problems of Foreign Relations," but carefully concealed its true purpose which was to study postwar problems. Made up almost exclusively of State Department officials, Under Secretary of State Sumner Welles served as chairman and

19. CSOP, "Fourth Report: Fundamentals of the International Organization," *International Conciliation* 396 (January 1944): 26–28.
20. "Statement by Under-Secretary of State (Stettinius), November 3, 1944," in VII, AA, #123883, CEIP Archives.
21. U.S. Department of State, *Postwar Foreign Policy Preparations, 1939–1945*, prepared by Harley A. Notter (Washington, D.C., 1949), pp. 18–20.

Hugh Wilson, formerly Ambassador to Germany, served as vice-chairman.[22]

With America's entry into the war, the burden of work on the State Department increased tremendously. Hull decided to reorganize the government's postwar planning activities. In December, 1941, he established an Advisory Committee on Post-War Foreign Policy which included various government officials including Welles, Leo Pasvolsky, Dean Acheson, Herbert Feis, and Myron C. Taylor. In addition to the State Department members, Hull chose various individuals from outside the government to serve on the committee. Norman H. Davis, chairman of the Council on Foreign Relations, Hamilton Fish Armstrong, publisher of *Foreign Affairs,* Anne O'Hare McCormick of the *New York Times,* Isaiah Bowman, president of Johns Hopkins University, Walter Reuther of the United Automobile Workers, and Shotwell all participated in the government's deliberations. Seeking to avoid Woodrow Wilson's mistakes during World War I, Roosevelt and Hull chose five senators, three members of the House of Representatives, and various members of other governmental departments and war agencies to serve as unofficial members of the Advisory Committee.[23]

The Committee met for the first time in February, 1942, but afterwards met only rarely in plenary session. Subcommittees, organized around specific problems of postwar policy, handled most of the important work. The Subcommittee on Political Problems took up the most crucial questions such as formal reestablishment of peace, international organization, national sovereignty, and the pacific settlement of international disputes. Because of its membership, which included Hull and Welles, and because of the nature of the problems it considered, the Subcommittee on Political Problems became the most important subdivision of the Advisory Committee. Other subcommittees considered such questions as economic reconstruction, economic policy, territorial problems, security problems, international organization, and legal problems. The work of the various committees was

22. Ibid., pp. 20–22; Cordell Hull, *The Memoirs of Cordell Hull,* 2 vols. (New York, 1948), 2: 1626–27.
23. U.S. Department of State, *Postwar Foreign Policy,* pp. 64–74.

coordinated by Leo Pasvolsky, who became the executive officer of the Advisory Committee and its director of research. All recommendations and reports from the subcommittees went directly to Hull, who usually discussed the most important issues with the President. Roosevelt also had frequent and lengthy conversations with Under Secretary of State Welles on a variety of postwar issues.[24]

Shotwell, who joined the Advisory Committee in June, 1942, not only served on the important Subcommittee on Political Problems, but also on the subcommittees concerned with security problems, legal problems, and international organization. He found the work, in general, similar to that undertaken by the Inquiry, but he felt much closer to the sources of power and decision-making now than he had during World War I. His close association with Sumner Welles probably accounted for his attitude. He was both impressed and somewhat overwhelmed with the importance of the questions with which he had to deal. Overall he seemed to delight in having an official position in government once again.[25]

Shotwell's own views changed somewhat as a result of his work on the Advisory Committee. In January, 1942, he questioned the feasibility of creating a universal world organization immediately after the war. Instead he leaned more toward the creation of a temporary "Anglo-American directorate." He saw little danger in this for he believed that "liberty loving people will not make themselves over into international police forces for any length of time." Six months later, after he joined the Advisory Committee, he still believed that a world organization had to be built slowly and in stages, but now included China and Russia along with Great Britain and the United States as policemen for the world in the immediate postwar period.[26] As a member of the Political Subcommittee and the Special Subcommittee on International Organization, Shotwell argued for a strong world organization, Austrian independence, and adequate control of Germany's heavy industry. He vehemently opposed the territorial divi-

24. Ibid., pp. 69–108, 124, 133; Hull, *Memoirs,* 2: 1634–40.
25. J.T.S. to Nicholas Murray Butler, July 1, 1942, Butler Papers; J.T.S., "Diary," June 23, 1942, pp. 7–9, Box 259, J.T.S. Papers.
26. J.T.S. to Albert Guerard, January 27, 1942, Box 231, J.T.S. Papers; J.T.S. to Ely Culbertson, June 31, 1942, Box 232, J.T.S. Papers.

sion of Germany, for he believed that strict controls over her economy would be just as effective and cause less antagonism in the long run.[27]

His participation in the government's postwar planning activities did not last very long. In July, 1943, Hull suspended the work of the Advisory Committee, and America's postwar preparations entered a second stage, one consisting of high level conferences within the State Department and with the President. While neither Shotwell nor many other persons outside the government participated in this advanced stage of preparation, a good many of the suggestions and principles worked out beforehand were incorporated into American foreign policy.[28]

Despite his deep involvement in both the Commission to Study the Organization of Peace and the Advisory Committee, Shotwell still found the time and energy to write two books, publish several articles, and make numerous speeches on the world situation and the requirements for the organization of a lasting peace. His wartime statements are important not only because they reveal his own thinking on a number of crucial issues, but also because his point of view had gained prominence in America after the outbreak of war. He no longer spoke for himself alone or for a small minority of internationalist-oriented intellectuals. His assumptions, views, and approach were now shared by those guiding America's destiny, as well as by an increasing majority of the American people. Instead of speaking as a minority critic, seeking to point out the fallacies and weaknesses inherent in America's foreign policy, he now articulated a world view and approach to international affairs implicit in the thought of those dominant both within the government and American society in general.[29]

Like most other Americans he viewed the war basically in idealistic and moralistic terms. "The fundamental issue of the present war," he

27. J.T.S., "Diary," June 23, 1942, pp. 3–4, 11–14, Box 259, J.T.S. Papers.
28. U.S. Department of State, *Postwar Foreign Policy,* pp. 163–67.
29. During the winter of 1943–1944 public opinion polls revealed that nearly a 73 percent majority in the country favored United States participation in an international organization which could maintain and enforce peace. See William A. Lydgate, *What Our People Think* (New York, 1944), p. 47. Polls taken in the early months of 1945 indicated that between 80 percent and 90 percent of the American people favored United States entry into a world organization. See Divine, *Second Chance,* p. 252.

declared a few months after President Roosevelt announced that the United Nations planned to compel the "unconditional surrender" of the Axis powers, "is not the maintenance of the independence of the peoples of Continental Europe, nor the British Empire, nor even the vast significance of the mastery of Asia; it is whether freedom itself can survive in nations which cherish it more than life itself, or whether those who have never lived securely under its benign regime will impose the contagion of their slavery upon the rest of the world."[30]

He did not, however, view Germany as inherently evil. In *What Germany Forgot,* published not long after the European conflict broke out, he argued that Germany's gravest mistake was in placing all the blame for its domestic troubles on the Treaty of Versailles instead of recognizing that the First World War itself, and not the settlement, was the cause of most of its problems. Germany forgot the great cost of the war and the fact that payments for waging a modern war did not end with the cease-fire but continued long into the future. By concentrating on the treaty, the German people failed to realize that war was no longer effective as an instrument of national policy.[31]

Viewing Germany's actions after the rise of Hitler as stemming from a failure to understand the true nature of modern warfare and believing a compromise peace with Hitler both impracticable and unthinkable, Shotwell reasoned that only unconditional surrender and total defeat could persuade the German people to renounce militarism. Since they respected power and would yield only to force, their defeat had to be so decisive that they could not again plot "to overthrow the decencies of life."[32]

Actually, the Anglo-American goal of unconditional surrender stemmed not from sheer emotionalism, but rather evolved logically from the collective security framework which Shotwell and his friends had so fervently promoted during the interwar period and which the Roosevelt administration gradually accepted during the war. The

30. J.T.S., "The Constitution and the Guarantee of Freedom," *Bulletin of the College of William and Mary in Virginia* 36 (June 1942): 3.
31. J.T.S., *What Germany Forgot* (New York, 1940), pp. 1–12, 64–81.
32. J.T.S., "Security, Welfare, and Justice: The Program of the United Nations," p. 9 (Unpublished address delivered in Toledo on May 21, 1943), in Vertical File on Shotwell, Carnegie Endowment Library, New York City.

enemies of peace had to pay the full price for their aggression regardless of any balance of power considerations. Total peace depended upon total victory.[33] While hardly anyone used the old Wilsonian phrase "war to end all war," Shotwell probably voiced the hope of most Americans when he declared:

> We do not want to go through this war again nor anything like it, either in the immediate future or at any time from now on. We want to end this business once and for all, and we know that it cannot be ended so long as the warlords east and west of us are in a position to remake the machinery of war and dominate once more the minds of those who think in terms of the enslavement of others.[34]

United States policy toward Germany, although important in itself, was only part of the general question of America's place in the postwar world. Shotwell dealt with this larger problem in his second wartime book, *The Great Decision.* His central thesis was that "war under the conditions of modern science" could not "be permitted anywhere in the world without endangering the peace of nations not parties to the dispute."[35] This argument, of course, had permeated most of his earlier work, but it now seemed to carry additional weight and appeared much more convincing than it had during the interwar period. The coming of World War II did not weaken his faith in the necessity of a viable collective security system, but it did alter his conception of the consequences of such a system. On the question of peace enforcement, he no longer maintained, as he had prior to the war, that economic sanctions alone could stop aggression. History, he now argued, proved that there was "only one sanction, not two, and that if the economic sanction is used it must be imposed by nations which are ready to take the consequences of that action." The organization of peace ultimately rested on the willingness of the "peace-loving nations of the world" to back it up with sanctions of an economic, political, and even military nature if necessary.[36]

33. Stromberg, *Collective Security,* pp. 160–64.
34. J.T.S., "Security, Welfare, and Justice," p. 9.
35. J.T.S., *The Great Decision* (New York, 1944), p. 226.
36. J.T.S., "Security," in Davis, ed., *Pioneers in World Order,* p. 34.

For Shotwell, as for many American officials as well, the best hope for peace lay in the continued cooperation of the United States, Great Britain, and Russia. This hope rested upon the assumption that having joined the Allies in defeating Germany, the Soviet Union would remain friendly to the West and help police the world for peace. Although Shotwell never leaned very far to the left, neither did he greatly fear the Russians or view them as a military threat. He believed that the war had so devastated their economy that the problems of restoration and reconstruction would occupy all of their energy. "The liquidation of the war," he proclaimed, "will present as great a challenge to the Soviet Government as that which it has met by victorious conduct on the field of battle. It will call for continued cooperation by the United States and Great Britain as well as by other members of the United Nations; and, if realism continues to reign at the Kremlin, the politics of the Soviet Government will be directed by its economic needs away from an adventurous course which would lessen sympathy for it or the desire to cooperate with it on the part of the other powers." He recognized that the Grand Alliance might dissolve after the war, but felt that continued cooperation was the only realistic choice for all concerned.[37]

Shotwell, in other words, sided with that small minority of American business and government leaders who supported a rapprochement with the Soviet Union based upon economic aid and cooperation. Instead of exploiting Russia's economic weakness in order to force Stalin to acquiesce in an American dictated postwar settlement (a policy which could only heighten antagonisms), he favored some kind of agreement with the Soviet leader on the questions of security and recovery. His easy optimism and firm commitment to collective action led him to dismiss, perhaps too hastily, the possibility that Russia might not prove as willing to cooperate with the West in peace as it had in war. But his suggestion that the United States meet Stalin's request for economic assistance as part of a general postwar agreement was neither naive nor unrealistic. It was rather a serious proposal for reaching an accommodation with the Soviets along lines consistent with the idea of a continuation

37. J.T.S., *The Great Decision,* pp. 40–41.

of the Grand Alliance during the postwar period.[38]

Even such a highly placed official as Secretary of the Treasury Henry Morgenthau, Jr., recognized the great importance which Stalin placed upon recovery and reconstruction. Shortly before the Yalta meeting he wrote to the President that "if we were to come forward now and present to the Russians a concrete plan to aid them in the reconstruction period it would contribute a great deal towards ironing out many of the difficulties we have been having with respect to their problems and policies."[39] Neither Roosevelt, Hull, nor their successors, however, made any serious attempt to negotiate with the Russians along these lines. Such an attempt might not have convinced the Soviet Union to abandon its influence in Eastern Europe or to acquiesce in all other American proposals, but it might have gone a long way in removing some of the distrust and hostility that had built up over the years and might have greatly altered subsequent Russian-American relations.[40]

Shotwell did not deny that the Soviet Union presented a challenge to the West, nor that the Russians hoped for the expansion of communism, but he conceived of the challenge more in terms of economics and social welfare than in terms of an arms buildup or military strategy. He believed that the answer to communism could not be found in the "policies of hostile intrigue." The expansion of communism could be prevented not by developing a preponderance of military power, but by spreading "prosperity both within each nation and among the nations so as to make the existing order of society and the whole body of the citizens the loyal defenders of a society in the prosperity of which they all share."[41]

Although his analysis offered a significant alternative to the containment policy later adopted by the United States, Shotwell proved unable to follow it through to its logical conclusions or offer any positive means for its implementation. His continued belief in the

38. For a general discussion of the debate over American policy toward the Soviet Union see William A. Williams, *The Tragedy of American Diplomacy* (Delta rev. ed., New York, 1962), pp. 204–9.
39. Quoted in William A. Williams, *American-Russian Relations, 1781–1947* (New York, 1952), p. 274.
40. Williams, *Tragedy,* pp. 228–29.
41. J.T.S., *The Great Decision,* pp. 81–82.

necessity of economic expansion clouded his perspective and weakened his argument. His prescription remained the same: international prosperity depended upon lower tariff barriers and a universal open door policy. "Common sense," he declared, "leads to but one conclusion, namely, that to secure prosperity at home we must enlarge the market for our goods, for prosperity depends not only on our capacity for production, but also on the capacity of others as well as ourselves for consumption."[42]

He failed to resolve the fundamental contradiction between his intellectual commitment to continued economic expansion guided by the Open Door policy and his support for a concert of power to deal with the new circumstances arising out of the Second World War. He refused to admit that the type of accommodation with the Soviet Union which he proposed demanded limitations upon American expectations and actions. Continued cooperation with the Russians depended upon economic stabilization as well as military agreement. Unfortunately, any sort of arrangement along these lines would necessarily limit America's freedom of economic action and force her to alter (or even abandon) her traditional policy.[43]

Instead of facing the new reality and shifting his approach accordingly, Shotwell simply reiterated his old arguments, maintaining that all would prosper through an expansion of trade. His faith in the Open Door strategy was never more clearly revealed than on the evening of May 21, 1943, when he addressed a Toledo audience:

> Economically the world has resources sufficient to guarantee the prosperity of all mankind. But no one nation can or should have a monopoly of the great store of riches. As a matter of fact, no nation has it. All of them need to exchange the goods they have for those which others have. Moreover in the raw materials of the world we are reaching a point where even so wealthy a nation as ourselves is within sight of the end of our great era of continental exploitation. . . . Therefore Secretary Hull's policy of reciprocal trade has more far-sighted statesmanship behind it than is generally recognized for it is to open for us as far as can be done through persuasion and argument, the things that other peoples

42. Ibid., p. 153.
43. Williams, *Tragedy,* pp. 204–6; Williams, *American-Russian Relations,* pp. 269–70.

have which we will need more and more and permit us to sell to them the things we have or make which they lack. . . .This is the first economic step towards the achievement of world prosperity and it is a proud chapter of our economic history that we are still leading in the effort to secure this form of economic emancipation from the economic warfare of the past.[44]

By 1944 the question of victory or defeat had become almost academic. Barring unforeseen developments, it was only a matter of time before Allied military power would break German and Japanese resistance. With victory in sight, the question of postwar planning became all the more urgent. In June, Thomas Watson, Nicholas Murray Butler, Shotwell, and Winthrop Aldrich, chairman of the board of the Chase National Bank, established the Committee on International Economic Policy. The committee was the result of the continuing cooperation of the Carnegie Endowment and the International Chamber of Commerce. The Committee hoped "to further the serious and competent consideration of the issues which confront all the free peoples of the world and which imply their useful cooperation in reconstructing their economy after the victory of the United Nations." In an effort to clarify some of the major issues, the Committee published a series of reports on such subjects as "World Trade and Employment," "Industrial Property in Europe," "Price Control in the Postwar Period," and "A Commercial Policy for the United Nations." Both the Office of Economic Affairs and the Department of State received copies of the reports and made extensive use of them.[45]

In addition to his work as chairman of the Commission to Study the Organization of Peace and as head of the Advisory Board on Economics of the Committee on International Economic Policy, Shotwell became involved with the New York Group, a small, intimate committee also concerned with postwar planning. Composed of several individuals who had directly participated in one way or another in the League of Nations or in the conduct of American foreign

44. J.T.S., "Security, Welfare, and Justice," pp. 15–16.
45. "Committee on International Economic Policy," n.d., Box 241, J.T.S. Papers; B. F. Haley to J.T.S., November 24, 1944, Box 241, J.T.S. Papers; J.T.S. to Leslie Paffrath, January 15, 1960, Box 235, J.T.S. Papers.

policy, the New York Group devoted most of its time and energy to drafting a proposed charter for a new world organization. Besides Shotwell, the group included Eichelberger, Malcolm Davis, Frank G. Boudreau, director of the Milbank Fund in New York and Shotwell's replacement as president of the League of Nations Association, Arthur Sweetser, a member of the League Secretariat, Huntington Gilchrist, also of the League Secretariat, Manley Hudson, an American judge on the Permanent Court of International Justice, and Professors Philip Jessup of Columbia University and Quincy Wright of the University of Chicago.[46]

In May, 1944, the Group completed its "Design for a Charter" and tried to get an interview with President Roosevelt. When this failed Shotwell sent the draft to Mrs. Roosevelt hoping that she would intercede with the President on their behalf.[47] Receiving no response from the White House, Manley Hudson, who served as chairman of the Group, decided to give it to *International Conciliation* for publication. Basically, the document called for the establishment of a modified system of collective security and an international organization consisting of all nations. Recognizing the predominant interest of the major powers in questions relating to security, it proposed that they each have a permanent seat on the "Council" and a veto on all Council decisions affecting security. The only limitation was that no Council member could vote on questions dealing with its own unauthorized use of force. The members of the New York Group hoped that such a qualification would remove some of the danger of the veto impeding collective action on behalf of peace enforcement.[48]

Shotwell strongly supported the "Design" arrangement. He personally accepted the need for the unanimity rule for the great powers "with reference to police action." He wrote to Representative J. William Fulbright of Arkansas that "the great powers should have the

46. Malcolm Davis, "Reminiscences," pp. 343–48.
47. Manley Hudson to Major General E. M. Watson, May 29, 1944, #5557, Roosevelt Papers; E. M. Watson to Manley Hudson, May 31, 1944, #5557, Roosevelt Papers; J.T.S. to Mrs. Eleanor Roosevelt, June 7, 1944, #5557, Roosevelt Papers.
48. "A Design for a Charter of the General International Organization," *International Conciliation* 402 (August 1944): 527–42.

right to withhold their consent to action in the repression of violence, because there might be circumstances under which police action would seem to them more dangerous than abstension." He opposed, however, the veto by great powers in cases which involved merely the investigation of whether there was really a threat to peace or not. In such cases, he supported majority rule.[49]

There was no way to determine the effect of the "Design" upon the President or Secretary Hull. It quickly became apparent, however, that it did represent the general trend of thinking within the State Department, for it closely paralleled the "Proposals" for a United Nations Charter released on October 9 by the United States, Great Britain, Russia, and China. The Proposals, which resulted from a conference held at Dumbarton Oaks during late summer and early autumn of 1944, called for the creation of a general international organization based upon the principles of the "sovereign equality of all peace-loving states," collective security, and the renunciation of war as an instrument of national policy. The principal organs of the proposed organization were a General Assembly made up of all the members, a Security Council composed of eleven members with the United States, Russia, Great Britain, China, "and, in due course, France" having permanent seats, a Secretariat, an International Court of Justice, and an Economic and Social Council subsidiary to the General Assembly.[50]

Shortly after the release of the Dumbarton Oaks Proposals, Shotwell and Eichelberger announced the formation of the United Nations Educational Campaign, sponsored jointly by the Commission to Study the Organization of Peace and the National Association for the United Nations. Through the Campaign they hoped to win support for the Proposals and organize public opinion behind American participation in the new world organization. In addition, they hoped to publicize the need for certain additions to the structure outlined by the representatives of the Big Four. Included among these additions were the creation of a trusteeship system for dependent people, the

49. J.T.S. to J. William Fulbright, November 28, 1944, Box 230, J.T.S. Papers.
50. The Dumbarton Oaks Proposals are printed in U.S. Department of State, *Postwar Foreign Policy,* pp. 611–19.

establishment of strategic air bases for United Nations' use, and the establishment of a commission on human rights. They also hoped to gain support for a compromise on the question of the veto, incorporating the principle that no nation on the Security Council should vote on issues stemming from conflicts in which it was a party.[51]

Between October 9, 1944, when the Dumbarton Oaks Proposals were released, and April 25, 1945, when the United Nations Conference on International Organization convened at San Francisco, the State Department did all in its power to supplement the work of the Commission to Study the Organization of Peace and other private groups seeking to educate the public on America's postwar plans and preparations. Officers within the Department accepted more than 260 speaking engagements and distributed approximately 1,900,000 copies of the Proposals. Both Roosevelt and Edward R. Stettinius, Jr., who had replaced Secretary of State Hull in late November, 1944, wished to avoid Woodrow Wilson's mistakes and sought to organize beforehand as much support as possible for American participation in the new world organization.[52]

In keeping with this general policy, Roosevelt appointed a completely bipartisan delegation to the San Francisco Conference. It consisted of Secretary of State Stettinius, Cordell Hull (who was too ill to attend), the chairmen and ranking Republican members of both the Senate Committee on Foreign Relations and the House Committee on Foreign Affairs, Commander Harold E. Stassen, U.S.N.R., a former Republican governor of Minnesota, and Dean Virginia C. Gildersleeve of Barnard College. In order to gain an even broader base of public support and placate the numerous private organizations seeking to send representatives to the conference, the Secretary of State also invited forty-two national organizations to appoint "consultants" to the American delegation. These "consultants" were to have the

51. CSOP, "Press Release, November 24, 1944," VII, AA, #123901, CEIP Archives.
52. U.S. Department of State, *Report to the President on the Results of the San Francisco Conference by the Chairman of the United States Delegation, The Secretary of State* (Washington, D.C., Conference Series 71, June 26, 1945), p. 27.

dual role of reporting a firsthand account of the proceedings to their constituents and to convey both their views and the views of their organizations to the delegation.[53]

Included among the groups invited to send representatives were leading national organizations in the fields of labor, law, agriculture, business, and education, together with the principal women's associations, church groups, veterans' associations, and civic organizations. The appointed consultants formed an impressive list consisting of prominent antiwar leaders, businessmen, and educators. Included among them were Clark Eichelberger, representing the American Association for the United Nations, Hugh Moore of the Americans United for World Organization Inc., Joseph M. Proskauer of the American Jewish Committee, Harper Sibley of the Chamber of Commerce of the United States, Henry Atkinson of the Church Peace Union, Thomas K. Finletter of the Council on Foreign Relations, Walter Van Kirk of the Federal Council of Churches of Christ in America, W. E. B. Du Bois of the National Association for the Advancement of Colored People, Robert M. Gaylor of the National Association of Manufacturers, William G. Carr of the National Education Association, and Jane Evans of the National Peace Conference.[54]

At their April meeting, the Executive Committee of the Carnegie Endowment for International Peace unanimously chose Shotwell to represent them at San Francisco. It was a well-deserved tribute to his long service in the cause of peace and recognition for his active participation in the work of postwar planning. The appointment pleased him tremendously. Although probably disappointed that the government did not name him directly to the American delegation, he gratefully accepted the chance to attend the conference as a consultant. He viewed the San Francisco meeting as a second chance to inaugurate the new world order promised by Wilson. He dramatically expressed his hopes for this new era—one based on economic and social justice—in a poem published shortly before the convening of the United Nations conference:

53. Ibid., pp. 27–28, 254.
54. Ibid., pp. 262–66.

Behind us, blood and sweat and tears,
Before us, like a veil withdrawn,
Light strikes the pathway of the years,
Is it the dawn?

In the distant lands the battle rages,
Will this bleak horror never cease?
Can we, who fought through all the ages,
Make lasting Peace?

A million years they fought and slew
With ruthless tooth and dripping claw,
In brutal hordes who only knew
The jungle law.

Now, lords of earth, as we aspire
To meet the sun at heaven's gate,
Is dust of Nineveh and Tyre
Our only fate?

Blind not the mind with ancient fears,
Time turns the glass; the sands have run,
Dawn on another million years
Has just begun.[55]

Whether intended or not the consultants became an active and influential part of the American delegation and succeeded in getting several of their proposals incorporated into the Charter. Stettinius, as well as the other delegates, kept them informed of the private meetings held between the various delegations and sounded them out on the different aspects of the new international organization. At their first official meeting the consultants appointed Shotwell as their chairman and agreed to hold periodic meetings to exchange views among themselves. With all the major delegations committed to collective security, Shotwell took the lead in emphasizing the need to strengthen the nonpolitical aspects of the proposed United Nations Organization. Most of his colleagues supported his efforts, and it was in this area that they devoted most of their attention and achieved most of their success.[56]

55. J.T.S., "Is it the Dawn?", *Think* (April 1945), p. 18.
56. "Notes on Plans and Program for the Consultant Organization at San Francisco," n.d., III, #61218, CEIP Archives; CEIP, *Year Book,* 1946, p. 105.

Shotwell and Eichelberger succeeded in getting both the consultants and the American delegation to back the proposals put forward by the Commission to Study the Organization of Peace on the question of human rights. These proposals, almost word for word, were adopted by the Conference and incorporated into the Charter. Most important were the additions to Articles 1 and 63. The former proclaimed as one of the major purposes of the United Nations the cultivation of "respect for human rights and for fundamental freedoms for all without distinction as to race, sex, language, or religion." The latter specifically called upon the Economic and Social Council to set up a commission on human rights. So great was the contribution of the consultants in getting these provisions adopted that Secretary of State Stettinius felt obliged to give them special credit in his report to the President.[57]

Under Shotwell's guidance the consultants also drafted several proposals for strengthening and broadening the scope of the Economic and Social Council. They succeeded in putting the fields of education and cultural cooperation within its domain and were primarily responsible for Article 71 of the Charter which provided for consultation between the Council and nongovernmental organizations concerned with economic and social welfare. In addition, Eichelberger and Shotwell met several times with Harold Stassen and argued successfully that strategic bases and nonstrategic trust territories should be handled separately and by different branches of the United Nations.[58] The success of the consultants in getting these various proposals included into the Charter marked one of the first occasions in history when an unofficial group at the scene of an international

57. U.S. Department of State, *Report to the President,* p. 114; Clark Eichelberger to Members of the Commission and Special Sub-committee on Human Rights," May 5, 1945, VII, AA, #123998, CEIP Archives; "Consultants" to Edward R. Stettinius, Jr., May 2, 1945, III, #61325, CEIP Archives; "Comparison of What Was Asked For and What Was Gained," pp. 1–2, in III, #61216, CEIP Archives.

58. U.S. Department of State, *Report to the President,* p. 120; Clark M. Eichelberger to "Chapters and Cooperating Groups of the Association and the Commission," June 11, 1945, VII, AA, #124004, CEIP Archives; "Comparison of What Was Asked For and What Was Gained," pp. 3–5, III, #61216, CEIP Archives; "Consultants" to E. R. Stettinius, n.d., III, #61317, CEIP Archives.

conference had significantly influenced the drafting of a treaty.[59]

Shotwell's leadership proved vital in many ways. Having served on the State Department's Advisory Committee on Post-War Foreign Policy, he knew personally many of the technical and political advisers to the American delegation and was able to gain a fair hearing for the consultants' point of view. He not only provided the consultants with direction and guidance, but also helped to mold their diverse suggestions into practical propositions. Allen D. Albert, a former president of Rotary International and a representative of that group at San Francisco, believed that Shotwell was the most important nonofficial member of the American delegation and furnished the consultants with leadership that was "inspiring, terse, [and] level headed."[60] Jane Evans of the National Peace Conference went even further in her praise and probably spoke for most of the group when she wrote that "Dr. Shotwell" was for all of them "a distinguished, gifted, beloved 'Elder Statesman' in the finest sense of that Japanese-abused term."[61]

59. James Frederick Green, *The United Nations and Human Rights* (Washington, D.C., 1958), p. 656, n16.
60. Allen D. Albert, "A Consultant at the Conference," *The Rotarian* 67 (August 1945): 13.
61. Jane Evans to J.T.S., May 25, 1945, III, #61020, CEIP Archives.

With portrait presented to the Carnegie International Center, 1956.
Courtesy the Carnegie Endowment for International Peace

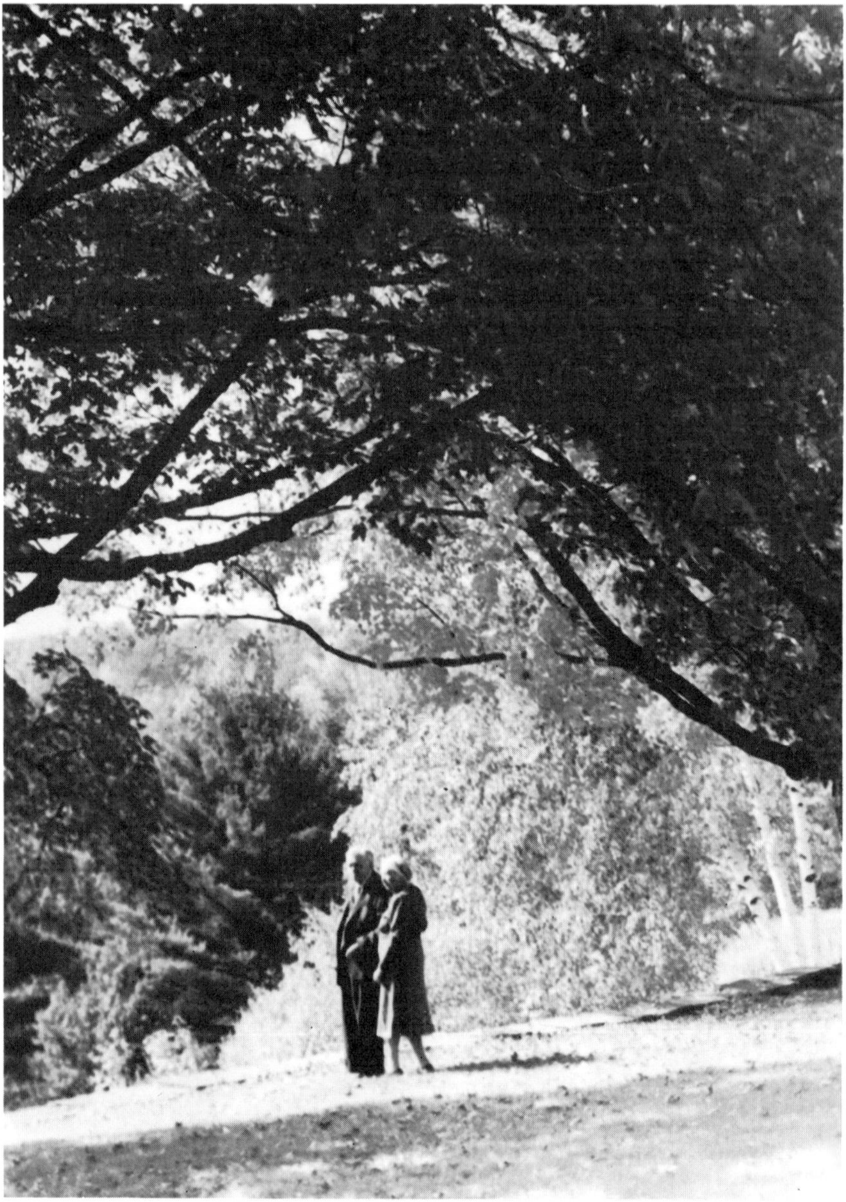

With Margaret at Woodstock, 1964.

14
World Peace or World Destruction?

Harry S. Truman received the news in the mid-Atlantic while returning from the Potsdam Conference on board the U.S.S. *Augusta.* His first remark to those crewmen around him was that "This is the greatest thing in history." His message to the nation made the evening newspapers. "Sixteen hours ago," he began, "an American airplane dropped one bomb on Hiroshima, an important Japanese Army base. That bomb had more power than 20,000 tons of T.N.T. It had more than two thousand times the blast power of the British 'Grand Slam' which is the largest bomb ever used in the history of warfare. . . . It is an atomic bomb. It is the harnessing of the basic power of the universe. The force from which the sun draws its power has been loosed against those who brought war to the Far East."[1]

Had he more information at the time, President Truman might have related to Americans that at exactly 8:15 A.M. on August 6, 1945,

1. U.S. Department of State, *The International Control of Atomic Energy: Growth of a Policy* (Washington, D.C., 1946), p. 95; Harry S. Truman, *Year of Decisions,* Vol. I: *Memoirs* (Garden City, N. Y., 1955), pp. 421–22.

a fireball one and one half miles in diameter had engulfed the city of Hiroshima, killing or injuring over 129,000 people and physically destroying approximately sixty percent of the city.[2] Three days later, about twenty-four hours after Stalin had declared war on Japan, American fliers dropped a second bomb, this time on the city of Nagasaki, with similar results. On August 14, the Japanese government accepted Allied terms, terms which were slightly short of unconditional surrender. The formal surrender ceremony took place on September 2, in Tokyo Bay on the battleship *Missouri.* World War II had come to an end.

The explosions over Hiroshima and Nagasaki ushered in the Atomic Age, and with it a host of problems both foreign and domestic. Despite America's monopoly in atomic power, the largest navy and air force in the world, and an economy second to none, Washington could not maintain harmonious relations between the victorious nations. Very quickly Truman and Secretary of State James F. Byrnes, who had replaced Stettinius in July, became suspicious of Soviet designs in both Central and Eastern Europe and the Middle East, and began to doubt the possibility of a continuation of the Grand Alliance. Stalin was similarly distrustful of the United States, with its global ring of strategic bases, its control of atomic power, and the increasingly hard line adopted by Washington. Stalin had cooperated with Roosevelt, but he had never overcome his suspicion that the United States was an antagonistic power. Truman's willingness to drop two atomic bombs on Japan, his abrubt end to lend-lease shipments, and his hard diplomatic stance played upon Stalin's fears that America not only had the potential, but the desire, to destroy his regime.

During the months following Japan's surrender important political negotiations between the United States and the Soviet Union took place on Germany, Central and Eastern Europe, Iran, and Asia. Equally important was the question of what the United States intended to do with her atomic secrets. The question, in fact, became a crucial factor in the general worsening of Soviet-American relations, for the Russians were becoming increasingly skeptical of America's

2. Joseph L. Nogee, *Soviet Policy Towards International Control of Atomic Energy* (Notre Dame, Indiana, 1961), p. 3.

atomic monopoly.[3] Truman talked abstractly of the future international control of atomic energy, but always followed these statements with a declaration that the United States had no intention of sharing its technical knowledge of the bomb's manufacture with anyone. The President, with the agreement of Clement Attlee of Great Britain and Prime Minister Mackenzie King of Canada, advocated the creation of a United Nations Commission to study the atomic problem and make suggestions as to how international safeguards against nuclear war might be devised. This, of course, meant that for the immediate future atomic secrets would remain in the hands of the western nations.[4] At Truman's request the Senate promptly established a special committee, chaired by Brien McMahon of Connecticut, to draw up a program for the domestic development and use of the new source of power.[5] The United Nations also responded by creating a special commission to study the international implications of atomic energy and to work out an international control agreement.[6]

In order to prepare for the United Nations meeting and to frame a coherent proposal, Secretary of State Byrnes established a blue-ribbon panel of political, military, and scientific advisers. He asked Under Secretary of State Dean Acheson to head the committee which also included John J. McCloy, a former Assistant Secretary of War, and the three men who supervised and directed America's atomic energy project, Dr. Vannevar Bush, Dr. James B. Conant, and General Leslie R. Groves. They, in turn, appointed a board of consultants to draw up a report "analyzing and appraising all the relevant facts and formulating proposals." David E. Lilienthal, head of the Tennessee Valley Authority, took charge of the consulting board. Believing

3. George Curry, *James F. Byrnes 1945–1947,* vol. 13 of *The American Secretaries of State and their Diplomacy,* ed. Robert H. Ferrell (New York, 1965), p. 159.
4. Ibid., pp. 159–60.
5. U.S. Department of State, *International Control,* pp. 17–21, 97, 109–12. The McMahon Committee held hearings throughout the winter and spring of 1945–1946 and in June submitted a bill to Congress. The bill, signed into law on August 1, 1946, vested all policy decisions relating to nuclear power in the hands of a civilian controlled Atomic Energy Commission.
6. "Resolution of the General Assembly of the United Nations," June 24, 1946, *International Conciliation* 423 (September 1946): 333–34.

that no systematic analysis or report could be made until the consultants had a functional understanding of what was involved in producing atomic energy, he and his committee spent the next several weeks inspecting various research and development laboratories in the United States.[7]

James Thomson Shotwell knew nothing of the American plan to develop an atomic bomb. Nor was he among the privileged few to travel to New Mexico on that day in July to witness the first great atomic explosion. The words "Los Alamos," "Manhattan Project," "Oak Ridge," "fission," and "reactor" had meant little to him until President Truman made his dramatic announcement on August 6, 1945, the very day he celebrated his seventy-first birthday. Yet the news neither surprised nor shocked him. For years he had predicted that science and not the military would determine the nature and scope of future wars. The development of atomic energy served only to strengthen his thesis and gave his arguments renewed vitality. Now more than ever intelligence had to be mobilized. Physical, social, and political scientists had to work together to control and direct the uses of atomic energy. Only if civilization could harness science and use it for peaceful purposes could it avoid devastation and chaos.[8]

Resting only briefly after the campaign for Senate ratification of the United Nations Charter, Shotwell jumped into the public debate over the control of atomic energy. In order to gain more knowledge of the subject, he convinced the Commission to Study the Organization of Peace to establish a subcommittee on atomic energy with himself as chairman. On September 15, 1945, more than a month before the Senate set up the McMahon committee, he presented a preliminary set of proposals for consideration. Emphasizing the United Nations as the only institution capable of effectively controlling the new force, he urged the immediate establishment of a special technical agency to advise the Security Council on both immediate measures and future policies. He further suggested that any adequate system of safeguards

7. David E. Lilienthal, *The Atomic Energy Years, 1945–1950,* vol. 2: *The Journals of David E. Lilienthal* (New York, 1964), pp. 10–26; U.S. Department of State, *International Control,* p. 34.
8. J.T.S., "Our Endless Frontier," *Survey Graphic* 34 (November 1945): 429–30.

must incorporate inspection and reprisals so that no nation could resort to war or the use of atomic weapons with impunity.[9]

What type of reprisals the Security Council might take he did not explain. Presumably it would have its own atomic force to stop aggression.[10] Such a thought, however, must have bothered even the most avid supporters of collective security. Nor did Shotwell make clear just how an effective inspection program would work. Despite the many unanswered questions, his proposals became the basis for the Commission's first public statement on the control of atomic energy. Receiving the support of several leading scientists who had taken part in the development of the bomb, the statement pointed to the United Nations as the appropriate authority for the international control of atomic energy, called upon the General Assembly to set up a committee to study the political, social, and economic implications of the atom, and proposed that the American government take the lead in restoring unity among the major powers.[11]

This last point had become a major concern to most supporters of the United Nations as the Second World War drew to a close. The hope for American-Russian cooperation seemed to fade in the aftermath of the Potsdam Conference. The Russian army controlled all of Eastern Europe and Stalin showed little inclination to pull back. It slowly became clear that Western conceptions of security and democracy differed significantly from those held by the Soviet leaders. Although Shotwell lost some of his optimism, he remained firm in his belief that the only hope for peace rested in reaching some sort of political agreement with Russia. If accommodation failed, he saw no alternative but "the division of the world into two great spheres of

9. CEIP, *Year Book,* 1946, p. 114; J.T.S., "Preliminary Suggestions for the Study of the International Control of Atomic Energy," September 15, 1945, III, #61386–61387, CEIP Archives.
10. In a revised draft of the "Preliminary Suggestions," completed on October 6, 1945, he made it explicit that he favored giving atomic weapons to an international air force as a deterrent to aggression. See CEIP Archives, VIII, P, #116478. That same month he published an article in *Survey Graphic* declaring that by giving an international air force "control of all bombs" it could "dominate the world of peace." See J.T.S., "Control of Atomic Energy," *Survey Graphic* 34 (October 1945): 407–8, 417.
11. CSOP, "Press Release, October 29, 1945," VII, AA, #124085, CEIP Archives.

influence each of which would be armed with weapons that could destroy the other, leaving nothing at all for either."[12]

Others in the academic and scientific communities shared Shotwell's interest in the control and future use of atomic energy. Political and social scientists throughout the nation expressed uncertainty and fear about the implications of scientific development. Leading nuclear physicists shared this concern and revealed far more social consciousness than had been customary among physical scientists previously. Albert Einstein and J. Robert Oppenheimer warned against minimizing the dangers of atomic energy and came out strongly for international controls as the only practical solution. Scientific organizations took a strong interest in the Senate hearings and helped organize a national education campaign carried on by the National Committee on Atomic Information. In addition, such organizations as the Social Science Research Council, the Council on Foreign Relations, the Foreign Policy Association, and the Institute of International Studies worked on various aspects of the atomic energy question.[13]

With so much attention focused on the question it was not surprising that Shotwell turned to the Carnegie Endowment for aid in setting up a high-level committee to make an intensive study of the problem. The Endowment Trustees appointed a committee made up of some forty physical scientists, industrial engineers, and political scientists, and appropriated a substantial sum to carry out the work. They named Shotwell as chairman and instructed the committee "to ascertain and report facts so that the process of development in atomic energy might proceed without danger of its misuse." In addition to Shotwell's usual team of Clark Eichelberger, Joseph P. Chamberlain, Raymond B. Fosdick, Manley O. Hudson, and Thomas Watson, other members of the committee included Joseph W. Barker, Dean of the Faculty of Engineering at Columbia, Everett Case, President of

12. J.T.S., "Implementing and Amending the Charter: An Address . . ., November 1, 1945," *International Conciliation* 416 (December 1945): 820–21.

13. Wittner, *Rebels Against War,* pp. 165–66; Merle Curti, *The Growth of American Thought,* 3rd ed., (New York, 1964), pp. 746–47; "The United Nations Atomic Energy Commission: Introduction," *International Conciliation* 423 (September 1946): 327–29.

Colgate University, Karl T. Compton, President of M.I.T., John Foster Dulles, Huntington Gilchrist of the American Cyanamid Company, Reuben G. Gustavson, Vice-President and Dean of Faculties at the University of Chicago as well as President of the Institute of Nuclear Research at Chicago, David Sarnoff, President of RCA, Paul F. Kerr, President of the Mineralogical Society of America, and Warren C. Johnson, Chairman of the Department of Chemistry at the University of Chicago.[14]

Although originally planned as a discussion group, the committee quickly turned to the work of coordinating and reviewing reports of specialists in various fields. In February, 1946, it released its first and perhaps most important report. Prepared by a technical subcommittee headed by Paul F. Kerr, the report dealt with the international inspection of radioactive mineral production. Besides surveying the possibilities of inspection, it outlined the type of authority needed to maintain adequate safeguards, listed the locations of important resources for the production of atomic weapons, and discussed the problems of camouflage and detection.[15]

The committee concluded that the technical control of raw materials was sufficiently feasible to justify a serious attempt at establishing a control system based upon inspection of known sources of raw materials and a detection program for new discoveries. It warned that such a system contained flaws, that economic and political devices would have to accompany technical ones for an effective inspection system to operate. But given these limitations, Kerr and his associates firmly believed that "a competent technical organization could establish a highly efficient world-wide raw-materials inspection for uranium and thorium" with modest facilities and a relatively small number of personnel.[16]

The report strengthened Shotwell's argument that the United Nations remained a viable institution for the preservation of peace. He

14. CEIP, *Year Book,* 1946, pp. 139–40; Finch, "History of the Carnegie Endowment," p. 251.
15. Committee on Atomic Energy of the CEIP, *A Conference Report on the International Inspection of Radioactive Mineral Production* (New York, 1946), pp. 1–14.
16. Ibid., p. 15.

used it to prove that an effective control system, directed by the United Nations and incorporating inspection backed by a firm policy of enforcement, was indeed possible.[17] Unfortunately, those responsible for making government policy in 1946 had neither Shotwell's faith in inspection nor his commitment to collective security. Having carefully studied and analyzed the problems involved in the control of atomic energy, they struck out upon an entirely new path. The results of their work were incorporated into "A Report on the International Control of Atomic Energy," drawn up by David Lilienthal and his Board of Consultants under the close supervision of Dean Acheson's State Department committee. On March 17, they transmitted their report to Secretary of State Byrnes, who released it to the press eleven days later.[18]

Shotwell's initial reaction to the Acheson-Lilienthal Report was one of surprise and dismay, for it completely rejected the major conclusions reached by his own committee. It stated that inspection and sanctions were insufficient safeguards for an international control system. It implied, moreover, that the Carnegie Endowment report had greatly underestimated the number of men needed for an adequate inspection system and had avoided the very serious social implications of such a plan. Instead of inspection and sanctions, international ownership of raw materials and managerial control of processing plants formed the basis of the State Department scheme. The report proposed the creation of an Atomic Development Authority which would have absolute control of all "dangerous" activities in the atomic energy field and would closely supervise through licensing and inspection all "non-dangerous" activities. In order to protect American security and minimize the danger of the premature release of atomic information, the report outlined a transitional period in which the United States would gradually turn over its secrets, atomic weapons, and processing plants to the Atomic Development Authority as the international controls tightened.[19]

17. J.T.S., "The International Implications of Nuclear Energy," *American Journal of Physics* 14 (May-June 1946): 179.
18. U.S. Department of State, *A Report on the International Control of Atomic Energy* (Washington, D.C., March 16, 1946), pp. vii–x.
19. Ibid., pp. 4–61.

Theoretically the State Department's report provided a much greater degree of security against the misuse of atomic power than the inspection scheme outlined in the Carnegie Endowment statement. But it too contained serious political liabilities. How, for instance, could the Soviet Union be induced to turn over its control of atomic energy to an international authority dominated by hostile states? Already suspicious of America's intentions, Russia could only view the proposal as an indirect attempt by the capitalistic states to gain control of its atomic energy plants under the guise of military security, but with the real aim of eliminating competition and checking Soviet economic growth.

But even if Russia accepted the proposal, the possibilities of Senate ratification were at best doubtful. Jealous of America's technological superiority and fearful of releasing atomic energy "secrets," many Senators saw no reason for the United States to turn over its bombs, processing plants, or knowledge to an international agency. Americans, as they assumed everyone knew, wanted peace and would never start a war. Why entrust such potentially dangerous knowledge to others who might not prove as peace-loving? Scientific data and methods might not remain America's monopoly forever, but through a nationally controlled development program as outlined in the McMahon bill, the United States might maintain enough technical superiority to make it senseless and futile for any other nation to contemplate the use of atomic weapons.

Fully aware of these political liabilities and firmly committed to the feasibility of inspection, Shotwell accepted at face value the statement made in the Acheson-Lilienthal Report that it offered not a final plan, but "a place to begin, a foundation on which to build."[20] Since the report only suggested an approach and did not represent firm administration policy, Shotwell felt no compunction about attacking it and continuing his committee's work. He agreed with Lilienthal that inspection had its limitations, but rejected the conclusion that international ownership of raw materials and managerial control of processing plants held the answer. A control system built around inspection might not prove one hundred percent perfect, but it could be made

20. Ibid., p. xii.

effective "up to the point of indicating that something seems to be wrong, or at least not normal, in either the scientific activities or the industrial activities of a nation." This was all the United Nations needed to know in order "to take over the problem and deal with it by international action on a political plane." In short, Shotwell reaffirmed the idea that international inspection was a "technical possibility" and an "effective guide to political action."[21]

Following his usual pattern, Shotwell became so entrenched in his role as advocate that he failed to analyze his own proposal with anything like the care and perception he reserved for suggestions with which he disagreed. He continued to speak in terms of sanctions and enforcement, but never made clear what type of action an international organization could take against a nation which only *seemed* to be violating the atomic energy control agreement. He failed to admit that the precedent of applying sanctions or taking direct action on the mere suspicion of wrong doing (the logical implication of his proposal) might endanger innocent nations at the same time that it deterred those contemplating aggression.

In mid-March, shortly before the State Department released the Acheson-Lilienthal Report, another figure entered the debate. Although Truman's appointment of Bernard M. Baruch as the United States representative to the United Nations Atomic Energy Commission won a good deal of public support, it greatly disturbed those already working on the problem. Lilienthal, perhaps a bit resentful that Truman had overlooked him for the post, became extremely depressed when he heard of the appointment. "When I read the news last night," he wrote in his diary, "I was quite sick. We need a man who is young, vigorous, not vain, and whom the Russians would feel isn't out simply to put them in a hole, not really caring about international cooperation. Baruch has none of these qualifications."[22]

Lilienthal took an even dimmer view of Baruch once they began discussing the atomic energy question. The "old man," as he usually referred to him, lacked scientific qualifications, was too proud, too

21. J.T.S., "Can We Put Brakes on the Atom?" *Survey Graphic* 35 (April 1946): 124–25, 137. See also J.T.S., "Enter an Atomic Authority," *Survey Graphic* 35 (May 1946): 158, 181–82.
22. Lilienthal, *Atomic Energy Years,* p. 40.

stubborn, and worst of all refused to accept completely the Acheson-Lilienthal approach. Baruch's objections to the report paralleled Shotwell's in some respects but diverged in others. His commitment to private enterprise led him to question the idea of international ownership of raw materials. While he agreed with the consultants that inspection would not suffice and that some form of managerial control was essential, he believed that Acheson and Lilienthal had placed too little emphasis on sanctions and enforcement. In line with this approach, he argued that the Security Council veto should not apply to questions concerning violations of an international control agreement. Abandonment of the veto and enforcement eventually became the central theme of his program, thus marking a major shift away from the Acheson-Lilienthal approach.[23]

While Baruch and his staff began to formulate a program to present to the United Nations, the Atomic Energy Committee of the Carnegie Endowment began drafting its own international convention for control of the new force. Despite the release of the Acheson-Lilienthal report and the announcement of the Baruch appointment, a legal subcommittee headed by George Finch, Director of the Endowment's Division of International Law, continued to work on a draft treaty based upon the feasibility of international inspection. They hoped that such a detailed treaty would clarify the major issues in the debate and add a new dimension to the discussion. By early May the committee had completed its treaty. It, too, differed sharply with the Acheson-Lilienthal Report. It failed to provide for the international ownership of uranium and made no provisions for the managerial control of all major processing plants. Instead it left ownership and operation in the hands of national commissions in each country. These commissions, however, would operate under the supervision of an international agency responsible for controlling and developing atomic energy. A further provision empowered the international commission to accept ownership of raw materials and plants in the event that a particular nation wished to turn them over.

23. Ibid., pp. 51, 58–61; Bernard M. Baruch, *The Public Years* (New York, 1960), pp. 366–68; Margaret L. Coit, *Mr. Baruch* (New York, 1957), pp. 565–70.

The plan did not raise the vexatious question of the veto. It empowered the international commission, in its routine activities, to take all necessary peacetime preventive measures against any nation planning war. If a nation actually resorted to an atomic attack, the police measures of the Security Council would come into force. In addition, all parties to the agreement obligated themselves to invoke Article 51 of the United Nations Charter and retaliate "immediately and with all the means at their disposal" against the aggressor state. In other words, if the Security Council failed to act because of the veto, the collective defense provisions of Article 51 would allow individual members of the world organization to take action together.[24]

Even before the legal subcommittee had completed its work, a debate arose over both the inherent value of the proposed treaty and the wisdom of releasing it in the light of the wide support for the Acheson-Lilienthal Report. President James B. Conant of Harvard attended several meetings and strongly urged that the Endowment back the idea of international ownership as the basis for a control agreement.[25] Quincy Wright, who had drawn up his own draft convention for the Atomic Scientists of Chicago,[26] also took a strong stand against the Endowment's emphasis on inspection. He argued that as long as the international authority did not own or operate the big manufacturing establishments, effective inspection would prove extremely difficult if not impossible. Any country having complete control of the atomic operation within its territories would have an excellent opportunity to evade inspection if it so desired.[27]

Eugene Staley, of the Exploratory Committee for an Inter-Organization Council on World Affairs, also criticized the Carnegie Endowment draft convention for its lack of adequate safeguards. "The thing that bothers me," he wrote to Shotwell, "is that I cannot see how the people of peacefully-inclined nations could get a real sense of security

24. Committee on Atomic Energy of the CEIP, *Utilization and Control of Atomic Energy* (New York, 1946), p. 19.
25. Lilienthal, *Atomic Energy Years,* p. 40.
26. "Draft for a Convention on the Development and Control of Atomic Energy by the University of Chicago Committee," *International Conciliation* 423 (September 1946): 397–407.
27. Committee on Atomic Energy of the CEIP, "Minutes of May 11, 1946," pp. 1–2, VII, P, #115319, CEIP Archives.

from a plan that depends on national control of atomic energy supervised and policed by international sanctions." He pointed out that a government acting in bad faith could disarm the rest of the world by pretending to go along with the plan yet surreptitiously building up a ready supply of atomic weapons. Even if this did not actually happen, the fear of such a development, well-founded or not, might induce violations and surprise attacks.[28]

Despite the many criticisms, Shotwell, with the help of Manley Hudson, Bemis Professor of International Law at Harvard University, and George Finch, director of the Division of International Law of the Carnegie Endowment, convinced a majority on the committee to prepare the draft for publication. He argued that the proposed treaty would add greatly to the public discussion by revealing that a substitute solution was both possible and necessary.[29] Before taking any action, however, he decided to send copies of the completed draft to interested government officials. He sent one to Senator Brien McMahon, who strongly favored the idea of national ownership with international supervision and had several times expressed his approval of the Endowment's work.[30] In addition, he sent copies to Acheson, Lilienthal, and Baruch, hoping to convince them of the political infeasibility of international ownership.[31] Neither Acheson nor Lilienthal found the treaty acceptable, and each in separate letters informed Shotwell that they believed his plan differed from their own "in points which are fundamental and essential." Although they admitted that the treaty deserved "the most open-minded and serious consideration," they suggested that if Shotwell decided to publish it he make the difference between the two documents clear and explicit.[32]

28. Eugene Staley to J.T.S., August 27, 1946, VII, P, #116461, CEIP Archives.
29. Committee on Atomic Energy of the CEIP, "Minutes of May 11, 1946," pp. 2–6, VII, P, #116461, CEIP Archives.
30. Senator Brien McMahon to J.T.S., April 25, 1946, VII, P, #116290, CEIP Archives; J.T.S. to Senator Brien McMahon, May 20, 1946, VII, P, #116291, CEIP Archives.
31. J.T.S. to Dean Acheson, May 16, 1946, VII, P, #116512, CEIP Archives; J.T.S. to David Lilienthal, May 23, 1946, VII, P, #116507, CEIP Archives.
32. Dean Acheson to J.T.S., n.d., VII, P, #116513, CEIP Archives; David Lilienthal to J.T.S., VII, P, #116508, CEIP Archives.

Early in June, several days before Baruch's scheduled address to the United Nations Atomic Energy Commission, the Carnegie Endowment's "Draft Convention" appeared in print. In answer to the many criticisms he recieved for his timing, Shotwell declared that the true responsibility rested with Baruch and to a lesser degree with Acheson, for they had both advised him to release the document.[33] To President Everett Case of Colgate University, who had complained that the draft would confuse public opinion and further lessen the already slim chance that Russia would give the American plan a real hearing, he stated quite bluntly that Baruch "insisted that it be published."[34]

It is possible that Shotwell misunderstood Baruch, who by June had become definitely committed to the Lilienthal approach of internationalizing both raw materials and processing plants. But it is more likely that Baruch did, in fact, make the suggestion.[35] His reason for proposing publication can only be surmised, but it is possible that he believed that it would give him a freer hand in carrying on negotiations with the Russians. Despite his acceptance of most of the Acheson-Lilienthal plan, Baruch brooded constantly over the fact that the report tied his hands and made him simply a "messenger boy."[36] He might have believed that publication of an alternative plan, especially one that contradicted the State Department report, would elevate his position and provide him with more freedom to formulate policy. In his letter to Everett Case, Shotwell stated that it was Acheson who suggested that publication of the draft treaty would give Baruch more freedom, but it seems more likely that the idea came from either Baruch himself or from one of his close associates.

33. J.T.S. to Maurice S. Sherman, June 13, 1946, VII, P, #116400, CEIP Archives; J.T.S. to the Trustees of the CEIP And Members of the Committee on Atomic Energy, June 17, 1946, VII, P, #115579, CEIP Archives.
34. Everett Case to J.T.S., June 25, 1946, VII, P, #115890, CEIP Archives; J.T.S. to Everett Case, June 27, 1946, VII, P, #115891, CEIP Archives.
35. Shotwell informed the Endowment Trustees that Baruch asked for one hundred copies of the first printing to distribute among the United Nations representatives and key personnel on the Atomic Energy Commission. See J.T.S. to Trustees of the CEIP and Members of the Committee on Atomic Energy, June 17, 1946, VII, P, #115579, CEIP Archives.
36. Harry S. Truman, *Years of Trial and Hope,* Vol. II: *Memoirs* (Garden City, N. Y., 1956), pp. 7–11; Baruch, *The Public Years,* pp. 361–65; Lilienthal, *Atomic Energy Years,* pp. 31–32, 44, 47.

When Baruch rose on the afternoon of June 14 to present the American plan to the United Nations Atomic Energy Commission, few people besides his personal staff and the President knew exactly what he was going to say. Even David Lilienthal, who had worked on the speech, sat anxiously in front of his radio with paper and pencil in hand to see how closely the Baruch Plan would follow his own.[37]

"My fellow citizens of the world," began America's elder statesman and park bench philosopher. "We are here to make a choice between the quick and the dead. That is our business. . . . Let us not deceive ourselves: We must elect World Peace or World Destruction."

Having set the stage, he presented a program very similar to the one outlined in the Acheson-Lilienthal Report. He proposed the creation of an International Development Authority entrusted with all phases of development and use of atomic energy, starting with raw materials and including the "managerial control or ownership of all atomic energy activities potentially dangerous to world security." The United States, he assured the Commission, was ready to set up safeguards and create an international law "with teeth in it." As soon as controls and punishments were agreed upon, the American government would end all production of bombs and begin transmitting to the international authority information necessary for the manufacture of atomic weapons. Baruch stated outright, however, that the United States would insist upon specific penalties for any illegal possession or use of atomic weapons, for illegal possession or separation of materials for use in a bomb, for seizure of any plant or property under the control of the international authority, for any willful interference with activities of the authority, and for the creation or operation of any dangerous projects, without the permission of the authority.

The Baruch plan deviated from the Acheson-Lilienthal scheme only in its strong emphasis on enforcement, punishment, and inspection. Baruch felt that punishment lay at the "very heart" of the security system and should not be hampered by any veto power. On questions involving the misuse of atomic energy the Charter had to undergo revision. "There must be no veto to protect those who violate their solemn agreements not to develop or use atomic energy for

37. Lilienthal, *Atomic Energy Years,* pp. 56–60.

destructive purposes," he told the Atomic Energy Commission. On this point he was adamant and unflinching: "The bomb does not wait upon debate. To delay may be to die."[38]

Reaction to the Baruch Plan in the United States was mixed. Newspapers and the public in general praised it highly. But strong criticism accompanied the praise. Lilienthal and his colleagues were pleased that Baruch had incorporated so much of their report, but they were also disappointed that he had made so much of sanctions, punishments, abandonment of the veto, and the outlawry of atomic weapons. Success depended upon winning over the Russians and this required a stronger emphasis on the constructive aspects of the plan. Questions involving enforcement, punishment, and the veto, they believed, could await further developments.[39] At least thirty Senators, moreover, reacted just as Shotwell had predicted and went on record as opposing the plan as neither tenable nor backed by public opinion.[40]

Five days after Baruch's address, Andrei Gromyko presented the Soviet position to the Atomic Energy Commission and sharply drew the lines of debate. Making no direct reference to the Baruch Plan, he called for the outlawing of atomic weapons, the destruction of those in existence, the exchange of atomic information, and the creation of a committee to study methods for supervision and enforcement of these covenants. His order of procedure completely reversed the one outlined by the American representative. Disarmament and exchange of information, according to Gromyko, had to precede the development of a control system. Although he did not come out directly against inspection (something he would do in later statements), he did not seem to favor the idea. He denounced, moreover, any attempt to abandon the veto and advised all members of the United Nations to resist efforts in this direction. Instead of relying upon an international commission to punish violations of arms control agreements, he suggested that each nation undertake to punish its own violators.[41]

The Russian proposal rested upon very sound power considerations

38. For the full text of Baruch's address see U.S. Department of State, *International Control of Atomic Energy,* pp. 138–47.
39. Lilienthal, *Atomic Energy Years,* p. 61.
40. Coit, *Mr. Baruch,* p. 586.
41. For the text of Gromyko's address see *International Conciliation* 423 (September 1946): pp. 367–76.

and not upon any desire to enter into an atomic armament race with the United States. The Baruch Plan would have allowed the United States to maintain its bombs and plants for an indefinite period—virtually as long as the American government felt it was necessary. At the same time it would have required the Soviet Union to turn over to an international commission its uranium and its chance to develop atomic energy for its own purposes. Under such circumstances the United States would have maintained not only a monopoly on atomic weapons, but also an important advantage in the development of atomic energy for industrial production. Moreover, Baruch's insistence on the abandonment of the veto would have allowed the Western powers to control the Security Council on all questions concerning atomic energy. It was not the type of plan designed to relieve Soviet suspicions.[42]

With the Atomic Energy Commission thus divided there seemed little hope for success. Ten of the twelve representatives gave their support to the Baruch Plan, but Russia and Poland consistently objected to its various parts. Publication of the Carnegie Endowment draft treaty had little effect on the discussion, although it did win some newspaper support as a possible compromise solution.[43] As soon as the United Nations negotiations began, Shotwell suspended all meetings of his committee. He believed that it would be unfitting and confusing for an unofficial body to continue formulating plans for atomic control in opposition to the avowed government approach. Although he believed that the Baruch Plan contained "many strange contradictions and inadequacies," he resolved not to push the Endowment plan too strongly. He neither wished to make things too difficult for Baruch by creating a controversy nor divide and confuse American public opinion.[44]

Despite his refusal to publicly criticize the Baruch scheme, he strongly condemned it in his personal correspondence. He viewed the introduction of the veto question as "a major diplomatic blunder."[45] Through Article 51 of the United Nations Charter each nation could

42. Lilienthal, *Atomic Energy Years,* p. 70.
43. Peter Kihss, "Carnegie Plan for Atomic Control," *New York Herald Tribune,* August 5, 1946.
44. J.T.S. to Douglas S. Freeman, June 18, 1946, VII, P, #116079B, CEIP Archives.
45. J.T.S. to Edward L. Ryerson, June 28, 1946, VII, P, #116352, CEIP Archives.

retaliate against violators of the peace. By incorporating this indirect approach the vexatious question of amending the Charter could be avoided and Soviet suspicions could be reduced. On this point he viewed the Carnegie Endowment plan as far superior to the Baruch scheme.[46]

The duality of Shotwell's position in regard to the Baruch Plan—his refusal to criticize it in public and his very strong personal and private comments—reflected the basic dilemma faced by many intellectuals and scientists who had studied the question. On the one hand, they fervently desired that atomic energy come under control and generally favored international supervision of some sort. They strongly sympathized, moreover, with the goals and ideals promoted by Baruch in his opening address to the United Nations. On the other hand, they believed that Baruch went too far on the question of the veto and American security interests. What was needed was a more flexible approach to Russia, one that would protect American interests and security, yet find common working ground with the Soviets.

Baruch and Gromyko, however, had forcefully presented their arguments and neither one seemed inclined to enter into serious negotiations which might involve fundamental changes in their proposals. On December 30, 1946, the United Nations Atomic Energy Commission adopted the Baruch Plan by a vote of 10 to 0, with Russia and Poland abstaining. The issue then went before the Security Council where Russia had her veto and felt no compunction about using it against a plan so obviously contrary to her interests. Baruch remained adamant throughout the negotiations; the United Nations would either adopt his plan or no plan at all. Shortly after the vote he resigned as the American representative, assured by Truman that the government would not alter his scheme in any fundamental way.[47] With both the Russians and the Americans holding firmly to their contrary positions, little hope existed for successful negotiations.

Interest in the United States shifted from the debate in the United Nations to the debate in Washington. In July, 1946, Secretary of Commerce Henry A. Wallace sent Truman a long letter condemning

46. J.T.S. to Everett Case, June 20, 1946, VII, P, #115889, CEIP Archives.
47. Coit, *Mr. Baruch,* pp. 602–7.

the increased army budget, the atomic bomb tests in the Pacific, and America's "insincerity" with the Soviet Union. As summer turned to fall, and then to winter, his statements became more open and extreme. Joining liberals and radicals in a loose entente, he accused the Truman administration of fomenting the Cold War by refusing to cooperate with the Russians. Regardless of ideology and interest, modern technology demanded peace between the interdependent parts of the world. He urged the President and the Secretary of State to alter their position in order to "allay any reasonable Russian grounds for fear, suspicion, and distrust."[48]

Shotwell at first sided with the President and Secretary of State. In November he published an article in *Survey Graphic* sympathizing with the desire to better relations with the Russians, but questioning their sincerity. He pointed to aggressive Soviet actions and argued that Stalin had violated his word to Roosevelt by refusing to allow free democratic elections in Southeastern Europe. He feared, moreover, that Wallace's criticism would lead to confusion and disillusionment similar to that which had occurred after the First World War.[49]

His support for the Truman administration stemmed less from a belief in the wisdom of the President's policy than from a desire to unify public opinion on the atomic energy question. Shortly after the vote in the Security Council, he began to criticize the doctrinaire and uncompromising attitude of the government. Americans had taken an "all or nothing" position, he complained. Progress toward peace and an end to international anarchy demanded "a readiness to find some formula of agreement at some future time which will permit the fullest amount of safeguard and not divide the world into two great areas with the atomic bomb hanging between them."[50]

By February, 1947, he moved very close to the Wallace position, although he never openly joined the Wallace camp. He now argued that Russia's seeming intransigence on the atomic energy question

48. Truman, *Year of Decisions,* pp. 555–59.
49. J.T.S., "Our European Policy," *Survey Graphic* 25 (November 1946): 387–89.
50. J.T.S. to Livingston Hartley, April 16, 1947, VII, P, #115746, CEIP Archives; J.T.S. to E. E. Minett, June 13, 1947, VII, P, #115767, CEIP Archives.

was largely due to American policy. "We are not without blame in our diplomacy," he told a friend, "for generally we have taken it for granted that Russia has some malevolent purpose. This I doubt. I think it is terribly embarrassed because the demands being made upon the Soviet Government are embarrassing to their own home economy as well." Once again he returned to the idea of reaching an accord with Russia by giving her economic assistance. The United States' "get-tough" policy weakened the more progressive and liberal forces in the Soviet Union and helped "the reactionary communist element to argue that the capitalist is an enemy which is simply whetting its weapons for a future attack."[51] The American government, he believed, had to maintain its strength and protect its interests, but it could not afford to place so much emphasis on its security policy that accommodation became impossible.[52]

Shotwell's hope that the United States would adopt a more flexible policy on atomic energy failed to materialize. The first Carnegie Endowment report had some influence in convincing diplomats and scientists of the feasibility of inspection. Total reliance on such a system, however, never gained much support. The Draft Convention on the Utilization and Control of Atomic Energy offered a compromise between the Russian and American positions, but neither side proved willing to deviate from their original positions. The United States remained committed to the internationalization of raw materials and the managerial control of atomic energy producing plants. It had no intention of giving away any of its secrets or destroying any of its bombs until an adequate system of controls was in operation. The Soviet Union, for its part, demanded disarmament as a first step and rejected the idea of inspection which would have permitted "foreigners" to enter its territory and atomic energy plants.

The Endowment's draft convention proved neither technically feasible nor politically adequate. It is doubtful that any plan could have bridged the gap between the Soviet and American positions. Russia's explosion of an atomic device in 1949 altered the entire question by

51. J.T.S. to Mark Grauband, February 17, 1947, VII, P, #116124, CEIP Archives.
52. J.T.S., *The United States in History* (New York, 1956), pp. 189–92.

removing the American monopoly. A race in atomic weapons and missiles heightened the conflict between East and West, and temporarily removed the incentive for an arms control agreement. In the United States talk of cooperation subsided, and containment, brinkmanship, and massive retaliation became the guiding principles of foreign policy.

The debate over the control of atomic energy marked the opening round in the Cold War. Russian suspicion, hostility, and aggressiveness in various parts of the world was quickly matched by American suspicion, hostility, and intervention. The dream of a postwar Grand Alliance, in which peace, cooperation, and friendship would reign, faded as the struggle in Europe, the Middle East, and the Far East revealed the persistence of power politics and international conflict. Nuclear fission had raised the stakes, but it could not change the rules.

15
A Strategy for the Cold War

Before the outbreak of the Second World War, Shotwell often referred to himself as an "academic war casualty." His real interest, he claimed, lay in the study and writing of history. America's entry into World War I, however, had forced him "to turn from those predilections of scholarship" to a study of the contemporary world and the problems confronting modern man.[1]

He was not entirely satisfied with the work. On several occasions he had become so discouraged with the peace movement that he withdrew to Columbia University determined to devote the rest of his years to teaching and research. For weeks, or perhaps a few months, his close associates would hear very little from him as he delved back into the medieval world which had so fascinated him as a young man. But inevitably one of them, usually Clark Eichelberger, Joseph Chamberlain, or Nicholas Murray Butler, would receive a telephone call,

1. *Addresses Delivered by Frank G. Boudreau and James T. Shotwell at the Annual Dinner of the League of Nations Association, January 29, 1940* (New York, 1940), p. 15.

and Shotwell's voice on the other end, deep and resonant, would be saying: "I have a memorandum I want you to read. . . ." Then he was off again, fresh, enthusiastic, and full of energy. He would organize committees, call meetings, set up interviews, and more often than not sail for London, Paris, or Geneva.[2]

Despite all his protests, Shotwell enjoyed the dual role of activist-scholar. He saw nothing contradictory in it. In fact, he believed that intellectuals had a responsibility to take an active part in the crucial debates of their own age. By the time he reached maturity as an historian, he had rejected the traditional role played by his profession. It was not enough for him to merely observe the past. Instead, he deeply desired to make history. He desired to face the challenges of contemporary society and actively promote those values which meant most to him. His approach lost him some respect among his more traditionally oriented colleagues, but it also made him something more than an historian or a scholar. It made him a "citizen" in the best tradition of the ancient Greek word.[3]

The quick ratification of the United Nations Charter appeared to Shotwell not so much an end as a beginning. It represented not the fulfillment of a lifelong dream, but only the first step toward its realization. Nor did he view the swift resumption of international conflict as reason for complete disillusionment. Instead, he saw it as further reason to work for an effective peace, one as dynamic as war itself. Four prerequisites remained for the establishment of a viable postwar settlement. Nations had to relinquish political and commercial imperialism; they had to eliminate special trading arrangements among themselves; they had to recognize and guarantee human rights by international treaty; and they had to somehow agree on the international control of weapons of mass destruction.[4] For the rest of his life, first as chairman of the Commission to Study the Organization of Peace, then as president of the Carnegie Endowment for International Peace, and finally through his personal writings, Shotwell tried

2. Clark M. Eichelberger, "James Thomson Shotwell," *Saturday Review* 48 (August 7, 1965): 16.
3. Howard Zinn, "Historian as Citizen," *New York Times Book Review,* September 25, 1966, p. 2.
4. J.T.S., "Alternatives for War," *Survey Graphic* 25 (June 1946): 204, 238.

to bring about the realization of these goals. Upon their achievement depended the establishment of a truly lasting peace, one devoted to the elevation of justice and freedom in all nations.

The first of these prerequisites, or "alternatives for war" as he preferred to call them, depended upon the swift implementation of the trusteeship provisions in the United Nations Charter. In order to bring this about Shotwell helped organize a vigorous campaign carried on by the Commission to Study the Organization of Peace. Through radio broadcasts, popular literature, press channels, and public conferences, the Commission urged the United States not to annex the Japanese mandate islands necessary for security, but rather occupy them "under the terms of the United Nations trusteeship." The Commission also called upon all nations with League of Nations mandates to transfer them to the United Nations trusteeship. Only by such actions, and the immediate establishment of regional commissions to deal with local problems relating to dependent people, could colonialism come to an end and the peoples of these areas made ready for self-government.[5]

Closely connected with the ending of political and commercial imperialism was Shotwell's second alternative for war, the "elimination of special trading arrangements among nations and the development of multilateral trade and financial agreements." Throughout the interwar period he had argued that both world peace and world prosperity depended upon the elimination of economic barriers. Following World War II, he urged the United States to do all in its power to revive the economy of Europe and extend aid to the rest of the world. In November, 1945, along with Carl Van Doren, Oswald Garrison Villard, and Russell Davenport, he helped organize the Citizens Emergency Committee for Overseas Relief which lobbied for Congressional appropriations for the United Nations Relief and Rehabilitation Administration and urged Congress to drop restrictions on extending aid to Russia and Eastern Europe.[6] He strongly

5. CEIP, *Year Book,* 1946, pp. 113–14; Eichelberger to Harry S. Truman, October 31, 1946, Official File, 85L, Truman Papers, Truman Library, Independence, Missouri; CSOP, "The Trusteeship System and Non-Self-Governing Territories," *International Conciliation* 426 (December 1946): 565–72.
6. *New York Times,* November 10, 1945, p. 6; J.T.S. to Robert A. Taft, December 4, 1945, Box 239, J.T.S. Papers.

favored giving a large loan to Great Britain in 1946, fully backed the Marshall Plan the following year, and supported Truman's pledge made in 1949 to help raise the standard of living of underdeveloped areas. "As long as two-thirds of the population of the world have a standard of living so low as to be unable to share in the economic and cultural advances of more favored peoples," he declared, "there can be no guarantee of ultimate peace and security. The welfare of nations is the fundamental basis of peace."[7]

During the late 1940s no question, except perhaps the control of atomic energy, interested Shotwell more than human rights. Both as a member of the government's postwar planning commission and as a consultant to the American delegation at San Francisco he had strongly advocated the inclusion of human rights provisions into the United Nations Charter. His success at San Francisco was merely a beginning. The establishment of a Human Rights Commission and the very difficult task of drafting an international convention for human rights still remained. As chairman of the Commission to Study the Organization of Peace, he played a major role in drafting a proposed "Bill of Human Rights," which, in January, 1947, he formally presented to the newly established United Nations Commission on Human Rights, headed by Mrs. Eleanor Roosevelt. The draft bill not only incorporated most of the provisions contained in the American Bill of Rights and the French Declaration of the Rights of Man, but also included such guarantees as social security, an adequate education, and the right of every person to receive assistance from the state in the exercise of his right to work.[8] Shotwell had no illusions about the force of a United Nations declaration. He realized that many governments would continue to ignore the basic civil rights of certain groups and citizens, but he firmly believed that the United Nations should define the ultimate principles toward which all nations might strive.[9] While the exact influence of the draft prepared by the Commis-

7. J.T.S. to Harold E. Stassen, March 9, 1946, VII, H, #99823A, CEIP Archives; J.T.S. to J. B. Condliffe, November 6, 1947, VII, H, #97265, CEIP Archives; *International Conciliation* 452 (June 1949): 459–564; *International Conciliation* 426 (December 1946): 565–72.
8. "Bill of Human Rights," *International Conciliation* 426 (December 1946): 559–64; "Bill of Human Rights," *Survey Graphic* 35 (December 1946): 461; J.T.S. to Mrs. Eleanor Roosevelt, February 4, 1947, Box 242, J.T.S. Papers.
9. J.T.S. to Monroe E. Deutsch, June 20, 1946, Box 242, J.T.S. Papers.

sion to Study the Organization of Peace cannot be determined, the United Nations' Universal Declaration of Human Rights, adopted by the General Assembly on December 10, 1948, included many of the same provisions.[10]

Neither Shotwell nor the other members of the Commission to Study the Organization of Peace restricted their work solely to the economic and social aspects of the United Nations. In June, 1947, they released the Commission's Fifth Report on "Security and Disarmament under the United Nations." Basically the report sought to strengthen the security arrangements of the world organization without revising the Charter. Shotwell and his colleagues strongly opposed the idea that atomic power and the American-Soviet conflict had made the United Nations obsolete. They believed that those calling for world government or the complete revision of the United Nations Charter lacked any sense of political reality.[11] Recognizing that Soviet-American hostility and the growing bipolarity in world affairs necessitated certain basic changes in the structure and functioning of the United Nations, they resisted the call for a general revision on the grounds that mutual antagonism between the United States and Russia would prevent any formal amendment of the Charter. As an alternative, they offered several reforms which conformed to the already existing legal framework of the United Nations Organization.[12]

The fundamental weakness of the United Nations, according to the Commission's Fifth Report, was its inability to reach decisions and carry them out. To overcome this inadequacy, the report proposed that the Security Council be given contingent forces, preferably a small air force under its own command, that international criminal law be codified, and that the organization establish an international criminal tribunal with jurisdiction to try individual offenders against the law of nations when a national tribunal proved incapable of dealing with the matter.[13] By far the most important and far reaching of

10. "Universal Declaration of Human Rights," in Eleanor Roosevelt and William De Witt, *U.N.: Today and Tomorrow* (New York, 1953), pp. 217–23.
11. For a discussion of the postwar World Government movement see Wittner, *Rebels,* pp. 170–81.
12. CSOP, Fifth Report: *Security and Disarmament Under the United Nations* (New York, June, 1947), pp. 13–17.
13. Ibid., pp. 18–21, 31–32.

the Commission's recommendations were those designed to increase the prestige and effectiveness of the General Assembly. Instead of trying to amend the Charter by eliminating the veto, the report proposed to shift security problems over to the Assembly where no veto could hamper actions. It suggested that any violations of armament agreements should be considered an "armed attack," thereby bringing Article 51 of the Charter into force. Moreover, it urged the American delegation to propose measures to permit the Assembly to function as a continuing body through the establishment of a permanent commission on security and disarmament policy. In cases of aggression where the Security Council failed to act, the General Assembly, on the advice of this commission, might pass resolutions pointing out the aggressor and recommending that its members—either individually or collectively—take whatever action they might deem necessary to halt the violating state.[14]

The American government did not go quite as far as the Commission suggested, but it did begin to introduce security questions into the General Assembly when it failed to get satisfactory action in the Security Council. While this policy proved effective in 1950 when North Korean troops invaded South Korea, it placed the United States in a very delicate position. The Assembly was a large and unwieldy body which the United States could not always dominate or control. The danger of the Korean incident was that it established a precedent which could be used at a later date to thwart American intervention rather than Communist aggression. Moreover, it placed a modicum of authority in a body whose control had little to do with the configuration of world power and thereby violated one of the basic principles of the United Nations security system—a system designed to link responsibility for international peace with the power to enforce it.[15]

The drafting of the Commission's Fifth Report seemed to end Shotwell's active career in the peace movement. By 1948 he had drastically reduced his commitments to the various committees, foundations, and institutions to which he still belonged. Only the Commis-

14. Ibid., pp. 23–27, 32–33.
15. Robert H. Ferrell, *American Diplomacy: A History* (New York, 1959), pp. 433–34.

sion to Study the Organization of Peace and the Carnegie Endowment for International Peace could justifiably list him as an active member. He even curtailed his activities in these two organizations. On December 28, 1947, he formally resigned as chairman of the Commission and turned over his position to Clark Eichelberger. He still attended meetings and read reports, but no longer did he guide and direct policy. His work for the Carnegie Endowment also diminished when early in 1948 Alger Hiss, who had replaced Nicholas Murray Butler as president two years earlier, reorganized the Endowment by dissolving the three separate divisions of Law, Education, and Economics and History. This left Shotwell with only his very light responsibilities as a Trustee and member of the Executive Committee.[16]

At the age of seventy-four Shotwell welcomed his approaching retirement. Increasingly he thought of returning to his books and to the writing of history. There was so much he still wanted to say and so little time to say it. But just as his wish seemed within reach, one of the strangest and most controversial cases in American legal history forced him into active service once again.

On August 3, during the hearings before the House Committee on Un-American Activities on alleged Communist infiltration of government, Whittaker Chambers, the senior editor of *Time* magazine, named Alger Hiss, among others, as having belonged to the Communist Party during the 1930s. Hiss categorically denied the charge, but Chambers made a more definite allegation of guilt. The resultant investigation soon shifted from the House Un-American Activities Committee to the federal courts where it was debated for more than three years.[17]

In order to avoid embarrassing the Endowment and to devote his full time to the case, Hiss resigned as president in December. The Trustees, however, tabled the resignation and granted him a three-month leave of absence.[18] Unsure how long the case would remain in the courts, the Trustees decided to appoint an interim replacement.

16. J.T.S. to Members of the CSOP, January 7, 1948, VII, AA, #124251, CEIP Archives; CEIP, *Annual Report,* 1949, p. 31.
17. Meyer A. Zeligs, *Friendship and Fratricide: An Analysis of Whittaker Chambers and Alger Hiss* (New York, 1967), pp. 3–4.
18. *New York Times,* December 14, 1948, p. 3.

As chairman of the Board of Trustees and chairman of the Executive Committee, John Foster Dulles had promoted Hiss to the presidency of the Endowment. Understandably, he now sought someone for the post who was widely known and respected in order to offset any adverse effects resulting from the trial. Shotwell's name came up immediately, and since he seemed best suited for the position, the Board of Trustees appointed him Acting President at a salary of $1,000 a month. Five months later, they formally elected him to the $20,000 a year position.[19]

Embarrassed by the Hiss-Chambers case, several of the Trustees urged the Endowment officials to remain completely silent on the subject. Shotwell, however, strongly sympathized with Hiss and testified on his behalf at the trial. He had worked with Hiss for several months during 1947 on a promotional campaign for the Marshall Plan and became convinced that a man who worked as hard for a policy which Moscow firmly opposed could not be pro-communist. While he could not testify as to what Hiss had or had not done before the war, Shotwell did state that since he had met Hiss through the Endowment he had become "thoroughly convinced of his absolute integrity." He was, moreover, very critical of the House of Un-American Activities Committee. The Congressional committee, he believed, held a very dangerous attitude in that it accepted the idea that "the assassination of one man's character" was nothing compared with its "own good motives of saving the United States."[20]

As president of the Endowment, Shotwell also broke with several of the Trustees over the question of constructing a new office building across the street from the United Nations. Rejecting as shortsighted the argument that such a costly enterprise should await the results of the trial, he convinced the Board to undertake the project. On December 12, 1949, Dulles formally announced the Endowment's plan to construct the new building. The Endowment hoped that it would not only house its own offices, but also those of most of the other major

19. *Ibid.;* CEIP, *Minutes,* 38: 228; Interview with Clark Eichelberger, December 28, 1966.
20. J.T.S., *Autobiography,* pp. 317–18; J.T.S. to Sumner Welles, October 5, 1948, Box 239, J.T.S. Papers; J.T.S. to Frank Warrin, September 22, 1948, Box 239, J.T.S. Papers.

American peace organizations.[21] Its completion in 1954 represented Shotwell's most important contribution as president. As recognition for his efforts, and for his long service to the Endowment as well, Joseph E. Johnson, who had succeeded him as president in 1950, suggested that they name the new Endowment Library after him.[22] On his eightieth birthday, at a meeting presided over by President Grayson Kirk of Columbia University, the Board of Trustees announced the opening of the James Thomson Shotwell Library and celebrated the occasion with a dinner in his honor. It was one of Shotwell's proudest days.[23]

It was not, however, the only honor he received. In 1951, shortly after he had become President Emeritus of the Endowment, Francis Harman of the Federal Council of Churches of Christ in America, Grayson Kirk, Joseph E. Johnson, and Clark Eichelberger organized a campaign to nominate him for the Nobel Peace Prize. Over one hundred prominant citizens supported his candidacy, including Mrs. Eleanor Roosevelt, Senators Joseph Sparkman of Alabama and J. William Fulbright of Arkansas, David Sarnoff, Adlai Stevenson, Sumner Welles, Thomas Watson, Arthur Hays Sulzberger, editor of the *New York Times,* and Allen Dulles of the Central Intelligence Agency. It was an impressive and prestigious list by any measurement. Professor John B. Condliffe of the University of California at Berkeley wrote directly to the Nobel Prize Committee, stating that Shotwell through his wide association with labor, business, farm leaders, womens' groups, journalists, and other scholars had profoundly influenced public opinion in America. "More than any other single person," argued Condliffe, "he is responsible for swinging American opinion from isolation to international cooperation."[24] Grayson Kirk, writing in behalf of all those supporting Shotwell's candidacy, reiterated much of what Condliffe had said. He, too, argued that few people had worked longer or more consistently in behalf of world peace. No

21. *New York Times,* December 13, 1949, p. 7; Interview with Clark Eichelberger, December 28, 1966.
22. CEIP, *Minutes,* 44: 209.
23. J.T.S., *Autobiography,* p. 331.
24. J. B. Condliffe to Nobel Prize Committee, November 26, 1951, Box 258, J.T.S. Papers.

other American, he added, had been more effective in preparing his countrymen and his government for assuming their international responsibilities.[25]

The campaign proved partially successful, for on March 6, 1952, the Nobel Peace Prize Committee nominated Shotwell, along with twenty-six other individuals and four institutions, for the award.[26] Unfortunately, however, the committee saw fit to make no presentation that year.[27] As Grayson Kirk pointed out, Shotwell's contribution to world peace had consisted of dedication, intellectual leadership, and consistency. He had made no single outstanding contribution in the crusade against war. Only those who knew him well and were familiar with his career understood the significance of his role in the peace movement. His influence and impact had been indirect and subtle. He had served as an adviser, publicist, critic, and initiator of ideas, a man usually behind the scenes and not one whose work was subject to specific measurement. He deserved the Peace Prize as much as any man, but the nature of his contribution precluded public acclaim and failed to bring him the recognition which was his due.

Shotwell's retirement as president of the Carnegie Endowment did not take him out of the public discussion over American foreign policy. Instead, it enabled him to devote even more time to it. He had anxiously awaited his retirement not because he wished to escape from the major conflicts and problems of the Atomic Age, but because he desired to spend his remaining years promoting an "enlightened" peace program. He might have viewed himself as an "academic war casualty," but he had no desire to become an ivory-tower intellectual.

Although he continued to use the rhetoric of collective security, he strongly supported the Truman-Acheson policy of committing American power against the "forces of aggression" when the United Nations failed to act. If the Russians would not help police the world

25. Grayson Kirk to Nobel Prize Committee, January 2, 1952, Box 261, J.T.S. Papers.
26. *New York Times,* March 7, 1952, p. 8.
27. Although it announced in October, 1952 that no one would receive the peace prize that year, the Nobel Committee reversed its decision in October, 1953, awarding Albert Schweitzer the 1952 prize and George C. Marshall the 1953 prize. See *New York Times,* October 4, 1952, p. 2, October 31, 1953, p. 1.

for peace, and if the British and French could not help, then the United States had no choice but to use its own power to prevent aggression. He advocated American participation in the North Atlantic Treaty Organization and interpreted the Korean War as a great victory for collective security despite the unilateral nature of President Truman's actions. On June 30, 1950, he and Joseph E. Johnson sent the President a telegram on behalf of the Endowment endorsing "the prompt and vigorous action taken by the United States . . . to support and defend in the present crisis the principles of collective security and of international law and justice under the United Nations."[28]

Yet Shotwell's support of NATO and of America's intervention in Korea did not prevent him from thoroughly disagreeing with the policy of containment. His major criticism of the Truman-Acheson policy, and later the Eisenhower-Dulles policy, was that it focused America's attention too narrowly on stopping Communist expansion by military means. By so doing it prevented "courageous, far-sighted thinking" during times of crisis. The United States, he admitted, had to resist Soviet aggression and develop a firm defensive policy, but it could not afford to ignore the possibilities of diplomacy and compromise. He felt certain that America could best meet the Soviet challenge not by resorting to force of arms, but rather by establishing a peace based upon social justice. "The only safety for democracy," he argued, "not only in these perilous times but in the long reaches of the future, lies in the capacity supplied by its heritage of freedom to deal with its vital problems without prejudice and with increased and self-disciplined intelligence."[29]

Shotwell's approach to international relations, as George Kennan and other political "realists" maintained, was extremely "idealistic" in that it upheld basic universal principles as both its criteria for judgment and its guideline for future action. The realists condemned

28. J.T.S. and Joseph E. Johnson to President Harry S. Truman, June 30, 1950, Official File, 471B, Truman Papers.
29. J.T.S., "President's Report," CEIP, *Annual Report,* 1949, p. 4; J.T.S., "The Study of International Relations," An address before the International Conference of Institutes of World Affairs, October 20, 1953, p. 7A, in CEIP Library, Vertical File; J.T.S., "Peace: A Challenge to Intelligence," *Think* 21 (June 1955): 7.

this approach as overly naive, if not dangerous. It ignored not only the importance of power in world affairs, but also the limitations of political action.[30] Yet Shotwell's analysis of American foreign policy cut through the rhetoric of Cold War diplomacy and astutely interpreted the fundamental challenge presented by Moscow and the ideology of communism. At a time when the attention of most American policy-makers had become fixed upon the security question, Shotwell recognized that the military threat posed by the Communists was only one aspect, and perhaps the least important, of the total challenge. During the Truman years, and at least during Eisenhower's first term in office, the United States held an overwhelming preponderance of military power and technological skill, a fact rarely disputed and never forgotten by the Kremlin. Soviet hostility toward the West, as even George Kennan later admitted,[31] manifested itself primarily in political rather than military terms.

As Shotwell viewed the situation, the real challenge presented by the Communists was social and economic. The United States had no choice but to ensure its own security by maintaining its military strength in the immediate future, but ultimately the success or failure in its rivalry with Russia would depend upon nonmilitary factors. Unless Washington could offer the depressed, exploited, and underprivileged peoples of the world a better alternative than Moscow, it could never claim victory over communism. Its strongest weapons were not the atomic and hydrogen bombs, but technology and the idea of freedom. These were the weapons which had to be deployed. Communism would then have to compete and make good its promises or share the fate of all previous military dictatorships. Soviet hostility, under such circumstances, might not dissolve, but the East-West conflict might transform itself from a destructive to a constructive rivalry, in which each system attempted to make good in its own way.[32]

30. See George F. Kennan, *American Diplomacy, 1900–1950* (Chicago, 1951), pp. 82–89; Hans J. Morgenthau, *Politics Among Nations: The Struggle for Power and Peace,* 3rd ed. (New York, 1963), pp. 3–26.
31. George F. Kennan, *Russia, The Atom, And The West* (New York, 1956), pp. 17–18.
32. J.T.S., "A New Way of Life for Asia," *Think* 19 (March 1953): 3–4; J.T.S., "The Last Frontier," *Think* 22 (June 1956): 3–5, 36.

Perhaps Shotwell overestimated the possibility of altering the course of the Cold War, yet he fully realized the futility of a military confrontation in the Atomic Age. He had no illusion about the difficulty or the enormity of the task he had outlined. Upon its fulfillment, however, depended the survival of the world. He had presented a program for the future. The alternative was catastrophe and holocaust.

16
The Road to the Hills

Throughout his thirty years of active service as an antiwar publicist, informal diplomat, and occasional State Department adviser, James Thomson Shotwell had most identified with the historical profession. His peace activities and his participation in public debates, he believed, had all stemmed quite logically from his scholarly inquiry. Now, during the years of his retirement, he desired to return to the writing of history. His scholarly concerns, however, little resembled those of the pre-World War I period. He had lost some of his earlier fascination with medieval manuscripts and early Church history. Two major wars and the discovery of atomic power had caused him to focus upon other problems. He now approached history as an elder statesman with a message and a faith he passionately desired to share with others.

From the time he retired as president of the Carnegie Endowment until 1962, when he sustained a serious injury in a fall which made all work extremely difficult, Shotwell published two major books, an autobiography, a book of poetry, and numerous articles. His work revealed a continued commitment to scholarship and historical truth, but it also demonstrated a desire to give his writings political and social importance. Unfortunately he could not have it both ways. His desire to promote political causes detracted seriously from his scholarship. Historical writing had become a means of conveying a message rather than a medium for helping others to understand the past.

The result of this shift in approach was revealed in 1956 when he completed *The United States in History,* the first volume of what he later claimed was his study of "freedom." Shotwell fully understood the implications of his approach, for at the outset he admitted that the book was not a general survey of American history, but rather a "commentary on it." It was a personal narrative "of one who has been privileged to watch from a corner of the stage itself the greatest drama of all history unfold its tragic course, through blunderings and heroic enterprises to a goal still hidden from us."[1]

Because he had written the book as a personal commentary rather than as an historical survey, he dealt mainly with issues that concerned him deeply. He devoted more than two-thirds of the volume to the twentieth century and to America's place in world affairs. As a personal narrative, the book was bold, imaginative, and incisive. Yet as a study of the development of freedom in the United States, its avowed purpose, it fell far short of the mark. Shotwell, unfortunately, failed to define what he meant by "freedom" and "justice," the book's two main themes. He ignored, moreover, some of the more important historical aspects of the problem. While he included chapters on prehistory and the Middle Ages, he omitted almost all mention of Jacksonian Democracy, touched upon slavery only in passing, devoted only three sentences to the immigration issue, and virtually ignored the reform movement before the election of Woodrow Wilson. Even in dealing with twentieth-century history, he hardly mentioned domestic questions despite their seeming relevance to his central theme. He made no mention of Red-baiting after either the First or Second World Wars, ignored the question of Japanese internment during the early 1940s, and said nothing about the civil rights movement. Yet he did find space to discuss German culture and history, the establishment of the International Labor Organization, the crea-

1. J.T.S., *The United States in History,* p. xiii.

tion of the League of Nations, the Geneva Protocol, the Locarno Treaty, the United Nations, and the Cold War.

In 1960, four years after the publication of *The United States in History,* Shotwell completed his magnum opus, *The Long Way to Freedom.* He declared that the book dealt "with the age-long history of a problem which, when viewed in all its aspects, outranks any other in the world today: that of the way by which the freedom of the individual can be not only maintained but increased, parallel with a continual, and apparently inevitable, increase in the scope of government." It sought to answer the fundamental question: "How can men be free and yet yield so much of their lives to the judgment of others as set forth in the laws and prescrptions of the State?"[2]

From Shotwell's point of view, the book was the most important he had ever written. He had begun working on it in 1948 when he received a $12,000 grant from the Carnegie Corporation and had finally finished it eleven years later. He believed the book countered the Communist charge that History was on their side. His study proved that the key to a successful and progressive future was freedom. No other political, social, or economic principle was as important. Communism, he argued, sought to alleviate economic injustice, but its approach denied individual freedom, as well as political and social justice. "All history," he believed, "shows that tyranny must govern by bureaucracies, which in the end fasten their dead weight on society, stifling initiative and progress."[3]

Like his earlier work, *The Long Way to Freedom* was more a profession of faith than a synthesis of historical scholarship. As Professor William McNeil of the University of Chicago pointed out, Shotwell seemed completely out of touch with historical material written since the First World War and constantly relied upon scholarship which had since been revised or expanded. McNeil felt that the book was little more than "a full throated affirmation of the liberal creed and view of history as formulated about the turn of the twen-

2. J.T.S., *The Long Way to Freedom* (Indianapolis and New York, 1960), p. 15.
3. J.T.S., "Address, March 9, 1960," Box 263, J.T.S. Papers; J.T.S. to Ordway Tead, February 6, 1959, Box 241, J.T.S. Papers; "Memorandum on the Carnegie Corporation Grant," n.d., Box 262, J.T.S. Papers.

tieth century." Even such a sympathetic reviewer as Professor Herbert J. Muller found Shotwell's handling of contemporary history extremely inadequate.[4] Not all reviewers were critical, but few found the book's chief strength in its historical scholarship. Joseph G. Harrison, writing in the *Christian Science Monitor,* stated that it was "a noble book written by a noble man." He believed that it would leave its readers both wiser and stronger.[5]

Whatever its failings, *The Long Way to Freedom* succeeded in creating a mood and in illuminating the didactic lessons of history as its author understood them. The most important of these was that a civilization based upon exploitation could not survive. Only through "justice" and "freedom" could mankind prosper and develop, and civilization perpetuate itself. Shotwell saw no hope for a society which set up obstacles before independent thinkers, nor did he feel that justice could develop under military regimentation. "There must be freedom for the individual," he declared, "to experiment and to explore, to think and to express his thought, and that freedom must be safeguarded by both law and custom so long as it is not anti-social." The true meaning of democracy was not the rule of the many, but rather "the safeguarding of their freedom, a freedom that justifies itself by providing disciplined intelligence in its leadership and a critical, open-minded citizenship."[6]

Fortunately, Shotwell's reputation as an historian did not depend upon his mid-century writings. His earlier works had revealed him as a painstaking scholar whose boldness and imaginative approach had impressed many within the historical profession. Although his last two major historical works seemed a bit antique and naive to readers of a younger generation, his faith, fortitude, compassion, and optimism served as a challenge to their easy pessimism and self-pity. These were the qualities which made his friends and associates defenders to the end, and his critics understanding and even sympathetic.

4. William McNeil, Review of *The Long Way to Freedom* in *Political Science Quarterly* 75 (September 1960): 443; Herbert J. Muller, "The Main Meaning of Man's History," *Saturday Review* 43 (February 27, 1960): 32–33.
5. *Christian Science Monitor,* March 3, 1960.
6. J.T.S., *The Long Way to Freedom,* pp. 165, 607.

The years after his retirement from the Carnegie Endowment for International Peace were extremely satisfying. A moderate annual pension from the Endowment and the money he received from books and articles proved more than sufficient to sustain his wife Margaret and himself during their final years. He kept his commitments down to a bare minimum and avoided new endeavors as much as possible. He did, however, become interested in the development of a settlement around Goose Bay, Labrador for displaced persons and migrants from Europe, the Middle East, and other areas. Promoted by his nephew John Shotwell, he became president and chairman of the Freedom, Labrador Settlement Foundation. The project, however, was mainly a Canadian enterprise and when his nephew died in 1962 Shotwell seemed to lose interest.[7]

Probably the most important event for Showell during his retirement was his return to Europe in the summer of 1955 after an absence of more than twenty years. Accompanied by his daughter Helen, he spent two months traveling on the Continent and in England. He visited with old friends and colleagues, attended the Strasbourg Conference on European unity in July, and even managed to give a few lectures. When he returned home it was with fond memories and a new optimism about the possibilities for European cooperation.[8]

His retirement also allowed Shotwell to spend complete summers with Margaret and Helen at their home in Woodstock, New York. The Shotwells had first come to Woodstock in 1907 to visit John Dewey. The following year they borrowed some money from Charles Beard and purchased a one hundred acre farm. Begun as an arts and crafts colony by Ralph Radcliffe Whitehead in 1902, Woodstock remains to this day committed to the arts. Shotwell viewed his modest house with its magnificent view of the Hudson Valley as his true home, much more so than his apartment in Manhattan. Built in 1910, the old house and its surrounding grounds had a solitude and serenity about it which he deeply loved. Perhaps it reminded him of the isolation and quietude of his boyhood days. Here he could escape from

7. For information on the Freedom, Labrador Settlement Foundation, see Box 260, J.T.S. Papers.
8. J.T.S., *Autobiography,* pp. 319–30; J.T.S., "European Journey, 1955" (Confidential Diary), CEIP Library, Archive 1013.

the swift pace of the twentieth century. "To me," he declared on his ninetieth birthday, "this is heaven, in beauty, peace and charm."[9]

He was able to relax at Woodstock. He enjoyed sitting on the porch of his home with Margaret, taking leisurely strolls, talking to neighbors, and showing guests around the grounds. He delighted in the frequent visits by his eldest daughter Margaret Grace and his granddaughter Peggy. Newspaper reporters always found him in high spirits in the country, and they rarely failed to describe how his silky, white hair blew in the breeze, or how his bright, blue eyes sparkled, or how his engaging smile, wit, and charm put even the most nervous at ease. He always seemed ready to discuss the prospects for peace, and his message was always the same: war in the Atomic Age had become so frightful, so terrible, that it had ceased to serve any rational purpose and would therefore eventually destroy itself.[10] On his ninetieth birthday he declared to a local Woodstock reporter: "What more can I say than what I have over the years, namely; that organized peace is the road to worldwide peace."[11]

During the last few years of his life he suffered greatly. A fall paralyzed him and only sedatives and narcotic injections administered by his daughter made the days tolerable. On July 9, 1965, his childhood sweetheart and wife for sixty-four years died. Six days later, and three weeks before his ninety-first birthday, he gave up the fight and quietly passed away in his sleep.

His death did not go unnoticed. There were many friends to mourn him, many to eulogize. Tributes flowed in from all parts of the country and from Europe. Grayson Kirk reminisced about his association with "Dr. Shotwell," recalling that "he had genuine wisdom, sympathy and warmth of personality that endeared him to all his many friends." The president of Columbia was certain that his death would leave the world poorer.[12] The London *Times* remembered him as "anything but the cloistered academic living on a diet of ideals." His work on behalf of peace, it pointed out, "sprang from first-hand

9. *The Woodstock Week Letter,* August 13, 1964; J.T.S., *Autobiography,* p. 334.
10. *New York Times,* August 7, 1957, p. 15.
11. *The Woodstock Week Letter,* August 13, 1964.
12. *New York Herald Tribune,* July 17, 1965.

experience of the riguors of peace-making and the frustrations and difficulties of setting-up international bodies."[13] The editors of the *New York Times* reminded their readers that "James T. Shotwell contributed mightily to the slow and sometimes painful shift in American public opinion from the isolationism of the nineteen-twenties to the internationalism of today." They also recalled that while his voice was often in the minority, his "diligent espousal of the cause of world peace as a practical ideal gave great stature to a long and distinguished life."[14]

In October, Shotwell's friends, family, and associates gathered at St. Paul's Chapel at Columbia University for a memorial service. Those who spoke had only the highest praise. Adolph Berle remembered him as an intellectual in action; Clark Eichelberger lingered on his eternal youth; Leslie Paffrath of the Johnson Foundation spoke of his great contribution to the cause of world peace; and Grayson Kirk recalled his life as an historian and teacher. But Norman Cousins, editor of the *Saturday Review* and an old friend, summed up the feelings of most of those present when he declared:

> Few men in our time have supplied more dramatic evidence of the range of human capacity and depth of feeling. Few men have displayed more gloriously the creative splendor that is the highest prize of life. Few men have given more fully of themselves to the ideas and ideals they believed in or to the people they believed in. Few men have demonstrated more consistently the evidence that man can continue to grow right up to the end of his personal odyssey on earth. Few men have imparted and implanted more of the best in themselves into the lives of others.[15]

Shotwell's legacy did not consist of any specific policy prescription or of any one great creative production. Instead, it consisted of his qualities as a human being and his approach to life. Many of his policy suggestions were of questionable value and rested more on idealism than on a sound understanding of political reality. Like so many other

13. *The Times* (London), July 17, 1965.
14. *New York Times,* July 17, 1965, p. 24.
15. Transcript of Memorial Service, October, 1965, p. 2, CEIP Office, New York City.

advocates of collective security in the United States, he defined a peaceful, progressive world in terms which were perhaps self-defeating in the long run. For to get peace on those terms, despite the rhetoric of collective security, meant the establishment of a kind of world-wide American imperium. Yet he did make a significant contribution in turning American thoughts toward internationalism and deserved a good deal of credit for helping to shape much that was valuable in the United Nations Organization.

More important, however, were the ideas he preached and the example he sought to provide for others. He devoted his life, both as an historian and as an activist, to the mobilization of intelligence and to the application of knowledge to everyday problems. He refused to surrender his optimism no matter how dim the future seemed. He fought tenaciously for the dignity of man. He seemed to understand the true meaning of citizenship in a democratic society. He understood both its responsibilities and its obligations. He offered a challenge to future generations to explore the unknown and to find solutions to fundamental problems. He was an idealist who sought to make his ideals living reality. Perhaps the battle was futile, but he enjoyed it and the world might have benefited a little from the struggle.

Today he lies beside his wife in the "artists" cemetery at his beloved Woodstock. Not far from the grave there stands a monument dedicating the cemetery to the artists and musicians who lived in the area. It is engraved with an inscription Shotwell wrote shortly before his death—an inscription which in its simplicity serves as a fitting epitaph for himself as well as the others:

> Encircled By The Everlasting Hill They Rest Here
> Who Added To The Beauty Of The World
> By Art, Creative Thought And By Life Itself

Bibliographical Notes

The books, committee reports, government publications, periodicals, newspapers, and unpublished manuscripts that have been of most substantial use in preparing this work are cited in the notes and will not be repeated here. Instead, this section is concerned with those manuscript collections containing important materials relating to the life and career of James Thomson Shotwell and to his own writings.

Manuscripts

By far the most important source for this study is the James Thomson Shotwell Papers at Columbia University. The collection is extensive, consisting of some 290 boxes. Unfortunately, as of this writing it is unorganized and uncatalogued. Each box, however, is labeled and in most cases the labels closely correspond to the enclosed materials. The collection includes most of Shotwell's office files from the Carnegie Endowment for International Peace, the League of Nations Association, the International Committee on Intellectual Cooperation, and the Institute of Pacific Relations. It also includes the complete editorial record for the preparation of the *Economic and Social His-*

tory of the World War. In addition to personal and business correspondence, there are notes, memoranda, clipping files, promotional material, organizational minutes, and published articles by Shotwell and others all relating to the peace movement. The major drawback of the collection is that it consists of hardly any correspondence prior to 1919. The Columbia University collection is by no means complete, for Miss Helen Harvey Shotwell has retained in her possession much source material as well as most of the family correspondence.

Another extremely valuable collection is the Archives of the Carnegie Endowment for International Peace, also located at Columbia University. In contrast with the Shotwell papers, the Endowment Archives are well catalogued and complete from 1910 to 1950. The Salmon O. Levinson Papers, University of Chicago, are particularly helpful for the 1920s. The Franklin Delano Roosevelt Papers, Franklin Delano Roosevelt Library, Hyde Park, New York, and the Harry S. Truman Papers, Harry S. Truman Library, Independence, Missouri, both contain some interesting correspondence. Other collections which contain some scattered but important material are the Newton D. Baker Papers, Library of Congress (LC); Tasker H. Bliss Papers, LC; Nicholas Murray Butler Papers, Columbia University; William H. Carpenter Papers, Columbia University; Norman H. Davis Papers, LC; William A. Dunning Papers, Columbia University; Edward M. House Papers, Yale University; Cordell Hull Papers, LC; Sidney Mezes Papers, Columbia University; David Hunter Miller Papers, LC; John Bassett Moore Papers, LC; Raymond Robins Papers, State Historical Society of Wisconsin; R. A. Seligman Papers, Columbia University; Munroe Smith Papers, Columbia University; Henry L. Stimson Papers, Yale University; William Allen White Papers, LC; and Quincy Wright Papers, University of Chicago. Less helpful were the Tom Connally Papers, LC; George Creel Papers, LC; and Elihu Root Papers, LC.

Of particular value for Shotwell's official activities are the Records of the Department of State at the National Archives, especially the Papers of the American Commission to Negotiate Peace: Records of the Inquiry, and the Papers of the National Board for Historical Service at the Library of Congress. The Papers of the American Institute of Pacific Relations at Columbia University also have some important information. The James Thomson Shotwell Library located in the Carnegie Endowment Office in New York City contains several Shotwell manuscripts. Most of these are reports and records of official business. Archives 1002 and 1013 are particularly revealing, for they contain Shotwell's diaries for his trips to Europe in 1931 and 1955.

Shotwell's Writings

Shotwell's writings are extensive and varied, reflecting his two major interests as historian and protagonist for peace. An unpublished "Bibliography" covering his work from 1904 to 1959 can be found in his papers at Columbia University and at the Carnegie Endowment Office. It contains a fairly complete listing of Shotwell's books, articles, newspaper editorials, and addresses. There are, however, a few significant omissions. Because this aid is reasonably accessible and because it would serve the needs of few scholars to list the more than 400 articles written by Shotwell before his death, this essay will try to categorize his voluminous writings and evaluate the most significant of them.

Because there is very little biographical material on Shotwell other than a short and completely inadequate sketch in *Current Biography* 5(October 1944): 53–56, and a short piece in *Who's Who in America,* 1961–1963, p. 2849, his own autobiographical accounts have proven extremely useful. By far the most important of these is *The Autobiography of James T. Shotwell* (Indianapolis and New York, 1961). While not extremely impressive as autobiographies go, the book does reveal Shotwell's cosmic view of history, his unbending faith in human nature, and his deep commitment to peace. It covers his activities during the 1920s and early 1930s very well, but is often superficial and leaves much to be desired in its treatment of the pre-World War I period and the period after 1935. The material contained in "The Reminiscences of James T. Shotwell" (Oral History Research Office, Columbia University, 1964), concentrates on his earlier years and ends in the 1920s. Two other brief autobiographical accounts which proved helpful were "A Personal Note on the Theme of Canadian-American Relations," *The Canadian Historical Review* 28 (March 1947): 31–43, and "Reflections on Peace and War," in the Carnegie

Endowment's *Perspectives on Peace, 1910–1960* (London, 1960), pp. 15–30.

Of his books, the most important were those published during the interwar period. Those published before or shortly after World War I reflect his interest in the New History. *The Religious Revolution of To-Day* (Boston and New York, 1913) and *Intelligence and Politics* (New York, 1921) emphasize the need to replace superstition and taboo with the scientific frame of mind. *An Introduction to the History of History* (*Records of Civilization: Sources and Studies,* New York, 1922), revised and reissued first as *The History of History* (New York, 1939) and later as *The Story of Ancient History* (New York, 1961), is his classic study of ancient and early Christian historiography. His interwar books reflect his deep concern with the League of Nations and the maintenance of peace. *At the Paris Peace Conference* (New York, 1937) briefly analyzes America's peace preparations and the work of the conference. The major portion of the book, however, is made up of his diary written at the conference itself. *War as an Instrument of National Policy and Its Renunciation in the Pact of Paris* (New York, 1929) traces the history of the Kellogg-Briand Peace Pact and explores some of its possible consequences, while *On the Rim of the Abyss* (New York, 1936) provides an astute critique of American foreign policy and suggests possible alternatives. In *Lessons on Security and Disarmament From the History of the League of Nations* (New York, 1944), co-authored by Marina Salvin, Shotwell explored some of the reasons for the failure of the League. He offered several provocative suggestions for the formation of a new world organization in *The Great Decision* (New York, 1944).

In his later years, Shotwell returned to the study of history and revived his interest in the development of critical thinking. Both *The United States in History* (New York, 1956) and his magnum opus, *The Long Way to Freedom* (Indianapolis, Ind., 1960), reflect this concern. Of lesser importance, but helpful in gaining insight into Shotwell's perspective and point of view are *A Study in the History of the Eucharist* (London, 1905); *The Heritage of Freedom: The United States and Canada in the Community of Nations* (New York, 1934); *What Germany Forgot* (New York, 1940); *Turkey at the Straits: A Short History* (New York, 1940), written with Francis Deak; *Poland*

and Russia, 1919–1945 (New York, 1945), written with Max M. Laserson; and *A Balkan Mission* (New York, 1949). An entirely different side of Shotwell's personality is revealed in his book of *Poems* (New York, 1953), while some of his best historical articles are brought together in an anthology entitled *The Faith of an Historian and other Essays* (New York, 1964).

In addition to his own published books, Shotwell helped edit many important academic projects and collaborated on several textbooks. One of his major achievements was editing the 150-volume *Economic and Social History of the World War* (1921–1940). He also served as general editor for the twenty-five volume study on *The Relations of the United States and Canada* (1936–1947), helped intiate and edit several volumes in the Columbia series *The Records of Civilization: Texts and Studies,* and directed the Carnegie Endowment series *The Paris Peace Conference, History and Documents.* In 1940, he collaborated with R. K. Gooch, Arnold J. Zurcher, Karl Lowenstein, and Michael T. Florinsky on the textbook *Governments of Continental Europe* (New York, 1940), and in 1946 he revised and enlarged James Harvey Robinson's *An Introduction to the History of Western Europe,* 2 vols. (New York, 1946).

Shotwell's articles, like most of his books, are mainly polemical in nature and reflect his deep commitment to international cooperation. While he published in nearly fifty different journals, the majority of his articles appeared in *International Conciliation* (1920–1959); *Survey Graphic* (1924–1947); *Current History* (1927–1952); and *Think* (1936–1955). In addition, he wrote numerous editorials and articles for the *New York Times* and the *New York Herald Tribune* between 1920 and 1945. References to his newspaper writing appear in the notes and will not be duplicated here. The following includes a selected list of his better and most representative articles and essays.

Before World War I Shotwell's major concern was with the Middle Ages and the promotion of the New History. His interest in the meaning and scope of history is revealed in his essay on "History" in the *Encyclopaedia Britannica* 13 (11th edition, 1910–1911): 527–33, and in "The Interpretation of History," *American Historical Review* 18 (July 1913): 692–709. Of his articles emphasizing the importance of science and technology in bringing about progress, the best are

"Social History and the Industrial Revolution," *Proceedings of the Association of History Teachers of the Middle States and Maryland* 9 (1911): 6–17; "Mechanism and Culture," *Historical Outlook* 16 (January 1925): 7–11; and "The Discovery of Time," *Journal of Philosophy, Psychology and Scientific Methods* 8 (April 15, 1915): 197–206, and 10 (May 13, 1915): 253–69; also 12 (June 10, 1915): 309–17.

In " 'Shall' or 'May': How We Handled Verbal Dynamite in Making the Peace Treaty," *The Independent* 99 (August 2, 1919): 154–55, he discussed some of the major problems faced by the peacemakers at the Paris Peace Conference. Most of his writing about the conference, however, concerns his own specialty, the International Labor Organization. These include "Labor Provisions in the Peace Treaty," *Monthly Labor Review* 9 (August 1919): 329–41; "Historical Significance of the International Labour Conference," in E. John Solano, *Labour As An International Problem* (London, 1920), pp. 41–66; "The International Labor Organization as an Alternative to Violent Revolution," *The Annals of the American Academy of Political and Social Science* 166 (March 1933): 18–25; "The Origins of the I.L.O.," in Spencer Miller, Jr., ed., *What the International Labor Organization Means to America* (New York, 1936), pp. 1–7; and "Recollections on the Founding of the ILO," *Monthly Labor Review* 82 (June 1959): 631–36. In connection with this topic, Shotwell edited an important source book entitled *The Origins of the International Labor Organization*, 2 vols. (New York, 1934).

As the leading advocate of collective security and American participation in the League of Nations, Shotwell wrote dozens of articles on the problem of security and on the League's efforts to strengthen the security system. The best of these include "Security and Disarmament," *Survey Graphic* 52 (August 1, 1924): 483–86; "The Challenge to Peace," *Our World* 6 (December 1924): 3–8; "The Problem of Security," *The Annals of the American Academy of Political and Social Science* 120 (July 1925): 159–61; and "A Turning Point in History," *International Conciliation* 229 (April 1927): 149–61. He examines the Geneva Protocol in "A Great Charter for Europe," *Survey Graphic* 53 (November 1, 1924): 145–47, and discusses the significance of the Locarno treaties in "Locarno and After," *Associa-*

tion Men 52 (February 1926): 269–70. In "A Strictly American Foreign Policy," *Proceedings of the Association of History Teachers of the Middle States and Maryland* 24 (May 1926): 16–25, he takes up the question of American participation in the League and urges closer cooperation.

Of his many articles on the question of disarmament, the ones most clearly expressing his point of view are "A Practical Plan for Disarmament," *International Conciliation* 201 (August 1924): 311–42; "Arms and the World, Problems that a Conference Must Face," *Century Magazine* 112 (May 1926): 24–31; "An American Policy with Reference to Disarmament," *International Conciliation* 220 (May 1926): 9–16; "The Problem of Disarmament," *The Annals of the American Academy of Political and Social Science* 126 (July 1926): 51–55; "Alternatives for War," *Foreign Affairs* 6 (April 1928): 456–67; "Disarmament Alone No Guarantee of World Peace," *Current History* 30 (September 1929): 1024–29; and "Drifting into Fog," *Outlook and Independent* 154 (February 5, 1930): 219.

Having originated the idea of the Kellogg-Briand Peace Pact, Shotwell naturally gave it his full support during the negotiations. His articles sought to clarify the meaning of the Briand offer and place it in the context of American foreign policy. The most important of these articles are "The Movement to Renounce War as a Diplomatic Weapon," *Current History* 27 (October 1927): 62–64; "Is the Briand Proposal Practical?" *Congressional Digest* 7 (March 1928): 85–86; "The Slogan of Outlawry," *Century Magazine* 116 (October 1928): 713–20; and "Ten Years After the Armistice: Effects on American Foreign Policy," *Current History* 29 (November 1928): 175–80. In "Divergent Paths to Peace," *New Republic* 54 (March 28, 1928): 194–98, Shotwell debated John Dewey on the need for a definition of aggression, while in "The Pact of Paris with Historical Commentary," *International Conciliation* 243 (October 1928): 445–49, he analyzed the implications of the Kellogg-Briand Peace Pact in terms of future world order and concluded that much more had to be done. A defense of his own draft treaty for the renunciation of war appears in "An American Locarno: Outlawing War as an Instrument of Policy," *Rotarian* 31 (December 1927): 6–7, 46.

Shotwell's internationalism extended to the field of economics. In

"Does Business Mean Peace?" *Outlook and Independent* 151 (March 13, 1929): 405–7, 436–37, he argued that continued economic prosperity depended upon the maintenance of international peace. After the depression he began to advocate the lowering of international economic barriers as a means of restoring prosperity and insuring continued international tranquility. These views are most clearly expressed in "Peas in the International Pod," *Outlook and Independent* 154 (March 12, 1930): 409–11, 433–37, and in "The Conditions of Enduring Prosperity," *International Conciliation* 261 (February 1931): 53–63.

For his treatment of Far Eastern questions see "The Strategy of Peace: What an Unofficial Conference Did in the Pacific," *Century Magazine* 116 (January 1928): 338–45; *Extraterritoriality in China* (Concord, N. H., 1929); "The Sea Powers and the League," *New Republic* 60 (September 11, 1929): 89–92; "China's Policy of Unrestricted Sovereignty," *Current History* 31 (March 1930): 1118–27; and "Sea Power and the Far East," *Current History* 41 (March 1935): 660–66. The Japanese aggression in the early 1930s and later the Italian adventure into Ethiopia caused him great anxiety. His analysis of the League's activities during this period appears in "Taking Stock of Peace and War," *Scribner's Magazine* 90 (July 1931): 1–8; "The League's Work for Peace," *Current History* 43 (November 1935): 119–24; and "What the World is Doing for Peace," *Think* 3 (January 1938): 7, 24, 26. In "Revising the Covenant of the League of Nations," *Proceedings of the Middle States Association of History Teachers* 32 (April 1932): 91–98, he offered several suggestions for revising the charter of the League in order to make it more effective and better prepared to deal with the growing lawlessness in the international community. In "A Plan for League Action," *The Independent Journal of Columbia University* 3 (October 4, 1935): 1, 4, he called for the convening of a new peace conference to make the necessary revisions in the League Covenant.

Throughout the 1930s Shotwell urged the creation of a more viable collective security system. In "The Issue in the Crisis," *Survey Graphic* 24 (November 1935): 522–23, 558, he argued that American participation in the application of sanctions was absolutely vital for the success of the League experiment. He became increasingly critical of America's "isolationist" policy and a staunch advocate of revising the neutrality legislation. In "Neutrality and National Policy," *Outlook and Independent* 151 (April 17, 1929): 620, he argued that American neutrality policy should discriminate between an aggressor and its victim. This became the central theme of many of his later articles including "Changing Conceptions of Neutrality," *Think* 1 (March 1936): 7, 20; "Neutrality," *Proceedings of the Institute of Public Affairs* 36 (*Bulletin of the University of Georgia,* July 1939): 1–19; and "A Study of Neutrality Legislation: Report of a Committee of the National Peace Conference with an Introduction," *International Conciliation* 316 (January 1936): 3–61. For his critique of the isolationist position see "The End of Isolation," *Journal of Adult Education* 3 (June 1931): 272–77; "Isolation and Nationalism Inherent Among Americans," *Columbia Alumni News* 27 (February 21, 1936): 3, 20; "Isolation and Nationalism," *Proceedings of the Institute of Public Affairs* 36 (*Bulletin of the University of Georgia,* July 1936): 2–33; and "American Foreign Policy," *The Wharton Review of Finance and Commerce* 13 (November 1939): 2–3, 10–11.

Almost as soon as the United States entered World War II, Shotwell began emphasizing the need to prepare for the future peace. In "International Organization," *The Annals of the American Academy of Political and Social Science* 210 (July 1940): 19–23, he discussed what steps should be taken during the war to facilitate the making of peace after it was over. This was also the theme of *Lesson of the Last War* (New York, 1942), a pamphlet containing an address delivered to the American Institute of Consulting Engineers on January 19, 1942. In "Setting the Pattern for Peace," *Rotarian* 63 (August 1943): 8–10, he urged the United States to give its full cooperation in the creation of a new world organization.

Shotwell realized that the creation of the United Nations Organization was only the first step in guaranteeing a lasting peace. Military security was only the foundation for peace; economic security and the promotion of human rights also had to be guaranteed. To educate the American people on these further needs and to help explain the significance of the United Nations, he wrote a series of eighteen articles for *Survey Graphic* entitled "Bridges to the Future," extending from February 1945 to March 1947. Political security, economic prosperity, social equality, and the control of atomic energy were among the many topics he discussed. Articles on these subjects of equal importance but not included in the series are "The Peace to Come," *Think* 11 (April 1945): 17–18; "Security," in Harriet E. Davis, ed., *Pioneers in World Order: An American Appraisal of the League of Nations* (New York, 1944), pp. 26–41; "Implementing and Amending the Charter," *International Conciliation* 166 (December 1945): 811–23; "Can Peace be Assured," *Think* 12 (April 1946): 14–15, 38; "The International Implications of Nuclear Energy," *American Journal of Physics* 14 (May 1946): 179–85; "A New Page in the History of Mankind," *Think* 12 (November 1946): 5–8; and "The Control of Atomic Energy under the Charter," *Proceedings of the American Philosophical Society* 90 (1946): 59–64.

The problem of peace in the Atomic Age is taken up in "The Faith of an Historian," *Saturday Review* 34 (December 29, 1951): 6–7, 24–27, and in "Peace: A Challenge to Intelligence," *Think* 21 (June 1955): 5–7. In "The United Nations: Strengthening World Government," *Current History* 20 (January 1952): 30–34, he argued that the United Nations remained the best means of preventing another international holocaust. This is also the theme of "The U.N. on its Eighth Birthday," *Think* 19 (October 1953): 3–5, 36, and "United Nations 1956: An Inventory," *Saturday Review* 39 (January 28, 1956): 9–10, 28. The threat and challenge of communism to the West is discussed in "The Meaning of it All," *Think* 19 (September 1953): 3–4, 28, and in "Red China—Knotty U.N. Issue," *Think* 20 (September 1954): 3–4, 31. In "Europe Faces a Great Decision," *Think* 20 (December 1954): 3–4, 36, Shotwell analyzes the movement for European unity, while in "The Commonwealth—New Pattern for Old Relationships," *Think* 23 (March 1957), he discusses the changes in the British Commonwealth of Nations.

During the last years of his life, Shotwell became very interested in the concept of freedom and the progress of individual liberty throughout the world. This interest is reflected in both "The Last Frontier," *Think* 22 (June 1956): 3–5, 36, and in "The Future of Freedom," *Saturday Review* 43 (March 26, 1960): 32. The general theme, however, was not something new, for it had appeared in some of his earliest writings and remained a major concern throughout his life.

Some of his earlier articles dealing with this problem are "Democracy and Political Morality," *Political Science Quarterly* 36 (March 1921): 1–8; "The Student and Citizen," *International Conciliation* 175 (June 1922): 213–29; "A New Era in World Affairs," *Outlook and Independent* 102 (July 24, 1929): 505; "Justice, East and West," *Pacific Affairs* 5 (May 1932): 393–403; "Freedom—Its History and Meaning," *International Conciliation* 350 (May 1939): 263–74; and "The Constitution and the Guarantee of Freedom," *Bulletin of the College of William and Mary in Virginia* 36 (June 1943): 3–21.

Index